A HERALD

to Jesus of Nazareth's Bride
in the United States of America

Gary Kuntz

OTHER BOOKS
Available at Amazon.com

BY GARY

- *Forerunner Messages – Volumes One, Two, and Three*
- *iThink*
- *Growing to Love Jesus: A Study of the Song of Songs*
- *David's Tent: Rebuilding It*
- *Alcoholic*
- *Two Joseph Stories*
- *This God's Grace: Knowing the True From the False*
- *Talking With Jesus*
- *The Kingdom Constitution: a.k.a. Sermon on the Mount*
- *The Passion Week*
- *Jesus' Return: Don't Be Deceived; Be Prepared*
- *Testimony*
- *The Original Gospel: the Gospel the Apostles Preached*
- *The Passion of Hosea*

TABLE OF CONTENTS

PREFACE

The voice of one crying in the wilderness: "Prepare the way for the LORD; make straight in the desert a highway for our God. Every valley shall be exalted and every mountain and hill brought low; the crooked places shall be made straight and the rough places smooth; the glory of the LORD shall be revealed, and all flesh shall see it together; for the mouth of the LORD has spoken." (Isaiah 40:3-5)

Today, within the United States of America there is an army of prophetic criers/forerunners who Jesus is sending out to call His Bride to repent and to prepare for His return to this planet.

And while this army is crying out with a message within the borders of the Christianized nation of the United States of America, our message is NOT to this nation. It is to The Church, to those who claim to be the followers of Jesus of Nazareth who live in this nation.

(There are other armies of forerunners who are being sent to other nations as well, for This Jesus' return will be to the entire planet, not merely to a small sliver of land that He came to the first time.)

For although Jesus has given VERY much to The Church in this country (Luke 12:48b), today, in spite of outward appearances, The Church in this country is mostly a barren, dry, empty desert, for she is devoid of the actual Presence of the Living God Himself. And worse, so very few are even aware of just how absent He is due to exchanging His Presence for mere Churchianity.

So, this writing is not about this nation's issues. This writing is about the serious issues which permeate The Church in this nation.

THE BACKGROUND

The Background

In the flesh I am an example of Paul's new man from Ephesians, chapter two. As my father was a Jew and my mother a Gentile, this provided me with the DNA of both. Thus, in the physical I represent the two types of human beings who make up The Church, the Bride of Jesus of Nazareth.

More irony.

When my mother was officially converted to Judaism, and she and my dad were then married, they moved to the newly born-again nation of Israel. This was sometime in 1951. My dad made pretty good money in those days, and after regaining a desire to live a serious Jewish life, and believing that the best way to do this was to live in Israel, he shipped things over there, such as furniture, appliances, and other general household items he knew were in short supply at that time.

In other words, this was not a vacation to the Holy Land. My parents fully intended to become Israeli citizens and to live in the Promised Land for the rest of their lives.

When my parents arrived in Israel, due to the enormous influx of Jews coming to the Land from all over the world after WWII and its Holocaust, living conditions were limited and difficult. In an attempt to accommodate all these people, the government created large tent cities to house them. My dad's mother was already living in one of these tents, so my parents moved in with his mother until he was able to obtain an apartment. And it wasn't long after they moved into their own apartment that they conceived me.

So, I was conceived in Israel.

However, five months into the pregnancy my mother had a checkup. She weighed some ninety pounds. The reason for this was that everything was rationed, especially food. I remember her telling stories about how they were allowed a pint of milk, two eggs, and a pound of meat per week. Again, this was due to the tsunami of immigrants and the country's infrastructure unable to provide for them all.[1]

At this prenatal checkup the doctor informed my dad that based on my mother's physical condition, the baby (i.e. me) was not going to

---

[1] Remember that Europe, as well as some other regions of the earth, were still rebuilding from the destruction of WWII, thus using lots of the world's resources.

make it without some significant improvement to my mother's nutriational needs. So my dad sent my mother back to her family in the States for them to nurse her back to health. In the meantime, realizing he was going to have to postpone his desire to live in Israel, my dad worked on settling his affairs and trying to find employment back here.

My dad knew a ton of people. And most of these people were successful businessmen. But out of all these many people my dad knew only one man had a job opening. His name was Davis Green. Mr. Green owned a chain of jewelry stores along the border of the United States and Mexico. And out of all his stores he had only one opening, that of a manager in his store in Corpus Christi, Texas. My dad then telegraphed my mother and told her to meet him in Corpus Christi.

And that's where I was born, in the city whose name is Latin for "Body of Christ." Was this just a coincidence? Maybe.

But the irony doesn't stop there.

From the time I was born I suffered with asthma, probably due to my mother's poor prenatal condition. And as the asthma increasingly got worse, when I was about two years old, the doctor suggested my parents move me to a higher and dryer climate where the air is thinner and easier to breathe.[2]

So once again my dad started contacting friends for employment and he found a job in El Paso, Texas. This is where I grew up, in the high desert of West Texas.

In the mid-1970's I moved to Houston, which was booming at the time with employment. Then on May 14th, 1980 Jesus of Nazareth – who as a Jew I certainly wasn't looking for, but who was looking for me – entered my life in a profound way.[3]

I grew up in a very conservative Jewish home, having my Bar (son of) Mitzvah (The Law) at age thirteen, attending Hebrew School as well as public school, and being quite involved in the synagogue and the Jewish Community Center. So as I said, I was certainly NOT looking for Jesus of Nazareth in ANY way.

To me, the words "Jesus Christ" was something one said when one hits his thumb with a hammer or stubs his toe. Further, there were no

---

[2] I don't know what happened, but when I was about nine years old, one day I just seemed to "out run" asthma, for I've never had an issue with it ever again.

[3] May 14th, 1948 is the day Israel was reborn after some 1,900 years.

big problems in my life at the time in which I needed the help of some "higher power." And neither did I have a fear of dying and going to Hell. In fact, I believed that just because I am a Jew Hell is not an issue.

Besides, I wasn't a bad person, much less an evil one. I wasn't perfect, but I was a good guy. And like most people I believed that because I was a good person there was no question I would end up in heaven. In fact, being a Jew and thus a member of the Chosen People, I believed I was guaranteed to be.[4]

So again, I was NOT looking to Jesus of Nazareth in ANY way. If anything, I was repulsed by just the thought of Him. After all, I had grown up with stories of how the followers of Jesus persecuted and murdered my people.[5] And the historical facts I heard from my elders was that since the Roman Exile in 70 AD, and up until the reestablishment of the nation of Israel, we Jews have been severely persecuted by people living in Christianized nations. Based on this fact, to me Christianity was one religion to avoid!

So when the person who told me the Gospel gets to the part in which he informed me that "the free gift of God is Eternal Life in Jesus Christ," I am NOT interested.

And yet...

———————

Yom Kippur (the Day of Atonement) of 1979. One of the holiest days in the Jewish calendar. Despite departing from practicing Judaism as an older teenager, I had decided that year to take this day seriously, doing the twenty-four hour fast and being present in the long service on Yom Kippur Eve as well as the all-day service Yom Kippur Day.

In the final hours of the day-long service the ark where the Torahs (first five books of Moses) are kept is opened and left opened. Out of respect for the Law of Moses, one stands when the Torahs are exposed like this. Wanting to be alone with my thoughts in a crowded place on such a holy day and at such a pivotal time in which we Jews ask the Holy One to forgive our sins and to give us another year of life, I positioned

---

[4] I like to tease Gentile Christians by telling them although there's no difference between Jew and Gentile in Jesus, we Jews get front row seats in Heaven. Calm down, I'm joking! There's no seats in Heaven.

[5] In typical Jewish thinking, there are only two types of people: Jews and Gentiles. And all Gentiles have a religion: Christianity, Hinduism, Islam, Buddhism, etc., just as we Jews have Judaism.

myself in a corner and pulled my tallis (prayer shawl) over my head to cover my face for some privacy.

In a moment...for some unknown reason...I began to become sort of emotional. And as I did I said, "God, who are you? I've been told lots of things about you, but who are you really? Is all this religious stuff really what you want? Can't I know you in some way?"[6]

Maybe it was just the impact of being in such an environment for so many hours, as well as not having any food, for by the next day I felt better, got busy with work, and promptly forgot the whole thing.

But, evidently the Living God did not forget.

———————

Easter weekend of 1980. I was at home alone; my wife was out on some errand. I had all the lights off and was watching television. This is long before cable TV, so there were only the three network stations and a few local UHF stations at the time. This was also before I had a remote control television, thus I was up at the TV clicking the channel changer looking for something to watch. I came upon something that seemed to be one of those cheaply made Hercules movies.

This being pretty much a guy-thing to watch, I sat on the floor and crunched on an apple trying to get into the story. The scene I had come in at had these ancient soldiers pushing what appeared to be a bad guy through a crowd. As I watched I assumed the man had done something for which these soldiers were going to torture or execute him. No big deal. Just part of the action that we guys like in such movies. Literally, I had NO idea what I was watching.

Finally, the soldiers got this man to wherever they were taking him, stripped off his clothes, threw him on the ground on top of a piece of lumber, and were about to torture or execute him. (I'm still crunching on my juicy apple.) I then hear the sound of hammering and the camera focuses on the pain-filled grimacing face of the actor. Suddenly, this thought hits me, "Why are they doing this to this innocent man?"

I nearly jumped out of my skin, for it was as if someone had actually said this to me!

---

[6] To this day I hate the question, "Where is your God?" (e.g. Psalm 42:2, 10). For there is something in me that wants to shout, "Behold, He's right here right now!", and then to have the manifest Presence of the Living God do His thing. Even back then I detested the God-vacuum of religion.

In an instant I had ALL the lights on and was looking for whoever or whatever had put this question to me. Again, I thought someone had somehow come into our apartment. Seeing that no one else was in the apartment, I calmed myself and wondered how in the world did I know this guy was innocent! I immediately changed the channel.[7]

Then, not long after that Easter, a business associate asked me one day over lunch what I thought a Christian is. I offered several things such as, going to church, being baptized, taking communion, and believing in Jesus. He responded to each of these by saying, "Yes, Christians do that, but what IS a Christian?" So when none of my answers answered his question, I said, "Okay, what's a Christian?"

To which he said, "I'll tell you about it sometime," and he returned to eating his hamburger. I thought that was weird, but I shrugged it off ...sort of. For every few days it bothered me that I didn't know what a Christian is. But every time I would remind this man that he promised to tell me what one is, he always had some reason why he couldn't tell me at that moment.

Finally, after several weeks of putting me off, I manipulated him (by lying to him) to get myself invited over to his house so I could "make" him tell me what a Christian is. And when I did, this man finally presented the Gospel to me, something no one had ever done.

And although I balked when he said the name of Jesus, because that name represented the persecution and even the murder of my people for 1,900 years of European history, this man's focus on my Sin (e.g. such as lying to him), and the eternal paycheck it qualifies me for, and what Jesus did to pay it for me, and thus Jesus' offer if I was willing to repent and to follow Him, was deeply convicting.

And due to conviction having its way with me, that was the night Jesus of Nazareth entered my life.

Thus, although I was NOT looking for ANY Jesus, like with Paul, Jesus of Nazareth sought me out.[8]

Several things began to happen to me within just a few weeks.

For example, I asked the man who had led me to Jesus, "Shouldn't I be doing something? I mean, aren't there things to do as a Christian?"

---

[7] A little over a year after Jesus of Nazareth entered my life I found out that that night I had been watching the movie "Jesus" which was produced by The Jesus Film Project in 1979.
[8] See Appendix A

He said, "Yes, yes there are."

I said, "What are they?"

He said, "Every day, read your Bible. This is one way Jesus will talk to you. Also, every day, pray, which is you talking to Jesus."

I was making some notes, beginning a to-do list by writing these first two things down. Then I said, "Okay, got it. What else?"

He said, "That's it. Talk to Jesus and listen to Jesus...every day."

I said, "C'mon. I'm Jewish. I've done lots of religious stuff. I can handle it. Tell me the real deal. Surely there's plenty to do in the Christian religion."

He said, "Gary, you're not in a religion. You're in a relationship with the Living God. So...you talk to Him and then you listen to Him. Trust me, if you do that every day, He will take it from there."

Thus, I began to read the Bible, and from the moment I opened it and began to read it, I began to consume it with an insatiable hunger and unquenchable thirst. I just could not get enough of it, for the Bible came alive! It was as if I could hear the people speaking, like I could smell the livestock, like I could feel the Judean dirt between my toes. I could see the looks on people's faces when the Living God encountered them. And when He touched them, He seemed to touch me.

I also began to try to pray to Jesus, which the man described as simply talking to Him. Initially I didn't know how to do this without a prayer book, for that's really all I knew about praying – reading prayers. But little by little, remembering what this man had told me about being in a relationship, I began to talk with Jesus like He was right there... for... He actually was right there.

And in doing just these two things this man was right. The Spirit began teaching me, encountering me, revealing Jesus of Nazareth to me, capturing my heart, making changes in my life, as well as putting me into a variety of ministry situations. In none of these was I the initiator. He was.

I can't emphasize this enough: One of the themes of my life, beginning with Jesus Himself, things I was NOT looking for or did NOT want came to me. Almost everything that has happened in my life since May 14, 1980 Jesus put me into, many times despite my initial rejection or intense reluctance. My plans for me have been trumped, trampled even at times by His plans for me.[9]

---

[9] Several significant events in my life have also tended to occur in the month of May.

As I said above, I wasn't a completely immoral guy, at least as I understood immorality in my un-transformed and un-renewed[10] thinking as an unregenerated person. Obviously, I would lie if it served my purposes, as I did with the man who presented the Gospel to me, but I can assure you that there were plenty of other issues that Jesus wanted cleaned up as well.

Not long after Jesus entered my life my wife told me that we needed to attend church. I suggested we go back to the Unity Church that we had been married in, for I thought the service there was nice. I of course had NO idea that the Unity Church was a New Age cult.

Then one Sunday morning as we were leaving to go to church, some neighbors we were friends with were also leaving to go to their Baptist church. They asked us if we wanted to come along, which my wife did, and so we went with them.

The service was nice enough. I noticed a little bit of a difference from the Unity Church, as in the pastor preached from the Bible. But other than that it seemed similar. My wife voiced her preference for this Baptist church, and since I had no preference, we began attending it. A few weeks later, at the end of the service when the pastor invited people to "receive" Jesus or to join the congregation, my wife expressed her desire to join.

I said, "Join?!?!? No way. Look at this place, I'll bet the membership dues are huge."

Westbury Baptist Church in Southwest Houston was a large church with very traditional buildings. The main sanctuary had a gigantic pipe-organ built into the front pulpit area.

My wife said, "Membership dues??? What membership dues?"

I said, "In the synagogue I grew up in people paid membership dues. In fact, the higher the dues, the better seat one was assigned on the High Holidays, you know, up front, near the rabbi."

She said, "We don't do that in Baptist churches. It doesn't cost anything to join a Baptist church."

I said, "You mean we can attend this place for free?!?"

She looked at me weird and said, "Yes."

I said, "Are you sure? Are you sure there aren't any hidden things we don't know about? We're not going to get a bill in the mail are we?"

---

[10] Romans 12:1-2

She said, "I'm sure, and no, there's no bill."

I said, "Okay! Let's join."

Then, some weeks later the couple who took us there told us that there was an open adult volleyball game in the gym on Tuesday nights, and they wanted to know if we wanted to go. So we quickly put on t-shirts, shorts, and shoes and showed up at the church gym to play.

It was fun, and we had an enjoyable time, and we got to do something that was bit athletic.

But then, as we were leaving, a couple of men came up to me, and one of them said, "We're glad to have had you here tonight, but in the future please do not wear," pointing at my t-shirt, "that t-shirt."

My t-shirt had one of many popular statements at the time printed on it. My version of this popular statement was, "Divers Do It Deeper." Lots of versions of this were all around, on t-shirts, billboards, bumper-stickers, etc.: Truckers Do It Longer, Cardiologists Do It Till Your Heart Stops, etc. And everyone understood that "do it" was a reference to having sex.

And so, what this man was addressing with me was that my t-shirt was an inappropriate thing for me to wear to church, but more importantly, is was not something a follower of Jesus should ever wear.

Initially his comments, although expressed to me very politely and quite gently, offended me. I thought, *What the heck, everyone wears stuff like this."* But when I got home the Spirit began to deal with me: "You know he's right. I don't like what you're wearing. It's vulgar."

And so began the process of Romans 12:1-2.

———

The following year to the month that Jesus of Nazareth entered my life He seemed to be asking me to do ministry on a fulltime basis. Another thing I did NOT go looking for and that I had NO interest in doing, even though I was already involved in doing some ministry in the form of a Bible study at a prison and a Sunday School class for single adults.

My pastor was the one who posed the question to me, noting all the things I had been doing (something I hadn't paid any attention to, thinking I was simply doing what all Christians did). But despite of my resistance to the idea, he told me to just go over to Houston Baptist University, apply for entrance, and just see what Jesus might do.

The thought of applying to a college was absurd, even a little intimidating to me. I am not a smart person. Never have been. Almost ten years earlier I graduated at the bottom of my high school senior class. I didn't read.[11] I could hardly write. (Which may still be true.) And as for Math, that is of the devil as far as I'm concerned.

In addition (no pun intended), I had no money. And when I found out the cost for this private university, I really had no money! And there was no way I was going put my family and I into debt by borrowing for college to get a degree in something I didn't want to do. If my poor grades and lack of education didn't disqualify me, not having any money to pay for college would surely nix my pastor's silly notion.

The HBU advisor who helped me complete the application told me it would take several weeks before I would receive an answer, as they had to get my high school transcript, and then the admissions committee had to meet to consider my application, etc.

A few days later the lady who I had spoken with called me to tell me they had obtained all the necessary information, the committee had met, and that I had been accepted. She also told me that there was money in my account to pay for my classes and books, and that I would start that coming Monday.

Money in my account?!?!? What account??? I'm starting Monday?!?!? So soon??? Books?!?!? I have to read books???

I was stunned! When I hung up the phone I just stood there trying to grasp what was happening. Jesus wants me in college? Jesus wants me doing ministry fulltime? What is this? Well, whatever it was...I did NOT choose it!

Beginning with my very first courses Jesus began teaching me how to learn. And for the next three years I took as many classes as I could so as to finish college as quickly as possible. And every time I registered there was money in my account for the classes and the books. I know Jesus was using someone to help me, but I never learned who.

Then at my graduation from Houston Baptist I was awarded a scholarship from HBU to Southwestern Baptist Theological Seminary. But about halfway through seminary I dropped out. I dropped out because I felt an intense spiritual dryness. It was as if I had lost sight of Jesus. He just wasn't around like He used to be.

I didn't realize it at the time, but I'd been learning lots of stuff about Jesus and about the Bible, however, I didn't know that knowing

---

[11] For example, in all my life up to that time I had only read five books from cover to cover. I still remember them: Court Clown, an eighth-grade version of the story of Ulysses, Winning Through Intimidation, How to Win Friends and Influence People, and I'm Okay, You're Okay. The last three I didn't really understand even though I read them.

stuff about Jesus is NOT the same thing as intimately knowing the One the stuff is about. And as it turned out this lesson was Jesus' doing. And truly, what a profound lesson!

The Pharisees and the Teachers of the Law, the Jewish sect with whom Jesus agreed the most theologically knew LOTS of stuff about the Scriptures. And yet, despite their abounding Bible knowledge, they did not recognize Him when He stood before them (John 5:31-47).

The "knowing" the Bible speaks of is not the knowing of information, not that knowing information is wrong. It is not. But knowing information is not the same thing as intimately knowing Jesus of Nazareth – as in Adam "knew" Eve and she conceived.

Also, at the beginning of my third year of college a little congregation in a small town about an hour northwest of Houston invited me to be their pastor. About two years later I moved to another small community west of Houston to pastor another small group. Neither of these pastorates went very well. But most importantly, in these failures I learned that I am not a senior-leader type person.

After these two pastorates I went to work for a counseling ministry named Rapha, then about two years later I joined a pastoral team I will say more about in a moment. Then since 1996 I have been at the same high school as a Special Education teacher.

———————

I should mention my extended family.

The first person I lead to Jesus of Nazareth was my younger brother.

My mother was next. I'd been talking with her, but it was a friend of hers who eventually led her to Jesus.

Some years later my mother came to visit my family and I for a few weeks. And in this visit she came with us for the first time to the congregation where the Presence of the Lord was quite present. (I'll provide more detail about this also in a moment.) A few minutes into the worship time I began to hear this certain kind of growl, a growl I had learned to recognize as being demonic. So I looked around to see from whom this growl was coming. It was MY mother!

There she was on the floor writhing and growling this low, angry growl, manifesting demons! The people in the row behind her were looking at her, then at me, then her, then me, wondering what to do, for this was the mother of one of the pastors! As I turned to move toward her to help her it seemed like Jesus said, "Leave her alone. This is between her and me." So I gave a hand signal to those people that it was okay, and I went back to worshiping Jesus.

At the end of the worship my mother was laying on the floor quite peacefully. I went to her, helped her into her seat, and asked her if she was alright. She looked at me (my mother could have been a successful standup comedian), smiled not only with her mouth but also with her eyes, and said, "Wow!!! Boy, do I feel better!!!"

I said, "I'll bet."

She asked, "What WAS that?"

I said, "I'll explain it to you later, Mom."

And truly, from that day forward my mom was a VERY different person. Gone were all the "psychological syndromes and disorders" she had struggled with all the years I knew her (she tried twice to kill herself), and for which various psychiatrists gave her pills that had no impact. And in the place of these "issues" was a joy and a passion to truly, openly, extravagantly worship Jesus! I had a new mom.

As for my dad, when I told him I had had an encounter with Jesus of Nazareth he immediately stopped all communication with me, claimed me as dead, and wrote me out of his will. However, for a while, and from time to time, he would do something to try to bring me back into the Jewish religion, as if he were trying to rescue me from a cult. Sometimes he would send me some information, or once he acquired the services of a rabbi in Israel who claimed to be an "expert refuter of Christianity" to get me to deny Jesus and to return to Judaism.

On one occasion my dad told me that if I'd become a Christian because I was afraid of going to Hell, that I didn't need to worry about that. As a Jew all I had to do was to find a single sentence in the official Daily Prayer Book that began with the first letter of my Hebrew name and ended with the last letter of my Hebrew name. Besides sounding rather like a lucky charm, trying to find such a sentence seemed a lot like trying to find the proverbial needle in the haystack. Amazingly my dad found just such a sentence, marked it, dogged-eared the page, and sent the entire prayer book to me. I was impressed to say the least.

And as it turns out, the sentence was Psalm 20, verse 7. The first thing that caught my attention was that I met Jesus of Nazareth when I was 27 years old. Then I looked up the verse. Here it is:

Some trust in chariots and some in horses, but we trust in the Name of the LORD[12] our God.

13

I thanked my dad and told Him that that would be a good thing to say to Jesus, that I was not trusting in any of my goodness or strength, but in the Name (i.e. character) and the blood of Jesus of Nazareth.

Some years later, when my dad was dying, he became willing to have conversation with me, which we did almost daily on the phone due to the physical distance that separated us.

One Friday morning as I drove to work it seemed like Jesus began to speak to me about my dad. It seemed He was telling me to ask my dad what "one thing" he would like for Him to do, and whatever my dad said, to then tell him He would do it for him for three days. This detail was too much to be my own thoughts.

And yet I was hesitant to bring this up with my dad when he called me at my office to talk that morning for fear of being wrong and thus looking stupid. But I finally got around to asking my dad what I thought Jesus told me to ask him.[13] I really didn't think my dad would have a response. But he was quick to answer. He said, "Oh, if I could just get rid of this pain!", for he was in great physical pain. Sometimes the pain was so intense he could barely speak.

I was surprised he had a response, but I half-apologetically told him what I thought Jesus told me to tell him – that He would do this for him for three days. My dad thought it a joke. I felt embarrassment, thinking what a fool I was to think Jesus would tell me such a thing.

This being on a Friday morning, and being especially busy, I did not get a chance to talk with my dad again that day. He does not use the phone on the Sabbath, which is Friday evening to Saturday evening. Then, he knew I would be in church on Sunday. So it wasn't until Monday morning before I called to check on him. An unknown, cheery voice I didn't recognize answered the phone. I asked to speak to my dad, thinking this was some friend of his visiting him.

IT WAS MY DAD! He was so light and cheerful as he told me he had been feeling really good. I was in shock!!! Doubt actually.

And without thinking, I said, "So Jesus took the pain away?!?!?"

This was like a lightning bolt striking my dad. He hadn't made the connection between what I had said to him according to Jesus' instructions to me and the pain subsiding. He just thought he was simply doing

---

12 In English translations of the Old Testament the publishers capitalize the word "lord" (LORD) to indicate that in the Hebrew text it is the name "Yahweh."
13 In our conversations I was always careful to use the words "God" and "Lord," and not the name of Jesus.

better. Further, when I said the name of Jesus...he was dumbfounded and speechless. He could not deny he had been pain free since that Friday morning. By lunchtime on Monday his pain was back.

During the time that I was at Rapha a friend told me about a Southern Baptist church that wasn't very typically Southern Baptist. My wife and I went to check it out, and it was a LITTLE different. We began attending and some months later the three pastors (one senior pastor and two associate pastors) asked me to join the pastoral team. (In the next few years we added two more pastors.)

Initially I came on staff part-time the first of August 1988. In January 1989 I was fulltime. And the first event I attended as one of the fulltime pastors was their annual, at-the-beginning-of-the-new-year Pastor's Retreat where they discussed and planned for the coming year.

Throughout most of the planning I remained quiet, seeing myself as the new guy who didn't know much. But at one point the senior pastor asked me if I had any suggestions. I did, and explained that even though I was certainly no expert on moves of the Holy Spirit, that one of the things I had noticed in my reading about this was that such moves always seemed to follow extensive and intensive times of prayer, prayer especially done by those who were fed up with religion and were desperate for the Real Thing (e.g. Joel 2:15-17).

My suggestion was that we four pastors set aside two or three mornings a week to pray. One of the associate pastors was adamantly against this, saying we were too busy to spend time like that in prayer. The senior pastor though had some interest. However, he didn't think we could do three mornings, but was willing to try two.

And so, beginning the next week and first thing in the morning, we went into the auditorium to pray.

Quite quickly we discovered...this was NOT easy! For after each one of us expressed some things to Jesus, we didn't know what else to say or to do. But it wasn't long before the Spirit not only began to draw our hearts but also to instruct us in what to do. And in this He showed us two things: first to combine prayer with worship as in Revelation 5:8, and secondly to pray the Scriptures.[14]

---

[14] Here is just a short sample list: Ephesians 1:17-19, 3:16-19; Philippians 1:9-11; Colossians 1:9-11; Romans 15:5-6, 13; 1 Corinthians 1:5-8; 1 Thessalonians 3:10-13; 2 Thessalonians 1:11-12, 3:1-5; Acts 2:17-21, 4:29-31; Luke 24:49-50. One caution: be

It wasn't long before we began spending all morning with Jesus. For with each appointed time with Him something was happening to us. To put it simply, we were becoming hungry and thirsty for the Living God. And in this, we began to become obsessed with having to have HIM and HIS Presence among us! Anything less than this was NOT acceptable. We didn't know it, but we had NO clue what such a thing would even look like, much less what it would cost.

Then, one Monday morning the second week of July 1989, we were in the auditorium praying, and we had only been praying for a short time when...Someone entered the auditorium.

This is a bit difficult to put into words, but it was like this: Have you ever been in a room with your back to the door when you became a-ware that someone had entered? You didn't become aware they enter-ed because you heard them enter, but because you sensed them. Well, this was sort of like that. There was no physical indication, and yet Someone besides the four of us was IN the room!

And after some time the Presence began to speak to us. And in His speaking it was something like having a conference call in our hearts. We didn't hear Him with our ears, we heard Him in our spirits. And the essential point He was making was this: Christianity is NOT about you; it's about ME.

We'd say, "We know that."

He'd say, "No you don't."

"Yes we do."

"No you don't."

"Yes we DO!"

"No you do NOT!"

"We know John 15:5, you're the vine and we're the branches, and we can't do anything apart from you."

"I know you know this theology; you're not doing this theology."

"Yes we are."

"No you're not."

"Yes we ARE!"

"No you're NOT!"

After some time, the senior pastor got so exasperated he blurted out, "God, are you telling me not to even preach?!?!?"

---

careful with taking promises made to Israel in the OT and applying them to The Church. In other words, context matters!

Now, maybe you need a little information on the Southern Baptist view on preaching in order to fully appreciate this. In those days, Southern Baptists DID NOT, not preach. Not preaching to a Southern Baptist was like some sort of unpardonable sin. Not preaching? It's utterly unacceptable. It's unthinkable. The church building can be on fire and no one is leaving until the sermon is over. So for the senior pastor to question Almighty God, who some Southern Baptists believe is a Southern Baptist, might be one of the greatest heresies known among men![15]

But at this question the senior pastor passionately voiced...the Presence suddenly left the room just as suddenly as He had come in. It was like a light switch had been switched off. This was a quite an unusual experience for all of us at that time. So we got up off the floor and went to our offices. I sat in my office wondering what in the world had just happened!

Over the next few of weeks we four continued to pray. Then, on the last Sunday of July, we were just ending the singing part (we were still just learning what worship is) of the early Sunday morning service (about 8:30) when that Presence suddenly stepped in.

In those days we four pastors used to sit on our little "thrones" (as I used to mockingly call them) up on the platform. When this Presence entered we recognized Him instantly, a couple of us prostrating ourselves on the pulpit platform. The congregation did not immediately sense Jesus's Presence. Their spiritual dryness made them unreceptive, sort of like a very dry sponge resists water at first.

We too had been just as dry. But unknowingly, in those hours and hours of seeking to lay hold of the Living God, to actually touch Jesus of Nazareth Himself, and in which we pressed Him with our ever-growing longing to actually and in our reality have Him present among us, we had been "soaking" in small amounts of His Presence.[16]

As for what was happening, I think the people must have been wondering what in the heck we pastors were doing stopping the service and laying on the platform on our faces...and in our coats and ties!

Maybe some might have said, "Look, Mildred. What are the pastors doing? Is this some new form of ministry? I don't think I like it. It's not becoming. It's not respectable. It seems odd and especially radical.

---

[15] Okay, maybe a little exaggeration and sarcasm, but hopefully you get my point: preaching is really, really, really important and nothing is allowed to stop it from happening. For if we're honest, preaching in Protestant/Evangelical services has replaced the Eucharist in the Catholic services.

[16] See Appendix B

I don't like radical. I like respectable, comfortable, nice, cute, nothing that really challenges me. Where's the special music? When's this thing going to be over? I'm hungry; what are we having for lunch? I sure hope pastor doesn't preach long!"

Time seemed to disappear, but I'd say some fifteen or twenty minutes went by. And with each passing minute a heaviness slowly filled the room. No one was moving. No one made any sound whatsoever.

Finally, the senior pastor stood up, turned on his lapel mic, and softly said, "I know the Lord is in the room, but I don't know what to do. So we're just going to wait on Him." And with that, he turned off his lapel mic and returned to his prone position.

Some more time went by.

And then...suddenly...all Heaven broke lose!

Numbers of people spontaneously began coming to the altar area, and being one of the "professional" ministers, I went to one lady to try to be of some help to her, after all I was one of the pastors who is supposed to know how to help people.

This woman was so overwhelmed, and was weeping so hard, that I felt like I should wait for a lull before I offered to help her. But the lull wasn't coming. She kept getting more and more intense. So I decided to break-in and to ask her what she felt like was happening to her. And when I did this, she turned herself to face me, grabbed my shoulders, and said intensely, "I'M LOST!!! I'M NOT A REAL CHRISTIAN!!!"

In short, what Jesus was initially doing was to deal with churched people's lost condition, sins, lukewarmness, and compromises with this World. And in this typical, middle-class, American congregation there were LOTS of these issues.

Further, it became quite clear quite quickly that we four little pastors were NOT in charge of what was happening – we hadn't started it, thus we had no control of it, and although we probably could have stopped it, we didn't dare.

So whatever this was, it was showing no sign of letting up or slowing down, even though it was past time for the first Sunday morning service to end and people were arriving for the second service. So we posted some deacons at the front entrances to try to help the arriving people. The deacons told these people that the Lord was doing something a little unusual that morning (what an understatement!) and instructed them to go in and to try to find a seat. And as some entered the auditorium, they too would be overwhelmed by this Presence.

Finally...at about 1:30 in the afternoon, the Presence lifted.

And when we came back for the 6:00 p.m. service the place was packed, for the news had spread.

But more importantly, for probably the first time we began to worship, for we had experienced The Jesus. Gone was this religious spirit in which people went through the motions of just singing songs. Now blown away by the Presence, the people sang their love for Jesus to Jesus. Truly, we had tasted something way beyond mere theology about Jesus. And when the worship time ended, the Presence again entered, and He did His thing to us until well past midnight.

The next morning, Monday, the senior pastor called us together for a meeting. As we sat around a table trying to understand what had happened, something suddenly hit me. I turned to the senior pastor and said, "You...you didn't preach!", which we had all overlooked. Instantly, the Presence drew close and pressed this truth into us:

> Christianity is NOT about you; it's about ME! I am able to accomplish what I want to accomplish. You serve MY purposes; I don't serve you and your programs. All you must do is to seek ME, follow ME, and fall deeply in love with ME, and I will do the rest.[17]

NOW...we were beginning, just beginning to understand.

AN IMPORTANT WARNING

A wise man used to repeatedly say that the Living God will offend people's minds to reveal what is truly in their hearts.

If you haven't seen This God do this many, many times throughout the entire Bible...you aren't reading very carefully nor accurately comprehending what you're reading. And if you're unaware of this in all of Church history...you don't know Church history very well either.

Jesus' "discussions" with the Pharisees, the segment of Jews whose theology was the most like His own, is probably the most obvious

----

[17] David Pawson wrote: "They [the disciples] were to wait in Jerusalem until the Holy Spirit came on them and then they were to go out. That is where the Kingdom lies now – wherever the Holy Spirit is. Wherever the Holy Spirit is filling people, you will see two things: the sovereignty of God being exercised – the same sovereignty Jesus exercised over demons and disease – and you will see people whom the Holy Spirit has enabled to be subjects of the Kingdom."

example of this. And if you think you are exempt from this...you're a fool. An arrogant fool even.

The FACT is: IF Jesus of Nazareth presents Himself to you person-ally or visits your group, He absolutely WILL do things, many things, that WILL offend you as He confronts any and all of your wrong theologies that He wants changed. If this doesn't happen, be assured that you are NOT experiencing THE Jesus.

So be prepared to have your beliefs and practices, and thus your hearts tested like this. My suggestion is that you hold everything with your palms up and open so that He can easily blow away what He does not like. If you doggedly grip the things He wants gone or changed, you yourself will be blown away with the chaff.

I present this warning to EVERY flavor of Christianity in this country. Whether you're Catholic, Protestant, Evangelical, Charismatic, etc., for when THE Jesus shows up He WILL confront what He does not like![18]

Imagine with me that you seek out some native tribe of people in the Amazon Jungle who have never encountered anyone or anything from outside their community. And to make friends with them, to show them that you are not a threat and have come in peace, you have some gifts for them. One of these gifts is a chocolate bar.

However, your interpreter informs you that these people have never seen chocolate, thus they don't even have a word for it in their language. Learning this, and as you unwrap the bar, you try to explain through the interpreter that what you hold in your hand is very tasty, it's something they're really going to like.

But no matter how much you try to assure them that this soft dark brown thing you're holding is good, the interpreter is telling you that these people are beginning to think you're playing a mean trick on them, for they have seen something dark brown and kind of soft before, as in human waste.

No, no, no, and you try very hard to explain that what you're offer-ing them is not only not that stuff, but it's really good. And the harder you try to explain this the angrier their faces become. Suddenly, in a moment of brilliance, you decide to read the ingredients listed on the

----

[18] See Revelation, chapters two and three.

wrapper, thinking what they need is some information to assuage their false judgment of what you are trying to graciously offer them.

Unfortunately, as you read the ingredients and the interpreter interprets, now nothing but confusion covers their faces, for hearing the ingredients is not doing much to help them understand. So in desperation, before the chief can deflect your hand, you shove a piece of the chocolate into the man's mouth.

At first the chief starts to spit this out, but then relaxes, smiles even, and asks for more. You are relieved, for you had heard these people are cannibals.

What made the difference?

The difference was simply this: the chief tasted, experienced the chocolate. Where all the assurances you gave, where even reading him the ingredients did not help...TASTING the chocolate made ALL the difference in the world.

And so it is with the Living God.

Explaining Him from the Bible is a good thing. BUT, when a person "tastes" or experiences Him for Himself... Wow! NOW they get it!

My point is this: the followers of Jesus of Nazareth in this country need far more than Bible lessons or theology, as good and as important as that is. They need to experience the Living God Himself in reality. In other words, the Spirit AND the Word.

And just as the First and the Greatest Commandment is first and greatest, coming before the Second Commandment, so the Spirit Himself comes before the Word. When one puts the Second Commandment before the First and the Greatest Commandment one gets humanism. And when one puts the Word before the Spirit one gets Informational Religion, maybe even Bible-olatry, that is, deifying the Bible.

Why is this? Because the Bible is not the Living God. It's His Word and it is important, but it is not Him. The Living God is the Living God. If the Bible didn't exist the Living God still does. Even more, putting the Bible before the Spirit is to make it something of the fourth member of the Trinity. Again, as vitally important as the Bible is, the Bible isn't the Living God. The Living God is the Living God.[19]

———————

———————

[19] Appendix C

This outpouring of the Presence of the Living God in that congregation in Northwest Houston went on for six years. It was profound. Jesus of Nazareth did a whole lot of things to a whole lot of people.[20]

———————

Before I move on, I'm not providing this very short summary about myself to try to validate what follows. I'm sharing these few things to give some personal background to what follows.

———————

For thou, O Lord, art high above all the Earth.
Thou art exalted far above all gods.
For thou, O Lord, art high above all the Earth.
Thou art exalted far above all gods.

Therefore...

I exalt thee, I exalt thee.
I exalt thee, O Lord.
I exalt thee, I exalt thee.
I exalt thee, O Lord.[21]

———————

[20] Sadly, a blindness to personal sin and character-issues in some of the leadership, which produced unhealthy staff relationships, brought the whole thing to a screeching halt. And as is so often the case, the Presence of the Living God left. I say this to express an important issue. As is one of the themes of this writing, Sin and even character issues WILL quench the Holy Spirit if not acknowledged and repented of (1 John 1:5b-6).
[21] "I Exalt Thee" by Pete Sanchez

THE TRAINING

The Training

In 1991 I had a dream. I call it "The Shaking Dream".

The dream began with me climbing up some steps which led up to a pair of large, heavy, and imposing wooden front doors of a church building. (Notice the direction I was going.) This entrance was sort of like the entrance to some European cathedral.

As I made my way up the steps, this building reminded me of one of those large inner-city church plants that in its day was full of people and activities – having a thousand-seat-plus auditorium, a multi-story educational building, and a gym – but today it stands more like a museum testifying to what used to be (which wasn't much of the Kingdom anyway) rather than being a place with the actual Presence of the Living God.

Once inside the doors I immediately noticed the showiness, gaudiness, glitziness, lavishness, extravagance, flamboyance, and the ostentation of it. And as I looked around, I felt utterly sick to my stomach by all this way-over-the-top design and décor, for the worldliness of it all was absolutely nauseating! It was grotesque and I was grossed out!

And as looked around I had the thought that whoever designed and built the place must have been completely ignorant of what Jesus said about Money and Materialism, as well as utterly being enslaved by the ways and the philosophies of the World. Surely these people did not know Jesus of Nazareth, for it seemed clear that they had missed the point of what His followers are sup-posed to be about (e.g. Matthew 5:3-10).

The place was so ugly, an abomination really, I desperately wanted to get myself out of there! But the Spirit spoke and told me that I was there to perform a wedding. (Note the issue of a wedding and not a church service.) As abominable as this place was, the assignment Jesus gave me held me. And so, I grudgingly began to make my way to the pulpit area, and as I walked I kept my head down partly to avoid looking at this sickening place, but also to look in my Bible for some scriptures to use in this wedding.

When I arrived at the pulpit area I found myself standing at the bottom of an incredibly tall staircase of two or three stories that led up to the platform. Now the sickening feeling I already had intensified. The pulpit area had been built FAR above the congregation.

And once again I had questions about those who had designed and built the place and how out-of-touch with the Scripture this was for leaders to be so highly elevated above the people.

Thus I wondered where was the evidence of what Jesus taught about those who want to be great in His Kingdom. Where was the reality that the way up in the Kingdom of God is down? What about the Living God giving His Grace to the humble (opposing the proud), His perfecting His power in weakness, and the fact that we must decrease for Him to increase? I wondered where was the concern about what Paul told the Corinthians in his first letter to them that The God would destroy the worldly wise, frustrate the intelligent, and shame the strong? And, how and why had these people's version of Christianity been more impacted by Americanisms than by the Word of God? I wondered where Paul's own example was that he expressed to the Christians in Corinth in the second chapter of his first letter to them.[22]

Half-heartedly, trying to stay focused on the purpose of performing a wedding, I climbed this enormous staircase and finally arrived at the top of the platform. And once again I returned to looking in my Bible for some scriptures to use in this wedding. Then, as I stood there doing this, I became aware that the pulpit area began to shake. The shaking started rather slowly, but it rapidly increased to the point that it knocked me down. When I tried to get back to my feet the shaking became even more violent. In fact, the harder I tried to get to my feet the harder and more violent the shaking became.

As this shaking was occurring I happened to look out at the people. They were experiencing none of it. They were even surprised at what they were seeing. Then, as it was becoming quite clear that I could not get myself onto my feet, I started to get scar-

---

[22] **And so it was with me, brothers and sisters. When I came to you, I did not come with eloquence or human wisdom as I proclaimed to you the Testimony about God. For I resolved to know nothing while I was with you except Jesus Christ and Him crucified. I came to you in weakness with great fear and trembling. My message and my preaching were not with wise and persuasive words, but with a demonstration of the Spirit's power, so that your faith might not rest on human wisdom, but on God's power.** (2:1-5)

ed, and in my fear I was just about to cry out to Jesus for help... when He appeared before me. But before I could say anything, He looked at me with resolute sternness, pointed over my head, and said, "Go! Find out why the pulpit is being shaken!"

Instantly I was taken to the first of three different places. Each place expressed a reason as to why the pulpit was being shaken.

In the first scene I was standing in the middle of a bus. When I looked to my left I saw a person I know who is a ministry leader driving the bus. I know this person to be a nice guy and a well-intentioned minister, but also someone who relies heavily on worldly versions to be "successful" in the ministry. Then I looked to my right and I saw another front of the bus. And in this driver's seat was the Lord. I looked back and forth at the two fronts of the bus that were of course facing opposite directions. The point was obvious: one direction is of man and the other is of the Lord.

Then I was taken to the second scene in which I was standing at the top of some stadium seats overlooking a racetrack like the Indianapolis Speedway. On this track was a great number of cars, more than the track could actually hold. They were all trying to race each other, and it looked ridiculous. In fact, the track was so crowded with vehicles that no one was able to go anywhere, much less determine who was ahead of whom. Some were even going in the wrong direction. Some were zig-zagging cross ways on the track. And others were just driving crazily. As I watched I realized that these were individual congregations and ministries. It was a sad sight, for it was all about trying to win something or to be something more than the others. As a result, there was almost nothing of Kingdom building, but rather effort to build individual kingdoms.

Then, I was taken to the third scene in which I was standing on top of a hill overlooking an ancient battlefield. To my right was the enemy's army who clearly knew what they were doing, for they were very prepared, very organized, very disciplined, and thus very purposed. To my left was a group of people who had some connection to some Jesus but who looked nothing like an army, for they were very unprepared, very unorganized, very undisciplined, and very un-purposed. If these were two football teams, one was from the National Football League and the other from Pop Warner Little League. Clearly these Christians were easy pickings, for the enemy was doing a much better job at his job than these followers of some version of a Jesus were at doing at their job.

After this third scene I was returned to the original church building. This time I entered the building by the backdoor by going down some steps, opening a door, and emerging into the auditorium again. (Notice the direction I was going.) Yet again I was grossed out by this place, but still being purposeful to perform this wedding I made my way toward the pulpit area.

This time when I arrived at the stairs to the platform, I was surprised to find that the pulpit area was now COMPLETELY different! There were just two or three steps to get onto it, as the pulpit had been GREATLY lowered!

And so, once again, I began searching my Bible for some scriptures to use in this wedding. And as I was doing this I heard a noise, and when I looked up I saw that the congregational part of the auditorium began to be shaken. And it was shaken just as violently as the pulpit had been. I waited, as the pulpit area was feeling none of this shaking. When the shaking of the congregation had finished, this part of the building was now UTTERLY different! Now the entire church had been changed! Even more, most of the people were gone, leaving only a small remnant. But the passion and the purity of this remnant was indescribable. As gross and as ugly and as nauseating as this place had been, the new simplicity and purity of the place was breathtakingly BEAUTIFUL!!!

As I stood there struck with awe and marveling over what had just happened due to the cataclysmic changes the shaking had produced, I felt Jesus come up behind me and whisper in my ear, "Now, do the wedding!"

When I awoke from this dream/encounter, Hebrews 12:25-29 stood before me:

See to it that you do not refuse Him who speaks. If they did not escape when they refused Him who warned them on Earth, how much less will we, if we turn away from Him who warns us from Heaven? At that time His voice shook the Earth, but now He has promised, "Once more I will shake not only the earth but also the Heavens." The words "once more" indicate the removing of what can be shaken – that is, created things (as in man-made instead of God-made) **– so that what cannot be shaken may remain. Therefore, since we are receiving a Kingdom that cannot be**

shaken, let us be thankful, and so worship God acceptably with reverence and awe, <u>for our "God is a consuming fire."</u>

Another thing that happened early on in Jesus' relationship with me, as "The Shaking Dream" illustrates, was His revealing of the Bridal Paradigm to me.

The Bible has several ways of describing those who belong to the Living God: His sheep, His children, His followers, His disciples, His workers, His servants, His warriors, etc. All of these are good metaphors. But the highest, the most important, the foremost description is that of the Bridal Paradigm – the Wife of the Bridegroom-King, Jesus of Nazareth. For one cannot get any higher revelation than the reason Jesus created Creation: so He could have a marriage-like relationship with the sons and daughters of Adam.[23]

Now, in order to begin to lay hold of the Bridal Paradigm, the first thing one needs to grasp is that the Son did Creation not the Father. John, chapter one (vs. 3) and Colossians, chapter one (vs. 16) tell us that it was the Son of God who created Creation. Once this biblical truth is understood then one can begin to see the Son's purpose for doing this. And the Son's purpose in creating Creation and making Adam in His image is revealed to us in the first two chapters of Genesis.[24]

In Genesis, chapter one, the Son gave Adam his job assignment, "You're the governor of this planet, so govern it (vs. 26-30)."

Adam says, "Gee, thanks Lord. That's pretty cool, but I don't know how to do that or what to do."

The Son says, "Yeah, I know you don't. Tell you what, why don't you show up here tomorrow morning early and I'll show you."

So Adam gets up early and meets up with the Son. He's enthusiastic and excited to get going. He says, "What should I do first, Lord?"

The Son says, "I think the first thing you should do is to name all the animals."

Adam says, "Sounds great! But...uh...two questions."

----

[23] When I speak of "revelation" like this I'm referring to having the "spirit of wisdom and revelation" as well as the "eyes of one's heart" being "enlightened" to "see" something deeper than with mere informational knowledge – Ephesians 1:17-18a.

[24] There is biblical evidence of the fact that throughout what we call the Old Testament it is mostly the Son who is interacting with humans and not the Father. For example, in Joshua 5:13-15 Joshua encounters the Captain of the Hosts. This is the pre-incarnate Son, for this Being is the Commander of the Armies of Heaven who we see again in Revelation 19:19.

"Yes, Adam," the Son says.

"First, what's an animal, and secondly what's a name?"

"I'll show you what an animal is in just a moment, Adam. As for what a name is, a name is what you call something. But more importantly, when you name something, Adam, you have authority over it."

Then the Son begins to bring the animals, two by two, before Adam so he can name them. This is intriguing. Why does the Son bring each animal, each creature as a pair, one male and one female? Why didn't He merely bring one of each creature, sometimes a male and sometimes a female? Why does the Son, very purposefully, bring each creature as a pair, one male and one female to Adam?

Now, Adam is new and thus he's not all that sharp yet. So it might have taken him a little while to notice this pairing, this coupling, this male and female thing. But eventually Adam notices this, and turning to the Son he says, "Lord, I've been noticing something here."

"Really Adam, what have you noticed," smilingly asks the Son.

"Well," says Adam, "I see that all of these animals are paired up, they have a companion that is like them, but not exactly (i.e. one is male and one is female), and yet they as a couple fit together."

"That's quite observant of you Adam," says the Son quite pleased.

Adam says, "So...Lord...where is my companion? Where is someone who is like me but not exactly? Someone who pairs with me?"

And this is where the Son creates Woman from Man, someone who is like Adam but not exactly, someone who fits Adam but isn't Adam, someone who will be Adam's companion and helpmeet...you know... EXACTLY like The Church was created from the Son and is to be His companion, His helpmeet, someone who fits with Him!

Paul told the Corinthian Christians in his second letter that he had been caught up to the Third Heaven, and that he heard and saw things he can hardly put into words, amazing, mind-blowing, tremendous things (12:4). And I believe Paul expresses one of these amazing, mind-blowing, tremendous things to the Christians in Ephesus when he's talking about the relationship between husbands and wives (5:22-33). For he quotes what the Son said to Adam in Genesis 2:24:

For this reason a man will leave his father and mother and be united to his wife, and the two will become One Flesh. (5:31)

And then, bursting with one of the surpassingly great revelations he was given in the Third Heaven, he says,

This is a profound mystery – but I am talking about Christ and The Church! (5:32)

The Son created Creation. And in this He created creatures that are like Him in that they have His image, but who are not Him, SO THAT the Son could have a companion, a helpmeet, a marriage-like relationship with these human beings. Not a servant-master relationship, not a teacher-disciple type of relationship, not a commander-warrior relationship, not even a relationship with children, as good as all of these are. But a mature, passionate marriage-like relationship with a Bride!

In the same way that THE highest human-to-human relationship is that of a marriage between one man and one woman[25], so the Bridal Paradigm is THE highest paradigm of the relationship between the Son and the humans who belong to Him.

As good and as important as the relationship parents can have with their children can be, or the relationship one has with one's parents, or the relationship between siblings, or the relationship between friends, etc., The highest and greatest of all the human-to-human relationships is the relationship between one man and one woman in marriage!

And THAT is EXACTLY what Jesus, the Bridegroom-King, wants! THIS is WHY the Son created Creation.

Thus, the Bible is more than a book of history about encounters between the God of Abraham, Isaac, and Jacob, the God of Israel, the One, True, Living God and human beings. The Bible is more than a collection of theological writings and spiritual advice. At its core the Bible is the Romance Novel of all romance novels. For its central topic, subject, and focus is about the Bridegroom-King and His Bride. Not quite sure about this? Well, the Bridal Paradigm shows up throughout the Bible. Here is a short list of examples.

When Yahweh gets Israel out of Egypt, Moses leads the people to the very spot where he himself had encountered Him at Mount Sinai. Then at Mount Sinai the God of Abraham, Isaac, and Jacob, the One, True, Living God conducts a wedding ceremony with Israel in which they

---

[25] Absolutely NOT between two men or two women. This form of intimacy is a perversion and Satan's mockery of the Son's one-man-and-one-woman model that He applies to Himself and The Church.

both exchange marriage vows. Yahweh says some "I will's" and Israel says some "We will's."

That was the day in which the Son married Israel, making her His Wife, becoming the God of Israel, which is like saying, Israel's Husband.

At the Final Party someone might ask, "So Honey, who here is your husband?"

Israel will point and say, "See that glorious hunk over there? I'm His wife."

"Who is he," someone might ask.

"He is Yahweh," Israel will say proudly, "But you may know Him as Jesus of Nazareth."

"Isn't this Jesus guy the Bridegroom-King?" someone may ask.

Smiling broadly, Israel will say, "Yes, yes He is!"

"Oh my Honey, you married VERY well!" someone will say.

"I sure did," Israel will say softly.[26]

As you know, when Israel committed idolatry the prophets confronted the people with the sin of adultery. To all the prophets, when Israel committed idolatry they said she was committing adultery. Idolatry and adultery are synonymous. Both are about being unfaithful to the One with whom one has a covenant, with whom one has vowed to be faithful and to love. Paul understood this paradigm as evidenced by what he told The Church at Corinth:

I am jealous for you with a godly jealousy. I promised you to one husband, to Christ, so that I might present you as a pure virgin to Him. (2 Corinthians 11:2)

When we get to John the Baptist he is literally the last Mosaic Covenant prophet, and yet he does not refer to himself as a prophet. John is also the forerunner to the Messiah with the spirit of Elijah on him. But again, he does not refer to himself as the forerunner. Instead, John had a very unique title on his business card: John the Baptist, Friend of the Bridegroom. John did not say he was a friend of the Lord, or the Savior, or the King, but rather the friend of the BRIDEGROOM.

Then, interestingly, the very first time Jesus of Nazareth demonstrated divine power was at...a wedding (John 2:1-11). Surely He could have shown such power at a variety of events, but quite purposefully I believe, He does so at a wedding.

---

[26] See the Song Of Songs and the "friends" the Bride interacts with.

Lastly, the last event in Revelation that transitions human beings from This Age into the Age To Come is not a meal for children, it's not a feast for warriors, it's not a supper for servants or a dinner for disciples. The last event is a wedding banquet! This is when the Son, Jesus of Nazareth, FINALLY gets what He has wanted from the very beginning and why He did all He did: a marriage-like relationship with humans!

I heard what sounded like the roar of a great multitude in Heaven shouting: "Hallelujah! Salvation and glory and power belong to our God, for true and just are His judgments. He has condemned the great prostitute who corrupted the earth by her adulteries. He has avenged on her the blood of his servants." And again they shouted: "Hallelujah! The smoke from her goes up for ever and ever." The twenty-four elders and the four living creatures fell down and worshiped God, who was seated on the throne. And they cried: "Amen, Hallelujah!" Then a voice came from the throne, saying: "Praise our God, all you His servants, you who fear Him, both small and great!" Then I heard what sounded like a great multitude, like the roar of rushing waters and like loud peals of thunder, shouting: "Hallelujah! For our Lord God Almighty reigns. Let us rejoice and be glad and give Him glory! For the wedding of the Lamb has come, and His Bride has made herself ready. Fine linen, bright and clean, was given her to wear." (Fine linen stands for the righteous acts of the saints.) Then the angel said to me, "Write: 'Blessed are those who are invited to the wedding supper of the Lamb!'" And he added, "These are the true words of God." (Revelation 19:1-9)

In the course of revealing the Bridal Paradigm to me, Jesus of Nazareth focused my attention on the process He uses to create a love-sick Bride (individually) as outlined in the Song Of Songs.[27]

During the time when Jesus showing me the SOS He used an event to form the Bridal Paradigm into the marrow of my bones. This began when a young woman showed up in our congregation.

After a few weeks of visiting, this attractive young woman came and asked if she could come by my office to talk with me. At the ap-

---

[27] See Appendix D

pointed time she arrived at my office, sat down, and started by saying, "I was a paratrooper in the Army."

I said, "Wait, wait, wait. YOU were a paratrooper in the Army?!?!?"
She said, "Yes."
I said, "You're kidding with me, right?"
She said, "No."
I said, "You trained to jump out of airplanes to kill people."
She said, "Yes."

I had the hardest time trying to reconcile this strikingly beautiful woman with someone in the military. I mean, beauty pageant contestant, absolutely; airborne paratrooper, no way!

She then told me that she had left the Army because she had had an affair with her commanding officer. She told me she even moved to Houston to get away from him, but she said this man was now coming to Houston to see her. She told me he would drive all night and show up at her apartment door wanting to spend the weekend with her, and of course, to have sex with her.

She told me that she knew this was Sin and she tried to resist him. But no matter what she did to have nothing to do with him he kept persisting, telling her he loved her even though he was married and had children. And because she couldn't get him to stop pursuing her, she came to me for help.

It took two letters and contacting this man's commanding officer, who was a deacon with this man in the same congregation, to get this man to stop chasing after this woman. Then, some months later I noticed that there was a young man sitting next to this young woman in church. And week after week I saw them sitting together, each time a little closer. So it wasn't much of a surprise when about a year later they came to me, told me they wanted to get married, and that they wanted me to do the ceremony.

When the Friday night rehearsal came we went through the whole ceremony practicing each person's part. We even practiced the soloist's song and the bride coming down the center aisle to the classic music of "Here Comes the Bride."

The next day at the real ceremony everything was going as planned and as practiced. We then came to the time in the ceremony for the bride to come down the center aisle. But when the young woman stepped to the top of the center aisle and began her walk, instead of hearing "Here Comes the Bride," the pianist played, and the soloist sang "My Jesus I Love Thee."

This is my very favorite hymn, for to me it seems to have a connection to the Bridal Paradigm. And although I love this hymn, hearing it at this moment confused me. I'm expecting "Here Comes the Bride" and I'm hearing "My Jesus I Love Thee." So I looked over at the pianist and the soloist wondering what they're doing, and they're just focused on doing their thing. I then looked back at this young lady who is walking down the aisle...and suddenly...I had a vision.

In this vision I see the Bride of Jesus of Nazareth!

Here is this Woman, once adulterous, now dressed in white, made righteous and holy, and she is breathtakingly, stunningly, knock-down gorgeous! A beauty I have no human words to describe!

And at the sight of this...I came utterly undone!

I began to weep SO hard that my tears were shooting out of my eyes and soaking the insides of the lenses of my glasses to the point that I could not see. I also began to tremble uncontrollably. The weeping and the trembling took such a strong hold of me I thought I was going to fall to the ground, so I dropped to one knee in an attempt to hold myself together in front of all these people.

But the harder I tried to get control of myself, the more I was unable to regain my composure. All I seemed able to do was to sob and to tremble at the redemptive beauty of the Bride.[28]

After some ten minutes or more, still weeping and trembling, I began to plead with Jesus to please back off so I could regain myself and finish this ceremony. Mind you, most of the people in the audience did not know me, and yet they sat there quietly, not understanding, but waiting patiently for me to get my act together.

Finally, the Holy Spirit slowly backed-off, having finished doing what He wanted to do to me, and I am finally able to regain myself enough to look at the young couple. The two of them are grinning at me. She spoke saying, "We wanted to bless you in some way."

She of course had no idea what an indescribable gift she had participated in giving me!

Yes, I completed the ceremony. But for me, I went home with something that became more than theology: The Bridal Paradigm.

---

[28] I.e. Revelation 5:4 and 21:2

My Jesus, I love thee, I know thou art mine;
For thee all the follies of Sin I resign;
My gracious Redeemer, my Savior art thou;
If ever I loved thee, my Jesus, 'tis now.

I love thee because thou hast first loved me,
And purchased my pardon on Calvary's tree;
I love thee for wearing the thorns on thy brow;
If ever I loved thee, my Jesus, 'tis now.

I'll love thee in life, I will love thee in death,
And praise thee as long as thou lendest me breath;
And say when the death dew lies cold on my brow,
If ever I loved thee, my Jesus, 'tis now.

In mansions of glory and endless delight,
I'll ever adore thee in Heaven so bright;
I'll sing with the glittering crown on my brow,
If ever I loved thee, my Jesus, 'tis now.[29]

---

[29] "My Jesus I Love Thee" by William Featherston

THE MESSAGE

The Message

One of the passages Jesus of Nazareth used to point me to His assignment as a forerunner is Isaiah 62:10-12.

In verse ten of this passage I am instructed to open gates and to build up the highway, that is, to make a way, a clear way for the King to enter deeply AND correctly into the lives of His people. And the way I am to make this clear way is by making the road passable by removing the stones that Jesus' followers in this country are tripping over.

Again, the ultimate reason for this road construction is to prepare Jesus' followers for Him and His return to this planet.

All forerunner passages have something like this. Sometimes the forerunner is to bring down the mountains and to raise up the valleys. Sometimes the forerunner is to make what's crooked straight. In other words, whatever metaphor is used – mountains and valleys, crooked ways, or stones in the road – the ultimate purpose of a forerunner is to call people to repent – to fix the things that need fixing and to remove the things that need removing – which prepares them to encounter Jesus of Nazareth Himself. For if they do not repent, things will not go well for them.

John the Baptist is of course an example. Here is a summary of John as a forerunner and his forerunner message:

In those days John the Baptist came, preaching in the Desert of Judea and saying, "Repent, for the Kingdom of Heaven is near." This is he who was spoken of through the prophet Isaiah: "A voice of one calling in the desert, 'Prepare the way for the LORD, and make straight paths for Him.'" John's clothes were made of camel's hair, and he had a leather belt around his waist. His food was locusts and wild honey. People went out to him from Jerusalem and all Judea and the whole region of the Jordan. Confessing their sins, they were baptized by him in the Jordan River. But when he saw many of the Pharisees and Sadducees coming to where he was baptizing, he said to them: "You brood of vipers! Who warned you to flee from the coming wrath? Produce fruit in keeping with repentance. And do not think you can say to yourselves, 'We have Abraham as our father.' I tell you

that out of these stones God can raise up children for Abraham.[30] The ax is already at the root of the trees, and <u>every tree that does not produce good fruit will be cut down and thrown into the fire</u>. I baptize you with water for repentance. But after me will come One who is more powerful than I, whose sandals I am not fit to carry. He will baptize you with the Holy Spirit [power] and with fire [purity]. His winnowing fork is in His hand, and He will clear His threshing floor, <u>gathering His wheat into the barn and burning up the chaff with unquenchable fire</u>. (Matthew 3:1-12)[31]

Notice what John is doing and saying as a forerunner.

First, John is living the fasted lifestyle of the Kingdom, that is, he is doing what he's calling the people to do.[32] Secondly, he's calling people to repent and thus to prepare to encounter the Bridegroom-King Himself. Thirdly, he's confronting and warning the religiously smug, and not very politely either. Fourthly, he addresses complacency. And lastly, John warns that there will be a judgment.

And notice that John is doing his forerunner ministry IN the Desert of Judea...not in the Temple...not even in the city of Jerusalem. In case you don't know, John deliberately found one of the loneliest and most secluded locations he could and just started preaching.

In other words, he didn't go looking for a "good" location, some place that was convenient, easily accessed, plenty of parking, a nice coffee bar, comfortable indoor seating with climate control, and a beautiful stage with all the latest bells-and-whistles of technology. Further, he did no advertising or publicizing. In short, John picked the most difficult and the most unlikely place he could.

Why did John do this?

Simple. He knew there would be a variety of people who would come out to investigate him – everything from those who seriously want the Living God, to those who were just curious, to those who liked to watch spiritual things from a distance, to those who would consider him to be crazy and would dismiss his message and ministry as being crazy. So John is purposely trying to sift out as many as he can who do not have ears to hear so he can focus on those who do, for John wasn't

---

[30] These two sentences are an affront to something of a once-saved-always-saved mentality of the Jews. This is true also for the followers of Jesus of Nazareth.

[31] Jesus of Nazareth also preached repentance. See Mark 1:15.

[32] See Matthew 5:19 – "...whoever **practices** and **teaches these commands will be called great in the Kingdom of Heaven**."

looking for a huge "congregation," and neither was he expecting revival. John was looking for The Few.[33]

Further, John didn't just tell people to repent,. Instead, he gave them specific examples of the kinds of things they needed to change in order to prepare for the Messiah's arrival.

> **"What should we do then?" the crowd asked. John answered, "The man with two tunics should share with him who has none, and the one who has food should do the same." Tax collectors also came to be baptized. "Teacher," they asked, "what should we do?" "Don't collect any more than you are required to," he told them. Then some soldiers asked him, "And what should we do?" He replied, "Don't extort money and don't accuse people falsely – be content with your pay." (Luke 3:10-14)[34]**

Forerunners are intense, and they intensely want to see everything cleaned up for the Living God. No exceptions. Everything. Thus, as John did, forerunners will surely always step on someone's toes...and suffer the consequences for doing so.

> **And with many other words John exhorted the people and preached the Good News to them. But when John rebuked Herod the tetrarch because of Herodias, his brother's wife, and all the other evil things he had done, Herod added this to them all: He locked John up in prison. (Luke 3:18-20)**

And in John's call to people, Jewish people, to repent, he demanded that they express their repentance with a unique and offensive-to-Jews public action, that of being immersed in water. This was not a Law of Moses ritual. The Jews adapted it from pagan religions, using it exclusively on Gentiles who wanted to convert to Judaism.[35]

Therefore, John's call for people to be immersed in the Jordan was incredibly vulgar to his Jewish audience. In a sense it was like saying that they weren't real Jews, calling them to do something that ONLY converting Gentiles were required to do. So even though there was

---

[33] Jesus taught and practiced this same issue: Luke 14:25-35 and John 6:60-70.
[34] Did you notice that every one of these examples Luke lists of the kinds of things John told the people to do as evidence of their repenting has to do with money?
[35] The synagogue I grew up in had a men's and a woman's baptism pool in the basement of the building. They were always bone dry, and I never saw them used.

some interest in John and his message, not all that many people responded by stepping into the Jordan. It was just too humiliating.

And take note that John did not soften his message to get more people to respond. John did not concern himself that his message and call to be immersed in water offended people, and neither did he look at the lack of response...for there was only a minimal response to his message. He wasn't expecting a large response, so he wasn't disappointed by the few who did. To John, like Jesus, he was more concerned with quality than with quantity.

And this is one of the characteristics of a true forerunner's ministry and message. A true forerunner is not popular and he's definitely not seeker-sensitive. His message is just too intense and too demanding of REAL change. For example, a person I know about had a dream. At the beginning of the dream the person saw a large group of Christians all facing the same direction crying out from Isaiah 64:1-3.

Oh, that you would rend the heavens and come down, that the mountains would tremble before you! As when fire sets twigs ablaze and causes water to boil, come down to make your name known to your enemies and cause the nations to quake before you! For when you did awesome things that we did not expect, you came down, and the mountains trembled before you.

Then the scene widened, and the person saw a multitude of angels standing behind these Christians. And every time the Christians cried out for the Lord to "rend the heavens and come down" and to do awesome things, the angels would, in unison, point at the Christians and say, "Rend your hearts and not your garments!" (Joel 2:13). The Christians would repeat, "Rend the heavens and come down" and do awesome things, and the angels would, in unison, point at the Christians and say, "Rend your hearts and not your garments!"

Over and over and over this went, the message being crystal clear: Christians just praying words and not changing their lifestyles will have NO response from Jesus of Nazareth.

Fact: There will NEVER be any of Isaiah 64:1-3 without Joel 2:13![36]

---

[36] And if you are one of those who is praying from 2 Chronicles 7:13-14, you have taken this passage out of its context. This was a promise Yahweh made to Israel, who was under the Mosaic Covenant, which had blessings and curses related to the land. This is NOT true for those under the New Covenant. Further, the United States of America is NOT some replacement for Israel either.

Also according to Isaiah 62:10, part of my assignment is to "raise the banner." And the ultimate Banner is Jesus of Nazareth Himself, as in who He is and what He's about, as oppose to the many false versions of Him (Matthew 24:5, 23-24).

Therefore, this herald to The Church in this country that you are reading is calling ONLY those who claim to belong to Jesus to earnestly repent based on the fact that the One, True, Living God is HOLY. And being Holy, He cannot dial-down His holiness, not for Love, not for ANY-THING! And definitely not for Christians in this country who seem to think they're special and thus they can give themselves to whatever they want with no concern of any consequence, even worse, ration-alizing all sorts of worldly evil with various Americanisms.

Two men had the almost indescribable experience of being brought into the throne room of the Most High. And one of the main things they saw and heard there were these weird looking creatures who never stopped saying day and night:

Holy, holy, holy is the LORD[37] God Almighty!

These creatures were NOT saying, "loving, loving, loving," or even "merciful, merciful, merciful," or "understanding, understanding, under-standing," etc. But rather, "holy, holy, holy!" The foundational quality and characteristic of This God, the God of Abraham, Isaac, and Jacob, the God of Israel, the One, True, Living God, is that He is Holy. Before e-v-e-r-y-t-h-i-n-g else He is, He is Holy. Unchangeably, unashamedly, uncompromisingly Holy.

So, while according to SOS 2:4 His banner over those who are in fact part of His Bride is "Love," the banner over He Himself is "Holy, Holy, Holy." And as a result, His holiness has specific ramifications not only for the Lost, but ALSO for those who belong to Him, for He cannot compromise or minimize His holiness. For example,

Make every effort to live in peace with all men and to be holy; without holiness no one will see the Lord. (Hebrews 12:14)

---

[37] Remember, this should read "Yahweh."

For I tell you that unless your righteousness surpasses that of the Pharisees and the teachers of the Law, you will certainly not enter the Kingdom of Heaven. (Matthew 5:20)

No one means no one. The Pharisees' righteousness was mere religious formality at the worse and human morality at the best. Jesus of Nazareth expects actual heart-change in those who have the Holy Spirit. For Jesus' followers their form of righteousness is to flow from a pure heart, which is the main ingredient of the Messianic Covenant that makes obedience a desire of a person's heart. They are absolutely not to have a form of godliness but denying its reality (2 Timothy 3:5a).

So my assignment is initially twofold: to remove the "stones" and to lift-up The Banner, namely, Jesus of Nazareth who is Holy.

And while I don't know all the "stones" The Church in this country needs to repent from, I know some of them. And I don't know these "stones" because I'm just so smart and figured them out. I know them because Jesus of Nazareth showed them to me over these many years.

Peter tells us that judgment begins with the House of the Lord (1 Peter 4:16-17). So, once again, Jesus of Nazareth is NOT dealing with the general population of the United States of America. He is NOT dealing with the Lost...at least not yet, for He does not hold Lost people, who do not have His Spirit, accountable to behave in ways that those who have His Spirit are to behave.

Therefore, if you are involved with any of the "stones" I'm about to address, and you are not being disciplined for not repenting, then you need to seriously consider Hebrews 12:5-13, and especially the possibility that verse 8 is true about you.

And have you completely forgotten this word of encouragement that addresses you as a father addresses his son? It says, "My son, do not make light of the Lord's discipline, and do not lose heart when He rebukes you, because the Lord disciplines the one He loves, and He chastens everyone He accepts as His son." Endure hardship as discipline; God is treating you as His children. For what children are not disciplined by their father? If you are not disciplined – and everyone undergoes discipline – then you are not legitimate, not true sons and daughters at all. Moreover, we have all had human fathers who disciplined us and we respected them for it. How much more should we submit to the Father of spirits and live! They disciplined us for a little while as

they thought best; but God disciplines us for our good, in order that we may share in His holiness. No discipline seems pleasant at the time, but painful. Later on, however, it produces a harvest of righteousness and peace for those who have been trained by it.

I have a much older half-brother who was a surgeon. When I was just a little kid I asked him one day exactly what kind of doctor he was. Trying to help me as a little boy understand without being too technical he said, "I cut people to heal them." I was probably five or six years old when he told me that, and I've never forgotten it. His statement has more meaning to me today than it did then, for it is a perfect descript-tion of what forerunners are called to do: cut people's consciences with conviction to heal them.

In Jesus' day the people too struggled with the repent-message, and He addressed this in Matthew, chapter eleven.

He told them that when John came preaching they all thought he was singing a dirge, a sad, heavy song no one likes to hear. Many also even thought John was demonized! Jesus then said that He came preaching the same message (i.e. repent, for the Kingdom is at hand), but that He did so with a seemingly happier song, which the people also didn't like, also saying He had a demon.

Jesus' point? It does not matter what the tune of the message is, hard and heavy, cheerful and light, those who don't want to hear it are going to find fault with the message AND with the messenger. And this is how it has always been. Some hear and most don't.

And so, in all that follows my purpose is to help the reader heed and respond to the warning Jesus gave to HIS followers at the end of His presentation of the constitution of His Kingdom:

Therefore everyone who hears these words of mine and puts them into practice is like a wise man who built his house on the rock. [When, not if] the rain came down, the streams rose, and the winds blew and beat against that house; yet it did not fall, because it had its foundation on the rock. But everyone who hears these words of mine and does not put them into practice is like a foolish man who built his house on sand. [When, not if] the rain came down, the streams rose, and the winds blew and beat against that house, and it fell with a great crash. (Matthew 7:24-27)

STONE NUMBER ONE: TWO TREES

There is a night-and-day, black-and-white, godly-and-demonic difference between the Tree of Life and the Tree of Knowledge of Good and Evil. And these two trees do NOT mix, no matter how hard so many people try to mix them together.

It has been my experience that when I ask people what the names of the two trees in the Garden are, some will know the name of the Tree of Life. And while some know there was a second tree, not very many are clear about what it was called. So they may say the name of the second tree either simply as the Tree of Knowledge, or they will say the Tree of Knowledge of good and EVIL, as if the good part of this tree is okay and that's it's just the evil part that's evil.

The truth is, as evil as the evil side of the Tree of Knowledge of Good and Evil is (although today even things that once were considered evil are no longer evil but considered to be good), the good side is even more so! Why? Because the good seems good. But the problem is, this tree's good is not the Living God's Good. It's Man's version of good.

And the problems caused by not knowing the difference have existed since Adam partook of this tree. When Adam and Eve decided that being innocently naked was evil and the good was to cloth themselves, when Adam and Eve decided that hiding from Yahweh was good and that being found by Him was bad, they were operating out of the Tree of Knowledge of Good and Evil, not the Tree of Life.

In Isaiah's day, in a list of curses ("woes"), he confronted Israel with their confusing of what the Living God says is good and what He says is evil with Man's version of good and evil by saying:

Woe to those who call evil good and good evil, who put darkness for light and light for darkness, who put bitter for sweet and sweet for bitter. Woe to those who are wise in their own eyes and clever in their own sight. (5:20-21)

Here's how Paul put it:

See to it that no one takes you CAPTIVE through hollow and deceptive philosophy, which depends on human tradition and the elemental spiritual forces of this world (i.e. the Tree of Knowledge of Good and Evil) **rather than on Christ.** (Colossians 2:8)

In this country there is a HOST of issues Man says is good and Man says is evil. And yet, in the vast majority of these the Living God says the complete opposite. Literally, the complete opposite! And this isn't happening just among the Lost, it is ALSO happening inside The Church.

For example, Man says homosexuality is good. The Living God says it's gross. Man says abortion is a woman's right. The Living God says its selfish murder. Man says divorce is okay for any old reason. The Living God says it is not. Man says Democracy and personal rights are what's best for mankind. The Living God says nothing about human rights but has a lot to say about human responsibility. Man says "natural" disasters are terrible. The Living God says He may be justifiably dealing with those people to bring them to repentance (e.g. Revelation 6:12-13 and 9:20-21). Man says always feeding the poor is the right thing to do. Jesus acknowledged that there are times not to feed the poor, as when they are missing the main point (John 6). And on and on and on and on the list goes.

As for inside The Church, in addition to many of the things I just listed, there is abundant theatrics and entertainment, the watering-down of the Gospel so as to make it appealing, the mixing of Psychology with the Word of God, Materialism galore, silly seeker-sensitiveness, Nazi-like Feminism, unbiblical Democratic Republicanisms, and on and on and on.

Similarly, all of the save this or that animal, or the walk, march, run, ride for the cure, the United Way, Habitat for Humanity, Red Nose Day, obsessive recycling to save the planet[38], climate change[39], etc., etc., etc. are all from the Tree of Knowledge of Good and Evil, that is, Man's version of good aimed at saving the world.

For all of these are done in the name of Man, not in the Name of Jesus, not just "g-o-d," but JESUS. Man's goodness, Man's compassion, and Man's wisdom are flaunted and publicized, glorified and adored, while Jesus of Nazareth is demeaned and ignored. The list of such

---

[38] What people are doing in this country isn't even putting a dent in the pollution problem due to what the people in China, India, and Russia are doing.

[39] This is not the problem some say it is. The pressure to make changes is rooted in greed, for most of the "solutions" are not solving anything, they're even making things worse.

47

things is virtually endless as Man seeks to make a better world WITH-OUT Jesus as their King!

The same Man-centered thing occurs inside The Church, as when leaders put on a good show in their services or do ministry without the actual Presence and power and the leadership of the Living God.[40]

And speaking of the power of the Living God: Why do the followers of Jesus of Nazareth seek healing from the medical industry and drug companies? All the very few references in the Bible to doctors speak of them in negative terms (e.g. Mark 5:6).

Why would the followers of Jesus waste their money on a pro-foundly overpriced medical profession which makes its people ridicu-lously rich? And don't get me started on the Drug Companies and their evil practices! The fact is the followers of Jesus seek out these worldly healers because Jesus doesn't heal them. What they should do is ask Jesus WHY He isn't healing them![41]

The reality is, if people, both non-Christians and Christians were honest, they'd say that Jesus of Nazareth is inept and impotent. And while SOME Christians would say out of their theology that Jesus is wise and powerful, they have little to no actual evidence of this, for He sel-dom if ever does anything among them that can ONLY be explained as the actions of the Living God.

For the message of The Cross is foolishness to those who are perishing, but to us who are being saved it is the power of God. For it is written: "I will destroy the wisdom of the wise; the intelligence of the intelligent I will frustrate." Where is the wise person? Where is the teacher of the Law? Where is the philo-sopher of this age? Has not God made foolish the wisdom of the world? For since in the wisdom of God the world through its wisdom did not know Him, God was pleased through the fool-ishness of what was preached to save those who believe. Jews demand signs and Greeks look for wisdom, but we preach Christ

---

[40] It irks me to see some local congregation outside of Wal-Mart or in some other setting asking the general public for donations. Why? Is Jesus of Nazareth unable to fund the things He wants to do? Maybe that congregation should consider the very real probability that Jesus is NOT in the thing for which they are seeking financial support.

[41] When the followers of Jesus are not manifesting the Power of Jesus that is NOT the time to turn to alternatives, to the things of the world. That is the time to get humble and to ask Jesus WHY this is. After all, The Church is commanded to heal the sick, cast out demons, raise the dead, and preach the Gospel... and all of that requires His Power! Otherwise, Christianity is just one more religion and philosophy among many.

crucified: a stumbling block to Jews and foolishness to Gentiles, but to those whom God has called, both Jews and Greeks, Christ the power of God and the wisdom of God. For the foolishness of God is wiser than human wisdom, and the weakness of God is stronger than human strength. Brothers and sisters, think of what you were when you were called. Not many of you were wise by human standards; not many were influential; not many were of noble birth. But God chose the foolish things of the world to shame the wise; God chose the weak things of the world to shame the strong. God chose the lowly things of this world and the despised things – and the things that are not – to nullify the things that are, <u>so that no one may boast before Him</u>. It is because of Him that you are in Christ Jesus, who has become for us wisdom from God – that is, our righteousness, holiness, and redemption. Therefore, as it is written: "Let the one who boasts boast in the Lord." (1 Corinthians 1:18-31)

The Greek word for "anti" in the New Testament most often means "no" and not "against" as most English-speaking people think. Thus, the meaning of the name "Antichrist" is "No-Christ." And that is one of the root issues of The Church's problems in this country. She has lots of theology about a christ, but no reality of Christ.

And as for the actual Antichrist, most Americans, including American Christians are going to LOVE this guy. Everything about him will be things Americans and American Christians value and worship. But, everything about him will be based on the Tree of Knowledge of Good and Evil, and with so much of what he will do seeming good, most Christians in this country won't recognize his good as not being the Living God's Good because they don't know the difference.

Because SO MANY followers of Jesus in this country have given themselves to the things of the Tree of Knowledge of Good and Evil, The Church in this country brings upon itself the deceptive consequences from its compromise with it and thus with the World to justify the obvious absence of His Presence being among them.

And even worse, there is a ton of unbiblical teachings permeating The Church that justifies, rationalizes, and condones so much of what comes out of the Tree of Knowledge of Good and Evil.

STONE NUMBER TWO: WHICH GOD?

My term for the kind of belief in a higher power that permeates this country, including most who claim to be Christians, is: Polytheistic-Monotheism. Which means: many versions of a god.

However, the God of Abraham, Isaac, and Jacob, the God of Israel, the One, True, Living God is NOT who and what a person wants to think He is. The God of Abraham, Isaac, and Jacob, the God of Israel, the One, True, Living God is who HE says He is as He has revealed Himself in the Bible (Genesis to Revelation only), and most especially in the Man Jesus of Nazareth (John 1:1, Philippians 2:5b-8a).

Humans may NOT come up with their version of a god, OR the God of Abraham, Isaac, and Jacob, OR Jesus. This is called idolatry, something MOST people in this country are guilty of...again, including those who consider themselves to be Christians.

Really, who doesn't believe that there is a higher power? The fact is there are very, very few true atheists. And while there are plenty of agnostics, one must work hard to deny the existence of Someone greater than humans. For Ecclesiastes 3:11 says that the One, True, Living God, the God of Abraham, Isaac, and Jacob, the God of Israel, the God and Father of Jesus of Nazareth put Eternity into the human heart. We ALL instinctively know that there IS a Person greater than us.

People wonder where He is or what He's doing, or why He doesn't solve some terrible issues that desperately need His involvement, or what He is truly like. But 99% of human beings know that there is a god, even one who will one day judge them. And yet, believing that there's a power greater than ourselves is NOT what the One, True, Living God is looking for. James wrote:

You believe that there is one God. Good! Even the demons believe that – and shudder. (2:19)

Believing in a higher power is not any better than what demons can do. In fact, demons know the One, True God and His Jesus of Nazareth by sight (e.g. Mark 1:23-24)!

In Hindu, Muslim, and Buddhist cultures people know who a person means when they refer to a deity. But in this country with the plethora of versions of a "god," very few who say "god" are talking about THE One, True, Living God, the God of Abraham, Isaac, and Jacob, the God of Israel, the God and Father of Jesus of Nazareth...even if they claim to be.

And in this Christianized country there are also a plethora of Jesuses. There's the American Jesus, the American Dream Jesus, the Hippie Jesus, the Country-Western Jesus, the Republican Jesus, the Democrat Jesus, the Conservative Jesus, the Liberal Jesus, the Psychology Jesus, each denomination's version of a Jesus, the Black Jesus, the Caucasian Jesus, the Jesus who looks like a woman with a beard, and on and on and on and on and on!

Truly, there is an ocean of false versions of a god in this country, even among those who claim to belong to The Jesus.

The biblical truth is that The God is specific about who He is, and thus He is quite deliberate about identifying and describing Himself.

So, when people use the word "god," who do they mean? "One nation under god." Which god? "In god we trust." Which god? "God bless the United States." Which god?

The English word "god" simply means a "higher power." The Hebrew word *"el"* also means a "higher power." The Greek word *"theos"* also means a "higher power." So the Living God's name is NOT "god." "God" is what He is – a higher power, and in The God's case He is The Most High Higher Power.

So in this country, which god are people talking about? Are they talking about the Baptist god? The Catholic god? The Charismatic god? This person's version of a god? That person's version of a god? Which God? Saying "god" does not clearly identify which god one is referencing, for even the Living God acknowledges there are lots of gods.

I am the LORD (Yahweh)[42] **your God, who brought you out of Egypt, out of the land of slavery. You shall have no other gods**

---

[42] In English translations of the Old Testament the publishers capitalize the word "lord" (LORD) to indicate that in the Hebrew text it is the name "Yahweh." Thus, it is easy to see that the writers of the Hebrew Scriptures were being VERY specific about who and which god they were talking about.

before me (meaning there are other higher powers to choose from). (Exodus 20:2-3)

So it's like this: Say a young boy bursts into a room where there is a men's meeting going on. And let's say that most of these men are fathers. When the young boy yells out, "Dad! I need you!", there is some confusion, for all these fathers turn to see who is calling for them. The boy sees his mistake, his lack of clarity as to which dad he needs, so he says, "Gary Kuntz! I need you!" Now he is identifying WHICH father/dad he's talking about.

In this country people capitalize the word "god," but we don't know which god they are referencing. For the Living God's name is not "God." G-o-d is what He is – a higher power. Just as I am a dad and my children call me "Dad," I still have a name and it's not "Dad." And this is EXACTLY the case in Genesis to Malachi. These writers were VERY specific about which higher power (i.e. god) they were talking about.

The One, True, Living God has been crystal clear about who He is, even specifically identifying Himself with specific names. He has NOT been vague or general in this. He is NOT simply "god." Thus, believing there is a higher power, even just one higher power, as James asserted, is NOT enough. Hell is full of people who believed in a higher power while living in this life. Why, they may even have prayed to their higher power, maybe even served him in some way. And yet, because they had the wrong higher power, they're now in Hell.

––––––––––

Although I'm going to use names such as "the Living God" or "Jesus of Nazareth" it is still virtually impossible to have clarity with the reader about which higher power I'm talking about.

So maybe I can say it like this: I'm NOT talking about the American higher power, the higher power of the founding fathers, the higher power of Money, the higher power of the American Dream, the higher power of Psychology, etc., etc., etc. And I'm certainly not talking about the higher powers or Jesuses of various pseudo-Christians cults such as the Mormons and Jehovah Witnesses. As for Jesus, I'm NOT talking about any denomination's filtered and infected version of Jesus[43], or

---

[43] i.e. Jesus of Nazareth is not a baby in a manger or a dead, broken man on a cross. Neither is Jesus of Nazareth powerless and in need of men's help. Neither is Jesus of Nazareth all about "love."

Oprah Winfrey's Jesus, or the Republican/Democrat Jesus, or the Money Jesus, the Hippie Jesus, etc., etc., etc.

I am talking about THE higher power – the Living God, the One, True God, the God of Abraham, Isaac, and Jacob, the God of Israel and His Son, Jesus of Nazareth, the Jewish Bridegroom-King as He has revealed Himself in Genesis to Revelation. As Paul wrote:

> **But I am afraid that just as Eve was deceived by the serpent's cunning, your minds may somehow be led astray from your sincere and pure devotion to Christ. For if someone comes to you and preaches a Jesus other than the Jesus we preached, or if you receive a different spirit from the Spirit you received, or a different gospel from the one you accepted, <u>you put up with it easily enough</u>.** (2 Corinthians 11:3-4)[44]

There are MANY examples of how Polytheistic-Monotheism gets expressed in this country.

For example, one of the founders of Alcoholics Anonymous saw a bright light. He's not the first to give such a testimony. But he never tells us the name of this light. Paul encountered a bright light on the road to Damascus that blinded him and knocked him to the ground. His testimony (Acts 9:3-5) is that when he asked the name of this light, and the light identified itself as Jesus of Nazareth.[45]

Seeing a bright light is not proof that one is experiencing the Living God. It IS proof of encountering a higher power though. The question is: Which higher power (2 Corinthians 11:14)?[46] So as in AA, in this country and in The Church in this country there is plenty of talk about a god. The problem is, which god?

When Moses came before Pharaoh he began by telling Pharaoh that Yahweh, the God of Israel, had sent him with a message (Exodus

---

[44] Marcionism taught there were two gods, the OT god who was mean and the NT god who was nice, as if Jesus had no standards of holiness and Yahweh didn't love Israel.

[45] Another example of Satan appearing as an angel of light is the book, <u>Saved by the Light: The True Story of a Man Who Died Twice and the Profound Revelations He Received</u> and <u>Secrets of the Light: Lessons from Heaven</u>, both by Dannion Brinkley.

[46] I have no doubt that Joseph Smith, the founder of Mormonism, experienced an angel with an ironic name (Moroni which is close to the word "moron"). However, because this angel presented a different Gospel and overall message than that of the Apostles (Galatians 1:8-9), I have no doubt this was a demonic angel (i.e. a demon).

5:1). Pharaoh must have said, "Yahweh? Who's Yahweh? Never heard of him." You see, Pharaoh was no atheist. He was a polytheist! He believed in many gods! He just had never heard about this Yahweh god.

But even more, Pharaoh had absolutely no fear or even concern about Israel's god, Yahweh, after all they had been Egypt's slaves for four hundred years. Surely this Yahweh god must not only not care about his worshippers, but he also must be rather wimpy and even afraid of Egypt's gods.

So, Moses is being exact and purposeful about who and which god he was speaking for. Moses is talking about Yahweh, the god who is Israel's god. In fact, even Israel had to be told which god was finally coming to their rescue. Moses informed them that the god who had appeared to Abraham, Isaac, and Jacob as the god Almighty is now revealing Himself as Yahweh, the god who is Always.

> **God also said to Moses, "I am the LORD.[47] I appeared to Abraham, to Isaac, and to Jacob as God Almighty, but by my name the LORD, I did not make myself known to them. I also established my covenant with them to give them the land of Canaan, where they lived as aliens. Moreover, I have heard the groaning of the Israelites, whom the Egyptians are enslaving, and I have remembered my covenant. Therefore, say to the Israelites: 'I am the LORD, and I will bring you out from under the yoke of the Egyptians. I will free you from being slaves to them, and I will redeem you with an outstretched arm and with mighty acts of judgment. I will take you as my own people, and I will be your God. Then you will know that I am the LORD your God, who brought you out from under the yoke of the Egyptians. And I will bring you to the land I swore with uplifted hand to give to Abraham, to Isaac, and to Jacob. I will give it to you as a possession. I am the LORD.'"** (Exodus 6:2-8)

And as Pharaoh will learn, Yahweh, the God Almighty, the God of Abraham, Isaac, and Jacob, the God of Israel is NO wimp! From then on ALL of Egypt would know not only the name Yahweh, and not only that Yahweh is Israel's god, but also that He truly is THE God Almighty.

---

[47] Remember, in English translations of the Old Testament the capitalized "lord" (LORD) indicates that in the Hebrew text it is the name "Yahweh." So as you read this passage insert the name Yahweh wherever you see LORD and note how This God is being VERY specific about who and which god He is.

In the New Testament there is something similar going on in which the writers are being clear about who they are talking about.

People of that time knew that the god of the Jews was not one of the gods they knew. In other words Yahweh had no connection to Zeus. So this was a specific distinction about which higher power the JEWISH apostles were preaching about.

As for Jesus, the apostles spoke of "the Christ," the Anointed One, who was a Jew. So again, people understood the specificity of which higher power the apostles were talking about.

For many centuries in Western Culture we have lost such clarity when people use the word "god" or the name "Jesus." And yet, it DOES matter who and which god and which Jesus a person is talking about!

So try this: The next time someone says something about a god, ask them if they mean Jesus. MOST people are good with or at least okay with speaking of a god, but when someone dares to get specific – Jesus – watch how uncomfortable people get.

This isn't true all of the time in this mostly Christianized culture, but sometimes it is. This is why the next step is to have more clarity about what attributes a person believes about the Real Jesus.

For example, to believe that the Real Jesus is the author of the supposed blessings of the American Dream would be false, for the Real Jesus had much to say about money and materialism (as did other writers of the NT letters – e.g. 1 John 2:15-17), all of which was highly negative (e.g. Luke 16:19-31). So if you believe Jesus of Nazareth is the source of the material wealth of this nation...you got the wrong Jesus.

Or, to believe that the Real Jesus invented Democracy, you got the wrong Jesus. The Real Jesus invented Monarchy. The pagan, perverted, pompous Greeks who thought themselves to be SO wise invented Democracy. And as the Real Jesus said, one can tell a tree by its fruit, and one of the pieces of fruit from the Tree of Knowledge of Good and Evil is Democracy. While this offends many Americans, THE JESUS said that a bad tree CANNOT – as in being unable – produce good fruit. And the Greeks absolutely were a bad tree!

Or, to believe that the Real Jesus is into Psychology, such as Self-Esteem, is an indication one has the wrong Jesus. The Real Jesus never, not one time, ever preached about the need for Self-Esteem. According to Psychology, Self-Esteem is one of the most important things a person needs to be a "healthy" human being. And yet, the One who created human beings, the Son of God, Jesus of Nazareth (John 1:3 & Colossians 1:16-17), never teaches this, much less even refers to it. Psychology is from the Tree of Knowledge of Good and Evil, not the Tree of Life (1 Corinthians 1:19-20, 25).

As important as it was in the days of the writers of the New Testament, today intimately knowing the Right Jesus is absolutely critical! For as this Jesus said, most people are going to be deceived by the plethora of false versions and false teachings about Him.[48]

One of the many causes for all this confusion about a god and a Jesus in this country is due to something most Americans, even most American Christians, believe is a good thing: Freedom of Religion. Freedom of Religion, among some other infections, has muddy the waters. For when there is no freedom of Religion, when the true followers of Jesus of Nazareth are persecuted...THEN we get clarity.

For example, the undeniable fact is that the god Americans believe in does not judge people based on Jesus' sacrifice.

So, in the movie, "Lone Survivor," did the three men who were killed by the Taliban go to Heaven? Did Chris Kyle of "American Sniper" fame who was a brave hero, a loving husband, a caring father, and a good guy go to Heaven when he was murdered? Did the Muslims these men killed go to Heaven?

MOST people living in this country, even many who consider themselves to be Christians, believe that of course these Americans went to Heaven because they're good Americans and thus good people, and of course the Muslims went to Hell, not because they're Muslims and not Christians, but because they were bad.

A biblical fact: If these men, as well as the Muslims they killed, were not correctly connected to the Real Jesus, they are all in the same Hell...no matter how good, how patriotic, and how religious they were.[49] Freedom of Religion would balk at this statement, for what Freedom of

---

[48] Matthew 24:5, 24

[49] In case you don't know this, NO ONE can be measured by their goodness or good deeds, for whatever "good" deeds an unregenerated by the Holy Spirit person does, they are the "good" from the Tree of Knowledge of Good and Evil and thus do not count. Isaiah put it this way: **All of us have become like one who is unclean, and all our righteous acts are like filthy rags.** (64:6a)

Religion ultimate wants is first tolerance of all religions and then one world religion for everyone.

Of course, the faithful followers of Jesus of Nazareth are not going to accept this, and as a result, the Freedom of Religion faithful will persecute these people. How ironic.

———————

The lack of crystal-clear clarity of which god is being spoken of in American culture is bad. But when there's confusion as to which god and which Jesus The Church in this country is talking about, THAT is beyond sad! It's shameful really as it exposes the terribly broken condition of the Bride in this country: She does not know her Husband!

And there are numerous reasons why people who attend "church" do not know the God of Abraham, Isaac, and Jacob, the God of Israel, the Living God, the God and Father of Jesus of Nazareth. One foundational reason is people giving themselves to what I call Churchianity instead of Apostolic Christianity.

What is Churchianity?

Churchianity is an entity that is considered to be Christian because it has SOME Christian elements. But, Churchianity is something that has compromised, secularized, modernized, politicized, materialized, and rationalized the basic and foundational elements of what the Apostles preached and taught and for which they were martyred.

In short, Churchianity, while presenting itself as Christianity that appeals to all people, minimizes the plain and simple teachings of the Word of God, mixing them even with numerous philosophies of the World in order to draw large crowds.

In fact, Churchianity measures its presumed success with size.[50] It even goes as far as to idolize its superstar human leaders, which have far more in common with the "super apostles" than with the apostle Paul. It uses technology to impress people, as if powerful sound systems and astounding visuals are the same things as having the actual Presence of the Living God.

What goes on in Churchianity is NOT the same thing as what Apostolic Christianity is about. Here is just one simple example: Those who are pursuing Jesus of Nazareth are hated. No one who participates in

---

[50] Jesus of Nazareth does not measure His version of success with quantity. He measures success by quality. See Matthew 7:13-14; John 6, Luke 14:25-35.

Churchianity would ever be persecuted for what they're doing, for what they're doing has very much in common with what the World is doing.

And yet, here's the biblical truth: If the World likes you...you are not following Jesus of Nazareth.[51]

In short, the World LOVES Churchianity. Churchianity fits the World and the religions of the world quite well, for it is more "enlightened," more "accepting," more "loving," etc. Churchianity does not have the "old fashion" ways and concepts of Apostolic Christianity (e.g. Sin and the absolute need for Jesus of Nazareth on HIS terms). Churchianity is more flexible and not so "hard-lined."[52] It's up to date with modern technology and modern messages for modern people. Etc.

In Paul's second letter to Timothy he stoutly warned what would be the condition of people in the Last Days:

But mark this: There will be terrible times in the Last Days. People will be lovers of themselves, lovers of money, boastful, proud, abusive, disobedient to their parents, ungrateful, unholy, without Love, unforgiving, slanderous, without self-control, brutal, not lovers of the good, treacherous, rash, conceited, lovers of pleasure rather than lovers of God – having a form of godliness but denying its power. (3:1-5a)

While this will certainly be the condition of all Lost people in the Last Days, the truth is that there will also be plenty of these exact same issues in those involved with Churchianity, the most basic of which will be having a **"form of godliness but denying its power."**

As I said, those who are living life as per Apostolic Christianity on the other hand are hated. Jesus said so, several times even!

Blessed are those who are persecuted because of righteousness, for theirs is the Kingdom of Heaven. Blessed are you when people insult you, persecute you, and falsely say all kinds of evil against you because of me (what Jesus of Nazareth stands for, His standards, requirements, and demands of those who want to follow Him). **Rejoice and be glad, because great is your reward in Heaven, for in the same way they persecuted the prophets who were before you.** (Matthew 5:10-12)

---

[51] Matthew 10:22, 24-25; John 15:18-25.
[52] Which is why **"If anyone loves the world, the Love of the Father is not in him"** (1 John 2:15b).

Bottom-line: Anyone who is not connected to Jesus of Nazareth in the way He says one must be, that person does not know the One, True, Living God. They may believe in a god, but they are NOT connected to The God.

For my (Jesus') **Father's will is that everyone who looks to the Son and believes in Him shall have Eternal Life, and I** (Jesus) **will raise them up at the Last Day.** (John 6:40)

Jesus said to them, "If God were your Father, you would love me, for I have come here from God. I have not come on my own; God sent me." (John 8:42)

I (Jesus) **and the Father are one.** (John 10:30)

Jesus answered, "I am the Way and the Truth and the Life. No one comes to the Father except through me." (John 14:6)

No one who denies the Son (Jesus) **has the Father; whoever acknowledges the Son has the Father also.** (1 John 2:23)

———————————

STONE NUMBER THREE: THE ACTUAL PRESENCE

———————————

Probably THE most important thing Moses ever said, among all the very important things he said, is this:

If your Presence does not go with us, do not send us up from here. How will anyone know that you are pleased with me and with your people unless you go with us? What else will distinguish me and your people from all the other people on the face of the earth?" (Exodus 33:15-16)[53]

———————————

[53] Immanuel means "God with US," not "GOD with us," or "God WITH us."

Every religion has buildings, music, holy writings, good deeds, expressions of love and kindness, morals, etc. So what ultimately distinguishes the born-again by the Spirit followers of Jesus of Nazareth from ALL the other religions?

Just one Thing.

The actual Presence of the Living God actually in and among His people. This is one of the MAJOR characteristics and benefits of the Messianic Covenant (Jeremiah 31:33; Ezekiel 11:19; Joel 2:28-29). And yet, amazingly and sadly, in this country He is clearly and obviously missing from the VAST majority of Christian's lives, as well as from the congregations they attend. For a few this reality is apparent. For most, no one even notices...or seems to care.

Moses isn't talking about having the theology of This God's Presence. Neither is he referring to This God's omnipresence. And the issue is not solved simply by people "believing" He's present. Moses is talking about the actual, felt, experienced, real Presence of the Living God. The very real reality that the Presence is vacant in The Church in this country is one reason people don't know the Living God, for they have never been around Him, substituting theatrical entertainment, or religious ritual, or mere informational knowledge (i.e. Bible teaching) for having His Presence in their services as well as in their personal lives.

———————

When Jesus said that where two or more are gathered in His Name (Matthew 18:20), He was not providing a formula to having His Presence.[54] Neither is Jesus guaranteeing His Presence just because the people gathered are Christians. For what goes on in LOTS of "Christian" gatherings all over this country has more in common with Ishmael (man's doings) than with Isaac (God's doings)...and Jesus of Nazareth WILL NOT give His approval to such things by being present.

In fact, just the opposite is true. His obvious vacancy is supposed to convict His people. His people should wonder why He's not among them doing what He does. But as I've said, sadly, very few know the difference or care. Once a person knows the difference, he or she cannot go back, for he or she cannot be satisfied or mollified, pacified or placated by the emptiness and silliness and showiness of Churchianity.

---

[54] In fact, there are NO formulas to Apostolic Christianity.

MOST of what goes on in this country that is called "Christian" reminds me of the scene in the movie "The Wizard of Oz" when Dorothy and the gang first enter the beautiful, awe inspiring sanctuary of the Great Oz. They're amazed at the grandeur and become quite religious. But what's going on is nothing more than a good show, an impressive production put on by a man.

People, even those claiming to belong to Jesus of Nazareth, are easily attracted to the show of religion, which is much easier to have than the Presence of Jesus. Listen to what Jesus said:

I know your deeds (The Church in Sardis); **you have a reputation of being alive, but you are dead. Wake up! Strengthen what remains and is about to die, for I have found your deeds unfinished in the sight of my God. Remember, therefore, what you have received and heard; hold it fast, and repent. But if you do not wake up, I will come like a thief, and you will not know at what time I will come to you.** (Revelation 3:1b-3)[55]

Alas, Christians in this country being SO long without the actual Presence of Jesus, or more likely, having never even experienced His actual Presence, have NO idea what they're missing. Fact: There is a gigantic difference between eating the Bread of Heaven and being fed Twinkies; there is also a great difference between taking long life-giving drafts of the Living Water and gulping Kool-Aid.

And in case you may misunderstand, I'm NOT talking about the difference between being charismatic and traditional. For every flavor of Christianity is devoid of the Presence of Jesus, preferring the Wide, Easy Way instead of the Narrow, Difficult Way.

———————

Further, when it comes to ministry Jesus commanded, not suggested, His followers preach the Gospel, heal the sick, cast out demons, and raise the dead, to name just a few things. These are demonstrations that are supposed to back-up the proclamation of the Gospel.

How do people know that the Good News that the Kingdom of Heaven is approaching and thus that they need to repent is true? Be-

---

[55] See Malachi, chapter one's good advice, for most should just shut the church doors and turn off the lights, for they're doing nothing but lighting false fires.

cause the kingdom of darkness is being abolished – people become followers of Jesus, as well as healed of diseases, set free from demons, and brought back to life in the Name of Jesus, all evidences of the actual presence of the Kingdom of Heaven.

Jesus of Nazareth is real. I mean really Real! Christianity is not a philosophy or a religion. Paul said:

For the Kingdom of God is not a matter of talk <u>but of power</u>. (1 Corinthians 4:20)

And yet, among SO MANY Christians and the church services they attend there is talk, talk, talk, and more talk. There's all this talk ABOUT the Living God, but nothing of the actual Presence of the Living God! Where are the realities of the Presence of Jesus in Christians' lives and in their congregations across this country?

––––––––

Some ten years ago or so a researcher named George Barna wanted to get a more accurate assessment of the condition of The Church in this country, so he did some extensive research using polling. He found some very disturbing yet illuminating things.

In his first round of research he found that 85% of Americans believe in Jesus, which includes plenty of people of other religions or spiritual beliefs, obviously. Well, that's nothing new. And yet, we all know that that figure doesn't tell us much.

So Barna went deeper.

In his second round of research in which he asked deeper questions he found that out of that 85% only 9% had a biblical worldview, that is, they knew some things from the Bible. But even with the big percentage drop, Barna sensed he was still not getting a clear picture of the condition of The Church in this country.

So he went deeper still.

In his third round of research he found that 4% of the 9% seriously sought to seek to follow Jesus of Nazareth, living life His way.

Assuming Barna's percentages, as with all polling, are off a bit, we're likely looking at a few million people in this country who are devotedly seeking to obey Jesus.

The next question to ask is: Would such a low number be backed up by anything in the Bible? Well...actually...yes.

Enter through the narrow gate. For wide is the gate and broad is the road that leads to destruction, and <u>most</u> enter through it. But small is the gate and narrow the road that leads to life, and only a <u>few</u> find it. (Matthew 7:13-14)

Note that I put the word "most" in this text. Here's my reason. The Greek word is *polus* which can be translated "many" or "most," with the context possibly indicating which word fits better. I believe the English translators chose the word "many" here because the idea of "most" just sounds too extreme.[56]

The thing is, the Jesus I know defines the word extreme! He is not one to soft-peddle something. He told people the truth, no matter how extreme it was. Thus, I believe Jesus meant "most" in this statement, not the softer idea of "many."[57]

And even more importantly, Jesus is NOT speaking to Lost people in Matthew, chapters five, six, and seven. He's speaking directly to HIS followers. This entire sermon, which is a presentation of the constitution of His Kingdom, is aimed at HIS followers (Matthew 5:1-2).[58]

Bottom-line: MOST, not just many, in this country have not chosen the Narrow Way. Instead, they have chosen the Wide Way that leads to destruction as evidenced by their choosing to live in compromise with the world, preferring Churchianity over Apostolic Christianity, and exchanging Jesus of Nazareth for some false version of Him. This is what Barna's research found even if the numbers are plus-or-minus some degrees of error.

---

[56] Compare the NIV translation of Matthew 24:12 with the NKJV translation.

[57] E.g. Most were destroyed in the Flood, and only a very few survived. Most were destroyed in Sodom and Gomorrah, and only a very few survived. Most of Israel was destroyed by Assyria, with only Judah and Benjamin surviving. Most of the Jews remained in Babylon (something of a prophetic example of the End Times and the impact the Harlot Babylon will have), with only a few returning to the Land. Most are destroyed by the three rounds of judgments in the Revelation. Etc.

[58] Jesus preached this sermon in a traditionally rabbinical way. That is, He stated His main points, of which He had eight (5:3-10). Then He began with the last point (5:10) and explains it (5:11-12). Then He takes the second to last point and explains it. And so forth as He works His way back to His first point (5:3 is explained by 7:13-14). Then he has some concluding remarks. Note that at the end the people were amazed at His teaching (7:28), not because it was new information or that He preached in a classic rabbinical fashion, but because He spoke as someone who was living what He was preaching about.

Need more information?

Okay, how about what Thom Rainer, president and CEO of LifeWay Christian Resources and the founding dean of the Billy Graham School of Missions and Evangelism at Southwestern Baptist Theological Seminary, wrote in his book, The Bridger Generation?

According to Rainer, of those born between 1927 and 1956, about 65% claimed to be Evangelicals.[59] Of those born between 1957 and 1964, only about 35% claimed to be Evangelicals. Of those born between 1965 and 1983, only about 16% claimed to be Evangelicals. And of those born between 1984 and 2006, only about 4% claim to be Evangelicals. And things have not improved since 2006.

First, this is a Southern Baptist, someone who is all about evangelism. He would love to report good news on the growth of The Church in this country, thus validating Southern Baptist church growth efforts. Secondly, Rainer's percentages are close to Barna's.

The actual reality of the situation is this: The Church in this country is utterly lacking the Presence of the Living God, and as a result MOST are living in Egypt along the River Denial about it!

STONE NUMBER FOUR: THE FEAR OF THE LORD

There were two initiations in biblical history in which the Presence of the Living God was profoundly manifest. The first one was when Israel began the process of taking her Promised Land. And as this began Yahweh told Joshua the following:

> **Be strong and courageous, because you will lead these people to inherit the land I swore to their forefathers to give them. Be strong and very courageous. Be careful to obey all the Law my servant Moses gave you; do not turn from it to the right or to the left, that you may be successful wherever you go. Do not let this Book of the Law depart from your mouth; meditate on it day and night, so that you may be careful to do everything written in it. Then you will be prosperous and successful. Have I not com-**

---

[59] To Rainer an evangelical is a born-again Christian.

**manded you? Be strong and courageous. Do not be terrified; do
not be discouraged, for the LORD your God <u>will be with you</u>
wherever you go.** (Joshua 1:6-9)

At its core, the taking of the Land was going to be a holy endeavor
because Yahweh Himself was going to be manifest among them (see
also Joshua 5:13-15[60]). And in preparation for this He had them conse-
crate themselves (Joshua 3:1-5). This consecration wasn't in preparation for battle, it was for being in the midst of the Presence of the Holy
God. Thus the warning, "Be careful to obey," for the Living God is Holy
and He cannot dial-down His holiness. Holy is what He is.

Well, everything begins VERY well. The walls of a formidable
citadel came crumbling down without Israel having to shoot a single
shot! Awesome!

However, one person – whose name we would never have known
if it weren't for what he did and the consequences that befell him and
his family – did one seemingly insignificant thing the Holy God forbade.
He kept a little of the junk of Jericho (Joshua 7:21a). And like Adam and
Eve, it wasn't merely that Achan disobeyed the Holy God, but that he
hid his sin (Joshua 7:19 & 21b).

Do you understand? The Holy God was right there! He is present.
Thus, He cannot – as in being unable – allow Sin to go undealt with...not
even for Love. It's not that Yahweh is being mean in what He commanded to be done to Achan and his family, it's that anything unholy
must be purged for the Lord is Holy.

Lest one might think this is Old Testament-ish, let's jump to the
second profound Presence of the Living God at the inauguration of The
Church as recorded in Acts.

Once again, the actual Presence of the Living, Holy God is actually
WITH them. And lots of wonderful things are happening. And as these
wonderful things are unfolding, Christians are experiencing the Living
God in such real ways that many of them begin to want to simplify their
lives and to express kindness to others by selling their possessions and
using the proceeds to help those who are in need.

Remember, the HOLY Spirit has been poured out. His Presence, His
HOLY Presence is actually right there WITH them.

---

[60] Ironically, this is the pre-incarnate Joshua (i.e. Jesus) son of David encountering Joshua
son of Nun.

Well, amid all this personal sacrifice, a couple – once again, people we never would have known their names if it wasn't for what they did and what happened to them – sell some property. Maybe they didn't think it was that big of a deal to say they gave such-n-such amount when they kept a little of it for themselves. And yet, Peter accused them of lying...to the Holy Spirit, not to him or to the people, even though their pretense of being generous givers was in front of people.

Once again, Ananias and Sapphira are hiding what they're really doing with a "little" misinformation. What they did wasn't all that bad, for it was their property and they had the right to keep some of the money from the sale if they wanted. It was their claim that they were giving more than they really did give that was untruthful. By today's standards FAR worse things go on in individual lives than what these two people did! And yet, as a result of their charade, the HOLY Spirit struck them both down. Again, not because He's being mean, but because He cannot dial-down His holiness. Sin must be dealt with.

———————

The lesson and the point is this: When Jesus' Presence is present He is Holy, for that is simply who and what He is. He cannot tweak this aspect of Himself. Thus, there can be serious consequences to what people may consider to be "little" sins. It's not that He demands Perfection, and He is willing to show Mercy IF a person is willing to confess his sins and repent. But, in the midst of the actual Presence of Holy God hidden Sin can be disastrous!

This is the Message we have heard from Him and declare to you: God is Light; in Him there is no darkness at all. If we claim to have fellowship with Him yet walk in the darkness, we lie and do not live by the Truth. But if we walk in the Light, as He is in the Light, we have fellowship with one another (the Living God and humans), **and the blood of Jesus, His Son, purifies us from all Sin. If we claim to be without Sin, we deceive ourselves and the Truth is not in us. If we confess our sins, He is faithful and just and will forgive us our sins and purify us from all unrighteousness. If we claim we have not sinned, we make Him out to be a liar and His Word has no place in our lives.** (1 John 1:5-10)

And notice that the result of Jesus dealing with His people like this was that the Fear of the Lord (a VERY critically important quality to have IF one wants to know the Bridegroom-King deeply) swept through the newly birthed Church (Acts 5:5b & 11), reminding the people that while the Gift of Eternal Life is free, holiness is not optional.[61] To have the Presence of Jesus requires certain things from those who would be around Him, namely, holiness. Not perfection, but honest holiness.

Some say that some people stress "grace" while others stress works. While this may be true, the Apostles stressed both. Every writer of the letters that make up the New Testament addressed the importance of righteous living...by Grace, that is, His empowerment. For example, James said it like this:

> In the same way, <u>faith by itself, if it is not accompanied by action, is dead</u>. But someone will say, "You have faith; I have deeds." Show me your faith without deeds, and I will show you my faith by my deeds. (James 2:17-18)

Paul said it like this:

> So I say, walk by the Spirit, and you will not gratify the desires of the flesh. For the flesh desires what is contrary to the Spirit, and the Spirit what is contrary to the flesh. They are in conflict with each other, so that you are not to do whatever you want. But if you are led by the Spirit, you are not under the Law. The acts of the flesh are obvious: sexual immorality, impurity, and debauchery; idolatry and witchcraft; hatred, discord, jealousy, fits of rage, selfish ambition, dissensions, factions, and envy; drunkenness, orgies, and the like. <u>I warn you, as I did before, that those who live like this will not inherit the Kingdom of God</u>. But the fruit of the Spirit is love, joy, peace, forbearance, kindness, goodness, faithfulness, gentleness, and self-control. Against such things there is no Law. <u>Those who belong to Christ Jesus have crucified the flesh with its passions and desires</u>. (Galatians 5:16-25)

And...

---

[61] See Appendix E

Do not be deceived: God cannot be mocked. A man reaps what he sows. Whoever sows to please their flesh, from the flesh will reap destruction; whoever sows to please the Spirit, from the Spirit will reap Eternal Life. (Galatians 6:7-8)

And...

What shall we say, then? Shall we go on sinning so that Grace may increase? By no means! We are those who have died to Sin; how can we live in it any longer? (Romans 6:1-2)

Jesus of Nazareth expects His followers to become like Him. And He is willing to provide the Grace (i.e. empowerment) to enable them to do that. For that is what biblical Grace is: empowerment on the inside to be holy and power on the outside to do ministry with the anointing of the Holy Spirit.

STONE NUMBER FIVE: THE TRUE GOSPEL

I am astonished that you are so quickly deserting the One who called you to live in the Grace of Jesus and are turning to a different gospel – which is really no gospel at all. Evidently some people are throwing you into confusion and are trying to pervert the Gospel of Jesus. But even if we or an angel from heaven should preach a gospel other than the one we preached to you, let them be under God's curse! As we have already said, so now I say again: If anybody is preaching to you a gospel other than what you accepted, let them be under God's curse! (Galatians 1:6-9)

For if someone comes to you and preaches a Jesus other than the Jesus we preached, or if you receive a different spirit from the Spirit you received, or a different gospel from the one you accepted, you put up with it easily enough. (1 Corinthians 11:4)

Obviously...the way a person is birthed physically has impact on his or her physical health. A healthy physical birth generally results in a physically healthy human being. The same is true spiritually. When a person is reborn correctly this has impact on the quality of their spiritual life. A proper spiritual rebirth has a better chance of producing a spiritually healthy follower of Jesus of Nazareth.

Fact: The Gospel has been changed not only in the Catholic Church but also in Protestant, Evangelical, and Charismatic congregations.

For example, many confuse the Living God's Mercy with His Grace. This God's Mercy is about not giving a person what they deserve IF that person repents. This God's Grace is giving a repentant person the power upon their heart to resist Sin AND to seek His righteousness. Thus, Mercy and Grace are not the same things.

> **For it is by Grace** (divine power upon the human heart) **you have been saved, through faith – and this is not from yourselves, it is the gift of God** (undeserved Mercy) **– not by works, so that no one can boast. For we are God's handiwork, created in Christ Jesus <u>to do good works</u>, which God prepared in advance for us to do.** (Ephesians 2:8-10)

The false gospel that is preached across this country allows people to feel that they are okay with the Living God even though they resist His righteousness and persist in deliberate Sin. In addition, people are told this is okay because God just loves them soooo much, as if love is the most important quality of The Living God.

So let's talk about John 3:16.[62]

There are some issues with this verse I wish to point out. First, all but one English translation translates verse sixteen incorrectly. Yes, incorrectly, as in not right. The second issue concerns who is speaking in verses sixteen through twenty-one. Then, there are some important resulting misunderstandings that need addressing.

———

I know only one English translation of the Bible, the Holman Christian Standard Bible, that even gets verse sixteen somewhat correct. Here's the HCSB version:

———

[62] I'm indebted to David Pawson's book, <u>Is John 3:16 the Gospel?</u>, and my Greek professor from Houston Baptist University.

For God loved the world in this way: He gave His One and Only Son [or "only begotten"]**, so that everyone who believes in Him will not perish but have Eternal Life.**

The first two words in this sentence in the best manuscripts we have of the Gospel of John are *houtos gar*.

The Greek word *houtos* means "so" and the Greek word *gar* means "for." So the sentence begins: So for loved God....[63] The word "so" is NOT modifying the word "love." Thus, it is incorrect to translate this as "God soooo (as in intensity or quantity) loved." That is NOT what is being communicated in verse sixteen.

The fact that the first two words in verse sixteen are "so for" (*houtos gar*), how would one smooth out that phrase in modern English? Wouldn't we say, "therefore" or "thus"? And that is EXACTLY the case here. The HCSB adds this footnote to their addition of the phrase "in this way":

The Greek word *houtos*, commonly translated in John 3:16 as "so" or "so much" occurs over 200 times in the NT. Almost without exception it is an adverb of manner, not degree (for example, see Matthew 1:18). It only means "so much" when modifying an adjective (see Galatians 3:3; Revelation 16:18). Manner seems primarily in view in John 3:16, which explains the HCSB's rendering.

Therefore, This God did NOT soooo love the world. Placing the word "so" to modify how intensely or how much He loved is incorrect. And translators know this. Why then don't the publishers correct this error? Simply because they know that they will lose sales of their Bible due to Americans thinking the correct translation is wrong, for people in this country are soooo used to hearing John 3:16 as God soooo loved.[64]

Here is a good English translation of John 3:16, which includes the verb tenses that are not clear in most English translations:

Therefore God loved (one time in the past) **the World and gave** (one time in the past, in a sacrificial way) **His only natural Son** (Jesus of Nazareth was a man) **so that all who believe** (go on

---

[63] Ancient Greek often puts the verb before the subject. In English we would say "God loved."

[64] And proof of this is in the reality that the HCSB is not a big seller.

trusting and go on obeying) **Him might never be ruined beyond recovery, but** (go on) **have** (-ing) **everlasting and abundant life.**

Secondly, if you have a red-letter edition of the Bible, verses sixteen through twenty-one are NOT the words of Jesus.

John stopped recording Jesus' conversation with Nicodemus in verse fifteen. Verses sixteen through twenty-one are John's words of commentary and explanation on what Jesus said to Nicodemus. And one piece of evidenced of this is the transitional phrase "therefore" of *houtos gar* that I just talked about. A.T. Robertson's Word Pictures in the New Testament explains:

> *Houtos gar* [so for]. This use is quite in John's style in introducing his comments (2:25; 4:8; 5:13, etc.). In verses 16-21 John recapitulates in summary fashion the teaching of Jesus to Nicodemus.[65]

But another smack-you-in-the-face obvious reason we KNOW verse sixteen and following are NOT the words of Jesus is also right there in verse sixteen.

It is the title "the one and only" (or "only begotten"). Jesus NEVER, EVER referred to Himself this way. Jesus' consistent title for Himself was the Son of Man. Jesus did NOT refer to Himself as the "the one and only" (or "only begotten"). But do you know who DID refer to Jesus as the "one and only" (or "only begotten") five times? John did.[66]

Next, many people in this country seem to think that John 3:16 is the ultimate message Lost people need to hear. And in thinking this they ignore the audience to whom John wrote this letter: to Jewish Believers, NOT unbelievers.

Jesus did many other miraculous signs in the presence of His disciples, which are not recorded in this book. But these are written that you may [keep on] **believe** [-ing][67] **that Jesus is the**

[65] See also AMG Complete Word Study Dictionary of NT and Vines Complete Expository Dictionary of OT and NT Words.
[66] John 1:14, 1:18, 3:16, 3:18, 1 John 4:9

Christ, the Son of God, and that by believing you may have Life in His Name. (20:30-31)

Further, when Christians begin sharing a gospel by telling unregenerated people that the Living God loves them, they are doing something that neither Jesus nor the apostles nor the early Church EVER did.

The telling of The Gospel does NOT begin with "God loves you," there are two words in this sentence that confuse an unregenerated person: "God" and "love."

The unregenerated person does not know The Holy God. They have what and who they in their unregenerated state think of a god. In other words, they have an idol. Additionally the best an unregenerated person knows about Love is some sort of human love, not Holy Love. Thus telling an unregenerated person that God loves them only serves to confuse them.

This is why the apostles never, ever told people that God loves them. Instead, The True Gospel, the one the Apostles preached, begins by confronting a person with the fact that they are a sinner (something even an unregenerated person CAN comprehend) who rightly deserves eternal separation from the Holy God. And the fact that this approach has fallen out of vogue due to our overly sensitive, politically-correct society should not change how The Church preaches the Apostolic Gospel. The Church is to tell people the truth, no matter how people "feel" about it.

And just to be clear about This God's Love, for there's lots of confusion about this even in The Church, let's look at it.

In English we have one word for Love: "love." So when I say I love my children or I love Five Guy's hamburgers, what does that mean? Do I love my children with the same love I have for Five Guy's hamburgers? Hopefully not! However, there is no way in English to know the difference based on the word "love." But in ancient Greek there are three words that express the idea of "love."

The first word is the word *eros*. *Eros* simply means passion, or love of the heart. Even though it is not used in the New Testament it is a good word, for Jesus has passion, LOTS of passion. And there's nothing wrong with passion, for what spouse, much less Jesus Himself, would want a relationship with a Spock-like robot?[68] Plus, passion is not only

---

[67] The Greek word is in the present tense, which means to believe and to keep on believing.

[68] Imagine a husband who comes home, presents his wife with a dozen red roses, and

love-passion, there is also anger-passion, something Jesus of Nazareth absolutely expressed on various occasions, for angry-passion shows that one cares deeply about something or someone.[69]

However, one downside to *eros* is that sometimes it wanes. Passion, or love of the heart, can have good days and bad days. It can be fickle, with ups and downs. Thus the writers of the New Testament did not think *eros* was a good general word to use for This God's Love, for although they knew Jesus had passion, what they experienced of Real Love from Him had more than just passion in it.

The next ancient Greek word translated "love" is the word *phileo*. This word is used in the New Testament.[70] This kind of love is love of the mind, and in English we tend use the word "like," as in we like somebody or something, which is a form of love. This Greek word is where we get the English word "fellowship," which entails hanging out with people we like and with whom we feel some commonality.

As good of a word as *phileo* is, love of the mind can also be fickle, for some days one may like a person, and then some days one may not like them. Once again the writers of the New Testament did not think *phileo* was a good general word to use for This God's Love, for although they knew Jesus liked certain things, as well as disliked others, what they experienced of His Love had more than just a form of liking to it.[71]

Then there's the ancient Greek word *agape*. The writers of the New Testament chose a Greek word that was seldom used in literature or common documents of the day, the word *agape*, which is love of the will, to express This God's Love. And I believe one of the primary reasons they chose the word *agape* was because it was NOT commonly used, thus it stood out as being different, which was what the writers wanted to emphasize about This God's Love: a love that was different from human love.

Some have said that the word *agape* means unconditional love. This is false. The phrase "unconditional love" is a phrase from Psychology; it is not the meaning of the word *agape*. The Living God's Love absolutely DOES have conditions – repentance and the right kind of

---

says, "Here. I read in a book that I should buy my wife flowers." She may accept them… and then beat him with them! Passion IS a good thing; passionless duty is what religion is.
[69] What spouse when finding out that their partner has been unfaithful, is calm, understanding even, as if that's the proper response of a healthy, loving person?
[70] E.g. John 21:15-17.
[71] For some of Jesus' likes and dislikes see His letters to the Christians in Ephesus, Pergamum, Thyatira, and Sardis in the Revelation.

belief, for example. In fact, Jesus gave a good example of *agape* in His parable of the Good Samaritan.

———————

Samaritans were half-breeds. They were part Jewish and part Gentile. They were the people who resulted from the removal of most, not all, of the people of the ten northern Hebrew tribes by Assyria. The Assyrians then brought people into that area from some other conquered regions. The Jews left behind intermarried with these Gentiles, producing Samaritans. Making things even worse, these Samaritans mixed Judaism with paganism creating a Jewish cult of sorts.

Thus to Jesus' Jewish audience it was shocking to be told a story in which the Bible teacher and the pastor, both presumed to be godly men, see this injured brother and yet looked the other way and walked right past him! And if that wasn't negative enough, how offensive it must have been to then hear that Jesus' hero in His story is a Samaritan, essentially a member of a pseudo-Jewish cult, who sees this injured Jew and steps up to help him!

One of the underlying points in this parable is that the Samaritan acted out of *agape*. That is, even though the Samaritan hated this Jew, and he knew the Jew hated him, he acted out of his will to do what this Jew needed. The Samaritan did not have love-passion of the heart (*eros*) for this Jew. And he did not have love of the mind (*phileo*), as in he did not like this Jew either. But as a charitable act of his will (*agape*) the Samaritan did what he knew this Jew needed.

———————

Translating *agape* with the English word "charity" is exactly what the old King James Version of the Bible does. And that is a good English word for *agape*, for the Living God does not have love of the heart for sinners, as in He just soooo loves them. Neither does He like sinners, as sinners are His ENEMIES.[72] Thus He hates them and the Sin they commit (e.g. Acts 12:21-23). It's not biblical to say, "God loves the sinner but hates the Sin."

---

[72] Romans 5:10; 1 Corinthians 15:25; Philippians 3:18; Colossians 1:21; Hebrews 1:13, 10:13, 10:27

Although Yahweh swore to never completely wipe out mankind as He did with the Flood, He IS going to purge the earth of those who refuse Him as their King. In fact, there are three rounds of purging.

The first purging is the period of time from Pentecost to the last three and a half years of This Age. During this period people have the opportunity to hear The Gospel of the Kingdom (Matthew 24:14) and The Gospel of This God's Righteousness (Romans 1:17) and to repent. Some will respond with repentance, but most won't. Those who don't will be purged.

The second purging is during the final three and a half years in which Jesus, the Lamb of God, pours out eighteen or so judgments (i.e. the Seals, the Trumpets, and the Bowls) upon the earth. Jesus' goal during this will be to reach the most people at the deepest heart-level to produce sincere repentance. Some will respond, most will not. Those who do not respond with sincere repentance will be purged.

The third purging occurs after a thousand years of Jesus' rule and reign on the earth (Revelation 20:1-3). Satan will be released from a prison and allowed to draw people away from Jesus. And there WILL BE people who will not like Jesus' kingship even after experiencing Him and His leadership for a thousand years. Thus, they will reject Him, and as a result, they will be purged.

To be crystal clear: Jesus, the Lamb of God, is giving people every opportunity to repent, to change their ways with the Holy Spirit's help, and to come under His authority as their King. Those who refuse will be tossed into the biggest crematory ever built – the Lake of Fire.

However...the Living God is willing to have *agape* (i.e. a charitable act of His will) to show undeserved Mercy to His ENEMIES who will repent and who will seek to obey Him because they LOVE Him, not just because they're trying to avoid Hell. In short, the Living God did for humans what He knew they could not do for themselves in crucifying Jesus. But, This God has terms and conditions as to a person accessing Him, His Mercy, and His Charity. And if a person does not accept His terms and conditions, that person is NOT accepted by this Holy God.

FOR THIS IS A RIGHTEOUSNESS-ISSUE, NOT A LOVE-ISSUE.

The Living God gave Jesus as a propitiation for Sin, not because He just soooo loved people. He did this in order to meet His righteous penalty for Sin – death. Certainly He understood that there is no way for ANYONE to make it without His charitable help but being charitable was not His point. Again, meeting the penalty for Sin was His point. For without such propitiation just being charitable would not have accomplished anything.

Why? Because Sin is a serious issue. No matter how loving, kind, merciful, or understanding Holy God is, He cannot compromise His Holiness by compromising with Sin. People's sins must be dealt with SO THAT it is POSSIBLE for the Living God to have a relationship with them.

This is the Message we have heard from Him and declare to you: God is Light; in Him there is no darkness at all. If we claim to have fellowship with Him yet walk in the darkness, we lie and do not live by the Truth. But if we walk in the Light, as He is in the Light, we have fellowship with one another (humans and This God), **and the blood of Jesus, His Son, purifies us from all Sin.** (1 John 1:5-7)

Certainly no one is perfectly Perfect.

But there is a difference between being a pig and being a sheep. And although both get into the mud...

The pig does so on purpose because he really does want the mud. Pigs seek the mud. Pigs live in the mud. Pigs love the mud.

Sheep on the other hand, when they get into some mud, which they sometimes do out of foolishness, they immediately know the mud is mud and thus a bad thing. So when a sheep gets into some mud they immediately begin to cry to the shepherd to come get it out of the mud. A sheep does not like the mud, want the mud, or considers the mud good in any way.

————————

It is This God's *agape* (i.e. undeserved Mercy offered as a charitable act of His will) that Jesus illustrates for Nicodemus in John, chapter three. Jesus does this when He refers to the bronze snake that was lifted up in the desert, saying that He too must be lifted up as a "bronze snake." In this one comment Jesus is pointing Nicodemus to the following lesson about Yahweh's Love found in Numbers, chapter twenty-one.

Here's that story.

The God of Abraham, Isaac, and Jacob, the God of Israel, the One, True, Living God had performed ten cataclysmic events – called plagues by the Egyptians, but miracles by the Hebrews.

Then This God provides His leadership to Israel with a pillar of fire by night and a cloud by day.

Then This God holds off the Egyptian army as He parts the Red Sea so His people can cross safely, then collapsing the walls of water to destroy one of the most powerful armies on the earth at that time.

Then Moses leads the people to the exact spot where he encountered This God, Mount Sinai, where This God marries Israel.

Then This God gives the people manna and quail, even water from a rock. But still the people are whining and wanting to return to Egypt, the World, and to the familiarity and stability of slavery.

Finally, This God's patience comes to an end. He sends hundreds, maybe thousands of snakes into the camp of Israel. Poisonous snakes. And the snakes are biting people – men, women, and children – and they're dying! And once the people realize this is a judgment, they run to Moses asking that he go to This God on their behalf and appeal to Him to stop the judgment.

Moses agrees to do this, approaches This God in the Tent of Meeting, and says something like, "Yahweh, the people are sorry. Would you please take away these snakes so that no more will die?"

Yahweh says, "No. Absolutely not!"

Moses must have said, "Uh...but Yahweh, the snakes are the problem. Can't you just take them away? The people are really sorry."

Yahweh says, "I said, no. The snakes stay. But here's what I'll do. Make a snake out of bronze, attach it to a pole, and go stick it on the top of that hill over there. Then tell the people that when, not if, they get bit by a snake, IF they look at that bronze snake on a stick and believe that I'll be charitable and show Mercy, they won't die."

Jesus' point to Nicodemus with this story?

This God does not owe anyone anything...except Hell. Everyone deserves to be bitten by the snake of judgment, to die as a result, and to be put out with the trash (Gehenna: a burning trash dump). THAT'S what everyone has earned and deserves.

However, as a charitable act of This God's will (*agape*) IF one looks to Jesus, the ultimate "snake on a stick," who took upon Himself what everyone deserves, and IF one then trusts that This God will be charitable IF they REPENT, This God will have Mercy (Romans 9:15-18).

So please hear this: This God's goal isn't to keep people out of Hell; His goal is to gather citizens for a Kingdom of Righteousness, and thus to have a pure, faithful Bride.

Jesus of Nazareth is NOT offering a Get-Out-of-Hell-Free Coupon and neither is He selling Fire Insurance for the Lake of Fire. These are NOT His offers. He IS, as a charitable act of His will, willing to forgive

Sin, to be charitable toward His ENEMIES, not because He's soooo in love with them or even likes them, but because he knows no one will make it if He doesn't offer His help.

However, His help comes with conditions, that of a person repenting and following Him, seriously seeking to live this life HIS way.[73] He knows no one does this perfectly, and yet He still calls people to seek to be perfect (Matthew 5:48)[74] and to seek to be great in His Kingdom (Matthew 5:17-20)[75].

In rebuttal to what I've just detailed there are surely those who would be quick to quote 1 John 4:8, affirming that This God is Love. Well, This God is Love...but...John says much more about who This God is in his first letter than the fact that He's Love.

John ALSO says that the Living God is Life (1:1-2, 5:11-12), that He's Light (1:5), that He's Faithful (1:9), that He's Pure (3:3), and that He's Righteous (3:7). Note that John makes three more references to This God's holiness than to His Love (Light, Pure, and Righteous).

So while it is true that This God is a god of Love, His Love is Holy Love. Everything, every quality and every characteristic about This God is founded upon the foundation of Holiness, not Love. Realize that there ARE things This God cannot do.[76] And compromising His Holiness is one of them. Thus, John 3:16 when translated correctly and explained correctly is wonderful. It's just not The Gospel in a verse.[77]

―――――――

How about yet another piece of shocking truth?

The word "love" is not in the writing called Acts, not even once. So consider this: Here is THE document the Holy Spirit includes in the Eternal Written Word which shows us the version of The Gospel the apostles preached...and the word "love" isn't in it AT ALL.

―――――――

[73] There is nothing in what I'm saying that ignores Ephesians 2:8-9. Just note Ephesians 2:10. Therefore, I am NOT preaching a gospel of works. I am preaching the same Gospel the apostles preached. The reason one may not recognize it is that the Apostolic Gospel has been watered-down into just "believing in Jesus," with not a word about repentance or living life in obedience to Jesus of Nazareth.

[74] The Greek word means to be mature, that is, to measure up to whatever one's level of maturity is and to keep on maturing.

[75] Note Jesus' comment about what happens to those who lower His standards, as well as what happens to those who seek to live up to His standards and then to teach others to do the same.

[76] E.g. Titus 1:2 (NKJV)

[77] Again, it says nothing about repentance or loving obedience (John 14:15, 21, 23, 24a, 15:10).

What does this mean?

Simply this: The apostles did not go around telling people that This God loves them. Why? Because:

But when Grace (i.e. Mercy) **is shown to the wicked, they do not learn righteousness; even in a land of uprightness they go on doing evil and do not regard the majesty of the LORD.** (Isaiah 26:10)

And there are at least two important reasons for this.

First, as I've hammered, The Gospel begins with the invitation to repent, to stop loving oneself, to regard the majesty of the Lord, and to turn to love the Living God (e.g. 1 Thessalonians 1:9b).

There are approximately 36,000 verses in the Bible. There are only about 36 verses which say that This God loves. But do you know what idea is FAR more often communicated in the Bible about Love? That humans are to love This God! Clearly Peter understood this, for not only did he NOT tell the people in his sermon on the Day of Pentecost that This God loved them, but He confronted them with their Sin, THEIR unloving act of murdering the Living God's Son (Acts 2:36)![78] The result? A critically important first step:

When the people heard this, they were cut to the heart and said to Peter and the other apostles, "Brothers, what shall we do?" (Acts 2:37)

In other words, the very first thing people need to feel when they hear The Gospel is the cut of conviction for their Sin, for their lack of loving the Living God...NOT that He loves them. When this critical part is removed from a gospel one is at best limiting the amount of Charity the person hearing a gospel will experience, and at worse one may be affecting whether the person is born-again by the Spirit.

When the "sinful woman" came bursting uninvited into a room full of men who had gathered to eat a meal and to have spiritual conversation with Jesus, then falling down before Jesus, weeping in brokenness

---

[78] Peter's sermon in Acts 2:14-39 is the first time the Gospel of Righteousness and the Kingdom is preached. In verse 38 Peter tells the people four things: 1. Repent. 2. Believe /Trust. 3. Be immersed in water. 4. Receive the Holy Spirit (which is evidenced by something bubbling up from inside them and coming out of their mouth in the form of tongues, prophecy, thanksgiving, or worship). Throughout Acts these are the four things the apostles were looking for, even if they were out of order. And if one of them was missing, that is the one they would focus on getting corrected.

over the wicked life she had created for herself, her tears wetting Jesus' feet, Jesus declared a PROFOUND principle. He told these "godly" men, especially Simon, the following:

...whoever has been forgiven little loves little. (Luke 7:47b)

The less conviction of Sin – of not loving the Living God – a person experiences when they are told a gospel, the less he or she will love Jesus and the less they will obey Him. The more conviction of Sin a person experiences when he or she is told The Gospel, the more he or she will love and obey Jesus due to realizing how VERY much Mercy He is extending to them.

The Living God gave the MOST valuable thing He had – Jesus. This SHOULD create even more of a sense of what a person's sins cost. So, DO NOT remove this part of The Gospel from people. It is critical to their spiritual health. And if they're offended by this step, then they're NOT ready for Jesus.

Secondly, the Unregenerated have absolutely NO idea what Real Love is. The ONLY way for ANYONE to know Real Love is to know the One who is Love. And the ONLY way to know Him is to know His Son.

When a person is willing to repent and to follow Jesus of Nazareth, and He responds to them with Charity, THAT is the very first moment a person experiences their very first taste of Real Love. Then, being born-again by the Holy Spirit, the Spirit begins the process of conforming the person into the image of Jesus of Nazareth (Romans 8:29). And one of the ways He does this is by leading the person through the maturing process in which the Fruit of the Spirit is formed in them.[79] And one of the Fruit is Real Love. Not human love, but the Living God's Love.

So, the Good News is NOT that This God soooo loves the world, or even that He gave His Son. The Good News is that although This God hates sinners and their Sin, which makes them His ENEMIES who He is going to destroy, He is willing to have Charity toward His ENEMIES...IF ...they are willing to repent. THAT is GOOD NEWS!

Trying to make a person feel good about being a sinner is just one reason SO many congregations in this country are primarily FULL of Lost people who go to church but have never been born-again by the Spirit. And one of the main reasons for this is this: People must get lost be-

---

[79] See Appendix D again.

fore they may want to be found and rescued; the Good News must begin with the Bad News, or else the Good News isn't good news at all.

Lastly, it's true, Jesus is a "friend of sinners." But there is a question in this: To which sinners is Jesus of Nazareth a friend?

The Pharisees and the Teachers of the Law did not consider Him their friend because they did not see themselves as sinners.[80] But the broken, those in-touch with their sins, those who knew they were sinners who needed help did consider Jesus their friend.

The issue which determines whether one sees Jesus of Nazareth as a friend or as a foe is the condition of the person's heart, not the softening of the Message.

And as for forgiving our sins, that is merely part – the initial part – of the process of making us fit for His Kingdom, fit to be His Bride. He then expects those forgiven people, those who have been shown such PROFOUND undeserved Charity to love Him and to obey Him, submitting to Him as their Bridegroom-King, seeking to live life His way.[81]

———

Now...once a person enters a relationship with the Living God through Jesus of Nazareth...THEN all the aspects of His Love begin to be opened to that person – passion, doing what's best for them, disciplining them, etc. For example, now it is possible for them to have what Paul prayed for the Christians in Ephesus to have:

> **I keep asking that the God of our Lord Jesus Christ, the glorious Father, may give you the Spirit of wisdom and revelation, <u>so that you may know Him better</u>. I pray that the eyes of your heart may be enlightened in order that you may know the hope to which He has called you, the riches of His glorious inheritance in His holy people, and His incomparably great power for us who believe.** (1:17-19a)

---

[80] Before Paul was confronted by Jesus on the road Paul did not consider himself a sinner (e.g. Philippians 3:4-6). After Jesus entered Paul's life he went through a thirty-year progresssive realization which resulted in him saying, **"Here is a trustworthy saying that deserves full acceptance: Christ Jesus came into the world to save sinners – of whom I am the worst. But for that very reason I was shown Mercy <u>so that</u> in me, the <u>worst of sinners</u>, Christ Jesus might display His unlimited patience as an example for those who would believe on Him and receive Eternal Life"** (1 Timothy 1:15-16). Paul focused on Jesus' patience with sinners, not His Love.
[81] See John 14:15, 21a, 23-24a, 15:10.

For this reason I kneel before the Father, from whom every family in Heaven and on earth derives its name. I pray that out of His glorious riches He may strengthen you with power through His Spirit in your inner being, so that Christ may dwell in your hearts through faith. And I pray that you, being <u>rooted and established in Love</u>, may have power, together with all the Lord's holy people, to grasp how wide and long and high and deep is the Love of Christ, and <u>to know this Love that surpasses knowledge</u> [mere information] – that you may be filled to the measure of all the fullness of God. (3:14-19)

Even MORE, listen to what Jesus of Nazareth asked the Father for those who rightly belong to Him:

Righteous Father, though the world does not know you, I know you, and they know that you have sent me. I have made you known to them, and will continue to make you known in order that <u>the Love you have for me may be in them</u> and that I myself may be in them. (John 17:25-26)

Jesus is working to reveal the Father to His followers "in order that" the Love the Father has for Jesus will be in Jesus' followers for Jesus! Wow! To love Jesus the way the Father loves Jesus! And this IS possible, for Jesus prayed for it.

IMPORTANT NOTE: Loving Jesus with the Father's Love comes from Jesus revealing the Father of Righteousness, not a god of love.

Okay, what is the Apostolic Gospel?

A simple way to see it is with the word "rubber," and then remove the two vowels so you have RBBR.

- R = Repent
- B = Believe/Trust
- B = Be Baptized
- R = Receive the Spirit

The very first time Peter preached The Gospel on the day of Pentecost, after receiving the Spirit himself, being born again and entering the New Covenant, he addressed all four of these steps.

"Therefore let all Israel be assured of this: God has made this Jesus, whom you crucified, both Lord and Messiah." When the people heard this, they were cut to the heart (convicted of their Sin) **and said to Peter and the other apostles, "Brothers, what shall we do?" Peter replied, "<u>Repent</u> and <u>be baptized</u>, every one of you, in the <u>Name of Jesus Christ for the forgiveness of your sins</u>** (i.e. Believe/Trust). **And you will <u>receive the gift of the Holy Spirit</u>.** (Acts 2:36-41)

Of the four parts to the Apostolic Gospel, being immersed in water (i.e. baptism) is the only one that is not mandatory, although it is important. Repentance, Believing/Trusting, and Receiving the Spirit are NOT optional.

REPENTING: While no one begins with perfect repentance, one should take this part of The Gospel seriously. In fact, in some cases, Jesus may expect a person to take specific steps to repent in which one does two things: turns FROM specific sins AND then turns TOWARD seeking to do what Jesus wants BECAUSE one loves Him. Zacchaeus is an example (Luke 19:8). If all a person does is simply acknowledge he or she is a sinner, but does not seek to want to love and obey Jesus, this is one of the reasons Jesus may withhold giving that person His Spirit, for He knows the person's heart and that he or she really does not plan to make any change, with His help, in their behaviors from living by the ways of the world to living life Jesus' way. This results in what can be called a spiritual "stillbirth" in which a person thinks they were born-again but have not been made truly alive.

BELIEVING/TRUSTING: While no one begins with perfect belief/ trust, one should take this part of The Gospel seriously also. For to simply "believe" in a "Jesus" without believing/trust Him and who He is results in what is called "Easy Believe-ism," which is NOT what The Jesus expects. The Jesus expects a person to believe who He is, and because they believe who He is, they want to trust Him with their lives. The person shows this trust in Him by how they then live to love Him and obey Him (James 2:14-26).[82]

---

[82] See again John 14:15, 21a, 23-24a, 15:10.

RECEIVING THE SPIRIT: IF one's repenting and believing/trusting are what The Jesus wants, He then responds by filling the person with His Spirit, that is, he or she receives the Spirit. One cannot "receive" Jesus because he is no longer here.[83] The Person one is to receive is the Person Jesus sent to take His place – the Spirit. The Holy Spirit is the foundation of the New Covenant (Jeremiah 31:31-37; Ezekiel 11:19-20a, 36:26-27). Without receiving Him, one is merely involved in some version of religious Churchianity. And when a person receives the Spirit something actually happens to them. In this experience in which a person receives the Spirit one of four possible things bubble-up from inside him or her and comes out of their mouth – some form of tongues, something prophetic, grateful thanksgiving, or spontaneous worship.

As for being baptized, this can be optional due to certain circumstances, whether immediate or postponed. However, this is a very wonderful thing because this gives the Spirit an opportunity to wash off of and out of a person some of the damaging consequences of their sins. Who wouldn't want that?!?!

STONE NUMBER EIGHT:
THE FIRST AND THE GREATEST COMMANDMENT

According to Psychology one of the most important things human beings need to be healthy mentally and emotionally is Self-Esteem. According to Psychology, Self-Esteem is CRITICAL to human well-being.

What baloney!

Never, not one time, did Jesus, the creator of human beings, ever teach on the need for humans to have Self-Esteem. If Self-Esteem is SO important to human health, one would think Jesus would have lots to say about this. But again, not even one time.

And please, do not reference Jesus' comment about loving others as we love ourselves as an example of Self-Esteem. First, Jesus says all the Scripture can be summed up with TWO commands – love the Living

---

[83] When John writes about **"to all who did receive Him, to those who believed in His Name"** (John 1:12a), he's referring to when Jesus was here and could be received, that is, accepted as being The Messiah.

God and then love others – not THREE commands, the third being to love oneself.

In other words, Jesus is saying that at the very least His followers are to take the love everyone most naturally has already for themselves and give that love to others. If anything, He's talking about Self-Denial, something He regularly taught as being an obvious characteristic of His healthy followers. And yet, no surprise, Psychology, as well as those Church leaders infected with the virus of Psychology, will insist humans need Self-Esteem.

————————

For Jesus of Nazareth, loving the Living God with all of one's heart, with all of one's mind, and with all of one's strength is THE first and THE greatest thing a human can do, even more than loving others, much less the foolishness of loving oneself. Loving others is important (i.e. 1 John 4:20), but it's still second. Loving the Living God is first and of greatest importance and is the foundation to EVERYTHING else in this life. It's the ultimate "key" to be a healthy human being, as well as a lovesick, faithful follower of the Jewish Bridegroom King.

So...how does a follower of Jesus of Nazareth grow in loving the Living God first and most? Well, it doesn't happen magically, as if all Jesus does is wave His hand over a person or twitch His nose like the witch in the old TV sitcom "Bewitched," and cha-ching, one loves This God first and most.

This God's Love, Real Love, the Love with which to love This God first and most is a fruit of the Spirit (Galatians 5:22a). And as with any of the fruit, growing in them is a process. And in this process the Living God has a part and the person has a part. The Living God won't do the person's part and the person can't do the Living God's part.

For example, how does a person acquire patience, a fruit of the Spirit? Simple: Jesus puts the person in situations which make them impatient and encourages them to choose to submit to Him. And in that choice to submit to Him the Spirit builds patience in the person. So, over time, involving situations that test a person's patience, the person learns to submit to the Holy Spirit, and as a result acquires the fruit of patience.

The same thing is true with Love...with a little difference.

The Scripture says that it's NOT that we love This God; it's that This God loved us first (1 John 4:10 & 19[84]).

So it's like this: The Living God reveals Himself and His Charity to a sinner. That person is overwhelmed by this incredible mercy he or she does not deserve. This experience then makes the person want to love Jesus back, which he or she does, even immaturely. Then Jesus expresses more of His Love – His Charity (*agape*), but also His passion (*eros*) and His liking (*phileo*) of the person – to the now born-again by the Spirit person, and they are blown away even more, resulting in an even greater desire in them to love Jesus back even more.

And back and forth this "dance" goes throughout the person's life. The more the person experiences and tastes Jesus' Love in all its forms (*eros, phileo, agape*), the more the person wants to love Jesus back. And without realizing it, just as fruit grows, the person grows in loving the Living God first and most. And then, secondly, again just as fruit naturally grows, the person WANTS to love others with this Love that they're getting from Jesus.[85]

Additionally, as with patience, Jesus will put the person into situations in which it's hard to love Him, things like suffering, losses, persecutions, etc. And yet, the Holy Spirit will encourage the person to keep loving Jesus of Nazareth...when it's HARD to love Him.[86] Just as Jesus noted that pagans can love those who love them, so is it with people who can love Jesus when life is going good and it's easy to love Him. But Mature Love is loving Jesus when it's HARD to love Him.[87]

And this is besides the situations Jesus puts His followers into in which it's also hard to love another person. These too help to develop Real Love in Jesus' followers, for the best kind of Love with which to love others is Real Love (which has both 1 Corinthians 13:4-8a and Hebrews 12:5-13), which can only be obtained from Jesus. But again, this expression of Love is secondary. Loving Jesus first is first. Doing the second commandment first is humanism, not godliness.

---

[84] Remember, these passages have the word *agape*, which is love of the will.
[85] Realize that Real Love, This God's Love has various expressions, sometimes it's tender (1 Corinthians 13) and sometimes it's tough (Hebrews 12).
[86] I was next to one of the big Hummer's at a traffic light. This Hummer had a lot of bells and whistles. When the light changed and the traffic moved I saw a bumper-sticker on its rear bumper that said, "I love Jesus." Sure he does, I write sarcastically.
[87] This is what I call the Weight Lifting Principle. The only way muscle gets stronger is by dealing with heavy weight. Do a thousand curls with a few pounds and all one will get is bored and tired. And so is the spiritual life with Jesus of Nazareth. For while His yoke is easy and light, the Way is hard and difficult. NOTE: there is much of this hard Love building in the process Jesus uses in the Song Of Songs.

Quite importantly, Jesus will never, ever force a person to love Him. He wants willing lovers, people who chose to love Him, not robots who are "programmed" to love Him. That wouldn't be honest love. Contrary to Calvin, people's wills were not impacted by The Fall. Their thinking and feelings were, but not their will. People ARE able to make choices. They have to be if Jesus is to be loved truly, and out of that love then obeyed willingly.

Even the Holy Spirit will not force a follower of Jesus to love Him and obey Him. Those who have the Holy Spirit can chose to love and to obey or not. Followers can choose to sow to the Spirit and reap life or sow to the flesh and reap destruction. I'm not saying that Jesus can't or won't press a person to choose to love and obey Him. But, He will not cross the line from pressing to forcing.

A willing lover is what Jesus is after.

No one, unregenerated or regenerated, is forced to do anything, especially whether he or she will love and obey Jesus. The willingness and the ability to choose to love Jesus first and most is what this life is all about. The question Jesus is seeking an answer to from every human being is not: Do you know that I love you? The question Jesus is seeking an answer to from every human being is: Do you love me?

The First and the Greatest Commandment is the foundation to EVERYTHING in the spiritual life with Jesus of Nazareth. Some people put ministry first, or family, or knowing the Bible, or a myriad of other things. But Jesus says that the first and the greatest thing one can do is the First and the Greatest Commandment.

Here is a fact: EVERY human being is very able to do what they truly love. In fact, we ALL always do what we truly love. Thus, others can tell what a person truly loves by how they live their lives. If a person loves Money, it's obvious. If a person loves this or that, it's obvious. If a person loves Jesus of Nazareth, this too is obvious.

Do not store up for yourselves treasures on earth, where moths and vermin destroy, and where thieves break in and steal. But store up for yourselves treasures in Heaven, where moths and vermin do not destroy, and where thieves do not break in and steal. <u>For where your treasure is, there your heart will be also.</u>

(What one truly loves is obvious.) **The eye is the lamp of the body** (what one focuses on). **If your eyes are healthy** (focused on godly things), **your whole body will be full of light. But if your eyes are unhealthy** (focused on worldly things), **your whole body will be full of darkness. If then the light within you is darkness** (worldliness)**, how great is that darkness! No one can serve two masters** (the Living God or the World). **Either you will hate the one and love the other, or you will be devoted to the one and despise the other. You cannot serve both God and Money.** (Matthew 6:19-24)

Love truly is a great power, for as I said, whatever a person truly loves, they are very able to give themselves to it, have plenty of time, energy, and discipline for it, and enjoy it. It is never a problem or a hardship, for the person loves it, whatever "it" is. Therefore:

Do not love the world or anything in the world. <u>If anyone loves the world, love for the Father is not in them.</u> For everything in the world – the lust of the flesh, the lust of the eyes, and the pride of life – comes not from the Father but from the world. (1 John 2:15-16)

As I noted above, there are approximately 36,000 verses in the Bible. There are only about 36 verses which say that This God loves. But do you know what idea is FAR more often communicated in the Bible about Love? That humans are to love This God!

While one needs to experience This God's Love first in order to have within them the Love with which to love Him, as well as the Holy Spirit who grows the fruit of Love in the person, loving This God first and most is absolutely critical to a healthy spiritual life. And this is possible, for Jesus ask the Father...

Righteous Father, though the world does not know you, I know you, and they know that you have sent me. I have made you known to them, <u>and will continue to make you known in order that the Love you have for me may be in them and that I myself may be in them</u>. (John 17:25-26)

———————————

STONE NUMBER SIX: MATERIALISM

Materialism: the true god of the United States of America, and one of the many gods of The Church in the United States of America.

Some of those who are in the Pro-Life Movement have said that the second largest abortion clinic in the world is located on the south side of Houston, Texas. They say the largest abortion clinic in the world is in Peking, China. I don't know if this is factual or not, but an illustration can still be made.

What is a fact is that not far from where this abortion clinic is located in Houston there is some property that could be purchased in which the "second largest" birthing center could be built. Other "second largest" facilities for such services as prenatal care, an adoption agency, daycare, employment help, etc., all staffed with top-notch professionals could also be built. And all of these could be offered to people at a very reasonable cost, and in some cases, free.

The question is: Then why aren't such Pro-Life ministries created?

The answer? No money.

Well, not exactly.

There is PLENTY of money just in The Church just in the Houston and surrounding area to do this, much less across the country, but....

While some Christians are willing to have the occasional prayer march asking Jesus to end abortion, the fact is that it is easier to pray and to march than to obey Jesus by denying oneself and living a fasted lifestyle, instead of living the American Dream, which would then free up financial resources to do what I just suggested.

In Jesus' day there was a similar example of the evil impact the god of Money had, and it was called "Corban" (Mark 7:11).

Here's the context: the Pharisees and the Teachers of the Law (i.e. lawyers), that is, the spiritual elite, confronted Jesus for not adhering to the Tradition of the Elders[88] and its interpretation of Moses' Laws on washings. To counter these guys Jesus brings up something – Corban –

---

[88] Today this is called the Talmud, a huge collection of rabbinical commentaries on the Law of Moses.

that they were doing that is a violation of SCRIPTURE, not merely relig-ious teaching and tradition.

Jesus points them to the Sixth Commandment which said to honor one's parents. And one way a person was to do this was to take care of their parents when their parents got old. Of course a person was to plan for this, sort of like setting aside funds for retirement. But what some of these big-time Bible scholars and spiritual elitists guys were doing was to declare these funds Corban, that is, "a gift to God."

Then here's something of what they would do. Let's just say they had $10,000. They would give the priest a $1,000 and they would give the Temple a $1,000. Bu the priest would record they gave $10,000. And the person would walk away with $8,000...and do NOTHING to help their parents! What wicked scoundrels! And Jesus knew they were doing this sort of religious-looking dung.

It's not that some of these guys Jesus is confronting with their Corban, their Gift to God, didn't actually give the entire amount to the Temple. And certainly, some of them even meant this as a Godly action. But, there was still for many the element of not letting one's left hand know what one's right hand is doing, that is, of giving in secret and not making a spectacle of what they were doing. Plus, they were still not taking care of their parents.[89]

So when the followers of Jesus of Nazareth march and pray but do not live His Kingdom's fasted lifestyle (i.e. self-denial and non-material-istic) so as to free up financial resources with which to help others in need, reflecting that they really do not care about the things of this world and do care about the agenda of the Kingdom, Jesus would say these people are hypocrites.

And...what about today? Well, here are some examples.

I know about a man who is a high-ranking person in his company and who has done very well financially with this company. Very well. He has his house, a lake house, and a beach house. He also has several especially nice vehicles, even some restored vintage ones. And he is seen by many as being a godly Christian. And while he may be a good guy, even a nice guy, what does Jesus of Nazareth think of his lifestyle? Does this man "need" three houses? Does he need these expensive vehicles? Did Jesus give this man his financial resources for his own personal benefit and pleasure?

---

[89] This is like what James is pointing out in 2:15-16.

Meanwhile, this man has an employee, a truly devout Christian, who does an incredibly important job for this same company. In fact, if it weren't for the job she does, a job that must be done perfectly, the company wouldn't make any money for anyone. And yet, her pay is quite pathetic. So while this man lives the American Dream, right in front of him is someone who lives barely above the poverty line, barely making it from paycheck to paycheck.

What's REALLY scary here is that there are MANY people who consider themselves to be "good" Christians in this country who see nothing wrong with this!!!

I know a husband and wife who are both pharmacists. Being involved in a modern form of sorcery (the Greek word for "pharmacy" means "sorcery"), they own their own pharmacy in a small northeast Texas town. And because they're the only pharmacy for some miles, they can charge pretty much whatever they want for the drugs they sell. As a result, they live very, very well in a big house on a hill...at the expense of sick people, even those on a fixed income who receive government assistance. And of course, they are perceived as being upstanding church members and respected citizens of their community.

I could give many, many, MANY more examples!

A grave and ominous warning from Jesus comes to mind:

There was a rich man who was dressed in purple and fine linen and lived in luxury every day. At his gate was laid a beggar named Lazarus, covered with sores and longing to eat what fell from the rich man's table. Even the dogs came and licked his sores. The time came when the beggar died and the angels carried him to Abraham's side. The rich man also died and was buried. In Hades, where he was in torment, he looked up and saw Abraham far away, with Lazarus by his side. So he called to him, "Father Abraham, have pity on me and send Lazarus to dip the tip of his finger in water and cool my tongue, because I am in agony in this fire." But Abraham replied, "Son, remember that <u>in your lifetime you received your good things</u>, while Lazarus received bad things, but now he is comforted here and you are in agony. And besides all this, between us and you a great chasm has been set in place, so that those who want to go from here to

you cannot, nor can anyone cross over from there to us." He answered, "Then I beg you, father, send Lazarus to my family, for I have five brothers. Let him warn them, so that they will not also come to this place of torment." Abraham replied, "They have Moses and the Prophets (i.e. the Word of God); let them listen to them." "No, father Abraham," he said, "but if someone from the dead goes to them, they will repent." He said to him, "If they do not listen to Moses and the Prophets, they will not be convinced even if someone rises from the dead." (Luke 16:19-31)[90]

Did you notice that this rich man was in the Abrahamic Covenant? In the watered-down theology of The Church in this country, this man "believed in Jesus," went to church, read his Bible, and did good things. He would have been a good American Christian. And yet, what he did with his money landed him in Hell.

Do those who claim to belong to Jesus of Nazareth in this country believe this would never happen to them?

Did you notice also that when this man asked for his family to be warned before it was too late for them, the answer he is given was that his family has the Word of God, thus they will have no excuse. Do YOU have a Bible? If you do, then you too will be without excuse concerning your living of the American Dream, your serving of the god of Money, and your treasuring of Materialism. Use whatever American excuse you want to "explain" living the American Way, just know that Jesus ain't going to buy it! (No pun intended.)

———————

There was once a senior pastor of one of the first-of-its-kind mega-churches here in Houston who used to collect vintage Ford Mustangs. He showed me the five or six he had had restored and kept in his barn, a building that was nicer than the little duplex my family and I lived in at the time. And he was quite proud of this hobby.

I'm also aware of a pastor of a congregation here in Houston who drives a yellow Hummer. Really, he needs a Hummer? And not the small one, but the big one! This leader likes to brag that he does not receive a paycheck from the congregation because he lives on the finan-

---

[90] Although the rich man is in Hell because of his American-like love of Money, if that idea is too extreme, then consider 1 Corinthians 3:12-15.

cial resources he made when he was in the business world. And he lives VERY well from these extensive resources.

And yet, IF it was Jesus of Nazareth who gave him these extensive financial resources when he was a businessman (and not the Devil to deceive him), He did NOT give these to him so he could live a luxurious American lifestyle. IF this man is a born-again by the Spirit follower of the Real Jesus he should have known that he is to live the fasted life-style of the Kingdom and to give MOST of what he made to help others. And if he didn't live such a lifestyle before he was a pastor, then he was absolutely NOT qualified to be an elder!

> **Here is a trustworthy saying: If anyone sets his heart on being an overseer, he desires a noble task. Now the overseer must be above reproach, the husband of but one wife, temperate, self-controlled, respectable, hospitable, able to teach, not given to drunkenness, not violent but gentle, not quarrelsome, <u>not a lover of money</u>.** (1 Timothy 3:1-3)

It does NOT matter to Jesus that this man is not collecting a pay-check from the congregation he's leading. What matters to Jesus, is the American materialistic lifestyle he's living and the resulting worldly ex-ample he is to those he's leading!

There are MANY other Church leaders just in the Houston area who live in some of the wealthiest neighborhoods in the city, some having chauffeur driven luxury vehicles take them to and from their plush offices, as if they're chief executive officers of their (not Jesus') church organization. Maybe their Bibles don't contain the following:

> **<u>...who have been robbed of the Truth and who think that godliness is a means to financial gain. But godliness with contentment is great gain.</u> For we brought nothing into the world, and we can take nothing out of it. But if we have food and clothing, we will be content with that. Those who want to get rich fall into temptation and a trap and into many foolish and harmful desires that plunge people into ruin and destruction. For the love of money is a root of all kinds of evil. Some people, eager for money, have wandered from the faith and pierced themselves with many griefs. But you, man of God, flee from all this, and pursue righteousness, godliness, faith, love, endurance, and gentleness.** (1 Timothy 6:2c-11)

Or maybe leaders today are unaware of Jesus' commentary and rebuke of the leaders in His day.

The Pharisees (i.e. leaders), **who loved money, heard all this and were sneering at Jesus. He said to them, "You are the ones who justify yourselves in the eyes of others, but God knows your hearts. What people value highly is detestable in God's sight."** (Luke 16:14-15)

Or, what about Jesus' sarcastic hyperbole?

Then Jesus said to His disciples, "Truly I tell you, it is hard for someone who is rich to enter the Kingdom of Heaven. Again I tell you, it is easier for a camel to go through the eye of a needle (which is impossible) **than for someone who is rich to enter the Kingdom of God."** (Matthew 19:23-24)

PLENTY of "serious" Christians in this country live a life that has MUCH more in common with the American Dream than with Jesus' Kingdom. To a vast majority of people who claim to know Jesus of Nazareth in this country, to live a non-materialistic lifestyle would be absurd, maybe even sinful...or worse...Communistic!

Besides the prolific individual abuses of money, there are also the abundant examples of individual congregations that spend MASSES amounts of money on buildings, payrolls, and utilities.[91] When Paul saw this "pursuit of happiness" based on materialism in his day, he said:

...as I have often told you before and now tell you again even with tears, many live as enemies of the Cross of Christ. Their destiny is destruction, their god is their stomach, and their glory is in their shame. Their mind is set on earthly things. (Philippians 3:18-19)

Is Paul being harsh? No!

Most Christians in this country see no problem with the American lifestyle, even believing it is proof of God's blessing, as if Satan wouldn't use the "blessing" of money to lead people off the cliff into Hell. Why isn't The Church in this country heeding these truths from Jesus?

---

[91] i.e. "The Shaking Dream"

Whoever can be trusted with very little can also be trusted with much, and whoever is dishonest with very little will also be dishonest with much. So if you have not been trustworthy in handling <u>worldly wealth</u>, who will trust you with <u>True Riches</u>? (Luke 16:10-11)

What seems obvious is that few American Christians think Jesus is talking to American Christians when He said the following:

Do not store up for yourselves treasures on earth, where moths and vermin destroy, and where thieves break in and steal. But store up for yourselves treasures in Heaven, where moths and vermin do not destroy, and where thieves do not break in and steal. <u>For where your treasure</u> (i.e. what you truly value) **<u>is, there your heart will be also</u>. The eye is the lamp of the body.** (Jesus is talking about what one's focus is.) **If your eyes are healthy, your whole body will be full of light. But if your eyes are unhealthy, your whole body will be full of darkness. If then the light within you is darkness, how great is that darkness! <u>No one</u> can serve two masters** (due to having a divided heart and thus divided loyalties). **Either you will <u>hate</u> the one and love the other, or you will be devoted to the one and <u>despise</u> the other. You <u>cannot</u> serve both God and money.** (Matthew 6:19-24)

Note that in Jesus' comments in both passages He doesn't refer to "the rich." In these passages Jesus is undeniably stating that whether one considers themselves rich or not, that if he or she does not handle worldly wealth by HIS standards (NOT by American standards) he or she will NOT be trusted with True Riches, and, that NO ONE (not even American Christians) can serve God and Money, for who or what someone truly loves and treasures is evidenced by how he or she lives.

With all the warnings Jesus of Nazareth gave about money, this should be a no-brainer. However, it seems to me, that as brainwashed as Americans Christians are, most of them in this country seem to think Jesus isn't speaking to them. Instead, most Christians in this country, without any hesitation, ignore ALL the things Jesus said about Money, choosing instead to believe that the material "blessing" they have is from Him. It never even seems to cross most of these Christians' minds that money is leading them away from Jesus and to the god of Money, which results in lukewarm Churchianity.[92]

What is wrong with The Church in this country? Has she taken a blow to the head? (Yes!) Why can't she see this? Answer? At the very least, because we're Americans, we're special, God just soooo loves us, thus we can do whatever we want...no matter how wrong it is...with no fear of any consequences. You know, grace, grace and we're Amer-I-cans-do-whatever-I-want.

But, there already ARE consequences unfolding upon The Church in this country for her love of the god of Money. The American Dream is about to become the American Nightmare for MANY who claim to know Jesus of Nazareth. You see, here's part of the problem:

When the sentence for a crime is not quickly carried out, the hearts of the people are filled with schemes to do wrong. (Ecclesiastes 8:11)

When Jesus doesn't deal with saved and unsaved sinners quickly, such people get the wrong idea. They think, "Well, nothing bad happened to me...so it must be okay." They forget that there IS coming a Day of Judgment when everything they have done WILL be judged. And at that time the consequences will be delivered. So it's not only a good thing when Hebrews 12:5-11 happens, for this gives a person the time to repent before That Day, but it is also evidence that one belongs to Jesus of Nazareth, for He does not discipline someone else's kids.

If you're not being dealt with concerning living the American Dream lifestyle, you should be profoundly concerned![93]

While the early Church minimized their lifestyles (Acts 4:32-37), The Church in this country seems to be in a race to see just how materialistic it can be. Let's be brutally honest. It IS true, one CAN tell a tree by its fruit and the fruit of American Christians is that they love money. Our lifestyles are vivid proof of this. Most Christians even buy into the belief that America is the greatest nation on the earth BECAUSE of our economy! Clearly such people are NOT measuring greatness with the same ruler Jesus of Nazareth measures greatness.

---

[92] **"I am rich; I have acquired wealth and do not need a thing"** (Revelation 3:17a).
[93] James 2:1-6

Here's a quick litmus test: If you give money and then deduct that amount off your income taxes...you are NOT giving. You loaned your money because you got your money back. You didn't give anything. Giving means giving, with no strings attached, and no way to recover what you gave. Jesus of Nazareth's followers are NOT to give to get. We're to give to give...like He gives!

Jesus said HIS people are to give in a way that they have no record of what they gave (Matthew 6:1-4). And one sure as Hell doesn't then get it back as a tax deduction! This kind of thing is good American thinking but terrible Kingdom thinking.

One of the many issues Yahweh confronted Israel with when she was praying for revival was how she was treating the poor. He told her:

The LORD takes His place in court; He rises to judge the people. The LORD enters into judgment against the elders and leaders of His people: "It is you who have ruined my Vineyard; the plunder from the poor is in your houses. What do you mean by crushing my people and grinding the faces of the poor?" declares the Lord, the LORD Almighty." (Isaiah 3:13-15)

Shout it aloud, do not hold back. Raise your voice like a trumpet. Declare to my people their rebellion and to the descendants of Jacob their sins. For day after day they seek me out; they seem eager to know my ways, as if they were a nation that does what is right and has not forsaken the commands of its God. They ask me for just decisions and seem eager for God to come near them. "Why have we fasted," they say, "and you have not seen it? Why have we humbled ourselves, and you have not noticed?" Yet on the day of your fasting, you do as you please and exploit all your workers[94]. Your fasting ends in quarreling and strife, and in striking each other with wicked fists. You cannot fast as you do today and expect your voice to be heard on high. Is this the kind of fast I have chosen, only a day for people to humble themselves? Is it only for bowing one's head like a reed and for lying in sackcloth

---

[94] See my example in this section above about the guy with three house and a profoundly under paid employee.

and ashes? Is that what you call a fast, a day acceptable to the LORD? <u>Is not this the kind of fasting I have chosen</u>: <u>to loose</u> the chains of injustice and untie the cords of the yoke, <u>to set free</u> the oppressed and break every yoke? Is it not <u>to share</u> your food with the hungry and <u>to provide</u> the poor wanderer with shelter – when you see the naked, <u>to clothe</u> them, and not to turn away from your own flesh and blood? THEN your light will break forth like the dawn, and your healing will quickly appear; THEN your righteousness will go before you, and the glory of the LORD will be your rear guard. THEN you will call, and the LORD will answer; you will cry for help, and He will say: Here am I. (Isaiah 58:1-9)

The Church in this country CANNOT have it both ways.

Just as Jesus said, one cannot – as in being unable – serve God and Money! NO ONE can live the American Dream, attend church in a comfortable, even a luxurious building, and think Jesus is receiving their worship and hearing their prayers, much less sending revival. And by the way, have you read this?

As Jesus looked up, He saw the rich putting their gifts into the Temple treasury. He also saw a poor widow put in two very small copper coins. "<u>Truly I tell you</u>," He said, "<u>this poor widow has put in more than all the others. All these people gave their gifts out of their wealth; but she out of her poverty put in ALL she had to live on</u>." (Luke 21:1-4)

When Jesus of Nazareth begins a comment with the phrase, "I tell you the truth" or "truly I tell you," one had BETTER pay attention to what follows. So if you're "tithing" while living the American lifestyle, you're not only NOT like this woman Jesus singled out to make a powerful point about giving, but you're also a joke! That is, you're fooling only yourself if you think you can "tithe" and that "tithing" somehow gives you permission to still live the American Dream:[95]

Do not love the world or anything in the world. <u>If anyone loves the world</u>, <u>Love for the Father is not in them</u>. For everything in the world – the lust of the flesh, the lust of the eyes, and the pride of life – comes not from the Father but from the world. The

---

[95] Similar to how some believe a diet soda and a Snickers bar cancel each other out.

world and its desires pass away, but whoever does the will of God [i.e. in how a person handles money] **lives forever.** (1 John 2:15-17)

Jesus of Nazareth does not need money. What He wants is followers who are free from the god of Money and Materialism. Living the fasted lifestyle of the Kingdom helps to produce this. Living the lifestyle of the American Dream produces the complete opposite. This is clearly a sowing and reaping thing.

Who doesn't enjoy Paul's letters, or Peter's, or John's, etc.? But, have you carefully considered Jesus' seven letters? (See Revelation 2 and 3.) Jesus wrote – dictated – seven letters, which John then sent out to seven congregations.

Out of the seven letters, in only two did Jesus have only good things to say to the leaders and to the people in those communities (Smyrna and Philadelphia).

Out of the remaining five letters, in four of them Jesus told those people some things He liked and then some things He did NOT like, calling them to repent of these (Ephesus, Pergamum, Thyatira, and Sardis).

In only one of the seven letters did Jesus of Nazareth have absolutely nothing – not one thing – good to say to the people in that community: Laodicea. And to them He commanded them to "earnestly" repent! Their single issue? The love of Money and what it produced.

At the core of what Laodicea was doing had to do with their wealth and the resulting comfortable lifestyle. Their comfort-filled lifestyles led them to think they did not need anything, even including being "hot" for Jesus and His Kingdom. And while being "cold" would have been better, for they would have at least been in touch with their low spiritual estate, instead, their American-like lifestyles made them arrogant and complacent. I don't know what it means but doing something that makes Jesus feel like vomiting can't be a good thing!

So contrast what Jesus said to The Church in Laodicea, who were living materially comfortable lives – **"you are wretched, pitiful, poor, blind, and naked"** with what He said to The Church in Smyrna, who was being persecuted – **"you are rich!"**

Additionally, in the five letters to the congregations in which Jesus had some issues, He told them what He would do for them IF they repented AND what He would do to them IF they did not repent. Of these five, four repented, for today, in those areas, there is still something of a Christian witness.

However, one congregation did not repent. How do we know? Because the community of Laodicea does not exist today. Today, where Laodicea was once located there aren't any interesting ruins to look at. The place is desolate. Truly, Jesus vomited them out of His mouth! And the sad thing is that Christians in this country think that Jesus wouldn't do such a thing here. If that's you, you don't know the Real Jesus.

Maybe Christians in this country don't think the word "rich" applies to them. This is not accurate.

When Jesus spoke of "the rich," He was NOT referring to the filthy rich, such as kings and nobles. Today the filthy rich would be those who have family wealth, corporate executives, Wall Street tycoons, those who have cashed in on technology, the music business, television and Hollywood, and professional sports. These are NOT the "rich" Jesus was talking about.

"The rich" Jesus was referring to were those who were merchants, artisans, tax collectors, etc. In other words, what we would call middle-class. These were the people the average person listening to Jesus wanted to be like, to have their kind of relatively easy and comfortable lifestyle. So when Jesus says, "the rich," He IS talking to Middle-Class American Christians, in addition to the filthy rich Christians.

Do you remember the "Jabez" fad from some years back (1 Chronicles 4:9-10)? Let's look at that.

Jabez's mother named him "Jabez," a Hebrew word that means "he causes sorrow/pain." The text says he was an honorable man, and yet he must have felt somewhat cursed by this name his mother gave him. Therefore he asks "the God of Israel" to give him two things: to bless him with wealth and to keep him from any pain. And this God granted his request.

Gee, who wouldn't want those two things?!?!

But, compare the temporal things Jabez got with what Phinehas got. First, here's the backstory.

Balaam was willing to curse Israel for a big paycheck. After trying to do this several times and was unable, blessing them instead, he advised the king of Moab to get Yahweh to curse them by getting Israel to sin sexually.

So Moabite women were sent to entice the men of Israel, successfully seducing many of them. And when this sexual immorality broke out throughout the camp, Yahweh broke out against Israel. Seeing the problem, a young man named Phinehas took action by driving a spear through an Israelite man and a Moabite woman while they were in the act of coitus. When Yahweh saw this, he told Moses:

> **Phinehas son of Eleazar, the son of Aaron, the priest, has turned my anger away from the Israelites. Since he was as zealous for my honor among them as I am, I did not put an end to them in my zeal. Therefore tell him I am making my covenant of peace with him. He and his descendants will have a covenant of a lasting priesthood, because he was zealous for the honor of his God and made atonement for the Israelites.** (Numbers 25:10-13)

Phinehas acted unselfishly; he did what was best for Israel. He had no thought about himself. And he did what he did because he was zealous for Yahweh's honor, not expecting anything in return. And while Jabez got rich and lived a life free from pain, two things Americans, even American Christians love, Phinehas and his descendants got a covenantal promise of a lasting priesthood.

So, do you want what Jabez got or what Phinehas got?

> **Large crowds were traveling with Jesus and turning to them He said: "If anyone comes to me and does not hate father and mother, wife and children, brothers and sisters – yes, even their own life – such a person <u>cannot</u> be my disciple. And whoever does not carry their cross and follow me <u>cannot</u> be my disciple.** (Luke 14:25-27)

Finally, the Rich Young Ruler is a perfect example of all I'm saying.

First notice the extremely high standard Jesus called him to: Give it all away; THEN come be my disciple! That's intense. And yet, I believe Jesus would say something just like this to most American Christians.

Secondly, the man wouldn't do it. Not that he couldn't do it, for he could, he was able, but he WOULD not do it. Why? Despite all his religious words and actions before Jesus (Mark 10:17, 20), the truth was that Money was what he treasured, not Jesus:

> "...he went away <u>sad</u> because he had great possessions."

Note also the additional lesson of the Rich Young Ruler Jesus gave to those who wanted to follow Him:

> **I tell you the truth, at the renewal of all things** (i.e. when Jesus establishes His Kingdom on the Earth)**, when the Son of Man sits on His glorious throne, you** (specifically the Twelve) **who have followed me will also sit on twelve thrones, judging the twelve tribes of Israel. And everyone** (i.e. all other followers down through the ages) **who has left houses or brothers or sisters or father or mother or wife or children or fields for my sake and the sake of the Gospel will receive a hundred times as much in this Present Age (homes, brothers, sisters, mothers, children, and fields – and with them, persecutions) and in the Age To Come and will inherit Eternal Life. <u>But most who are first will be last, and the last will be first</u>.** (Matthew 19:28-30; Mark 10:29-31)

Most of those who have financial ability and comfort in this life, and thus are "first" in this life, will at the renewal of all things find themselves at the end of the line receiving no rewards...or possibly worse. This is the Great Reversal of Jesus' Kingdom. As Craig Keener puts it:

> **For the love of money is a root of all kinds of evil.** (1 Timothy 6:10a)

STONE NUMBER SEVEN: PSYCHOLOGY

"Fairy tales do not tell children that dragons exists. Children already know that dragons exist. Fairy tales tell children the dragons can be killed." – G.K. Chesterton

Let's say you are having some terribly painful stomach pains and decide to go see your doctor about it. And when the doctor comes into the little examining room, looks at the chart the nurse handed him, he says, "I see you're having some stomach pains."

You say, "Yeah, Doc, I am." And you begin to tell him about your terribly painful stomach pains. The doctor listens with his or her best patientcare listening skills. And when you're finished describing your terribly painful stomach pains, the doctor thinks for a moment, and then says, "Well, it's obvious you have stomach cancer. We need to immediately get you into radiation and chemotherapy. These therapies won't heal you, but they will at least help you to live a reasonable life with your incurable disease."

"Radiation and Chemotherapy!?!?!" you exclaim. "But Doc, first, how did you come to such a diagnosis without doing any actual medical tests? And secondly, how can you then prescribe these incredibly body-damaging treatments without some medical tests?"

The doctor, putting on his or her best professional demeanor and speaking quite expertly says, "I know you have stomach cancer just from the symptoms you've described. And you will have great difficulties from this if you don't immediately begin this specific drug therapy."

Would you be okay with such an approach to medical treatment? And yet, this is EXACTLY what Psychology does.

In most other medical specialties, diagnoses are bound by biological markers, and thus outcomes can be more easily quantified. However, in Psychiatry, there are no biological markers that separate a patient with a "disease" from someone without it, which renders Psychiatry more vulnerable to bias, since it relies more heavily on subjective judgments for making diagnoses and assessing symptoms.[96]

So here is a bibliography for you to check-out for yourself the evil pseudo-science of Psychology.[97]

Jay E. Adams. The Biblical View of Self-Esteem, Self-Love, Self-Image

Fred A. Baughman, Jr. The ADHD Fraud: How Psychiatry Makes "Patients" of Normal Children

Peter R. Breggin. Toxic Psychiatry

Peter R. Breggin. Your Drug May Be Your Problem

Peter R. Breggin. The Anti-Depressant Fact Book

Peter R. Breggin. The Ritalin Fact Book

Paul Brownback. The Danger of Self-Love: Re-Examining a Popular Myth

Lori and Bill Granger. The Magic Feather: The Truth About Special Education

Karl Menninger. Whatever Became of Sin?

Ray Moynihan & Alan Cassels. Selling Sickness: How the World's Biggest Pharmaceutical Companies Are Turning Us All Into Patients

Thomas S. Szasz. The Myth of Mental Illness

Thomas S. Szasz. Psychiatry: The Science of Lies

Thomas S. Szasz. The Medicalization of Everyday Life

Thomas S. Szasz. The Myth of Psychotherapy

Thomas S. Szasz. Schizophrenia: The Sacred Symbol of Psychiatry

David Tyler. God's Funeral: Psychology – Trading the Sacred for the Secular

David Tyler & Kurt Grady. Deceptive Diagnosis: When Sin Is Called Sickness

David Tyler & Kurt Grady. ADHD: Deceptive Diagnosis

Paul C. Vitz. Psychology as Religion: The Cult of Self-Worship

---

[96] Psychiatry Under the Influence, page 139.
[97] Even though some of these sources are dated, the facts they're providing have not changed. Psychology is still a pseudo-science.

Robert Whitaker. Anatomy of an Epidemic: Magic Bullets,
    Psychiatric Drugs, and the Astonishing Rise of Mental Illness in
    America
Robert Whitaker and Lisa Cosgrove. Psychiatry Under the
Influence: Institutional Corruption, Social Injury, and Prescriptions
for Reform.[98]

Given such results, our society can only conclude this: The APA
(American Psychological Association) has provided us with a diagnostic manual that, from a scientific perspective, cannot lay claim
to being reliable or valid, which are the twin requirements for a
medical manual to be clinically useful. However, as this chapter
documents, the manual has proven to benefit the interests of the
pharmaceutical industry and the guild interests of the psychiatric
profession, and DSM-5[99]will continue to nurture those ends.

What distinguishes psychiatry from other medical disciplines is that
it does not have biological markers for its conditions, which means
that it is more vulnerable to commercial influences when making
decisions about diagnostic criteria.

In a 2011 interview, Robert Spizter[100] spoke of how the drug companies understood that a new commercial world would unfold with
the publication of the DSM-III, as its new disease model was certain
to trigger a "gold rush." The pharmaceutical companies, Spitzer
said, "were delighted."[101]

There are few things in this world as wicked and as deceptive as
Psychology.[102] It is one thing for the masses of foolish people in this

---

[98] Freud and his Jewish associates, even Carl Jung the token Gentile who chose science
over Jesus in spite of his father's (who was a pastor) attempt to lead him to Jesus, all hated
Christians. Freud's stated goal was to find a "scientific" explanation for human behavior,
thus eliminating Sin, which he knew would then make The Church obsolete.
[99] Diagnostic and Statistical Manual of Mental Disorders
[100] Spitzer was the head of the task force in 1980 that developed the DSM-III, a diagnostic
manual that was based on the disease model of mental illness, something that to this day
has not been proven scientifically.
[101] All three quotes are from Psychiatry Under the Influence, page 115.
[102] Three very wicked deceptions were unleashed on the world in the 1800's by three Jews:
Charles Darwin – Evolution, Carl Marx – Communism, and Sigmund Freud – Psychology.

country who are in love with pills and quick-fixes, but it is profoundly sad when those who are supposed to have the Spirit of Discernment are duped and deceived by such obvious falsehoods.

Here are some FACTS about Psychology.

First, there is virtually NO truth in it. Secondly, it attempts to replace Sin with "medical" problems. And thirdly, no matter what it claims otherwise, it essentially removes human responsibility for choices and behaviors.

I say that Psychology has "virtually" no truth in it because in ALL deception there is just enough truth to hook people. After all, that's how deception works. Deception must have some truth in it or else it doesn't deceive people. Criminals don't counterfeit fifty-five-dollar bills, and the reason is obvious – there aren't any real fifty-five-dollar bills.

Further, at its VERY best Psychology is a Band-Aid on a broken bone. It's like taping a piece of paper over the Check Engine light on one's dashboard. One doesn't see the warning light anymore, but the problem is still there. When Dr. Phil helps people without dealing with their Sin through Jesus, he's putting a Band-Aid on their broken bone or taping a piece of paper over the Check Engine light of their life.

Neither kind of Psychology – talking or biological – has any basis in actual science, much less medicine. Here is a fact: NONE of Psychology's diagnoses result from some scientific or medical test.[103] So, there is no such thing as being bipolar, schizophrenic[104], ADHD, and a whole lot more. There isn't even a blood test for the false label of a "chemical imbalance." Etc. Again, there is virtually NOTHING scientific or medical about anything in Psychology.

Further, the pseudo-science of Psychology, claiming it knows best what ails Man's soul and/or body, has in this country quite successfully replaced Sin with the unsubstantiated idea of a chemical imbalance or genetic malfunction. If these are true, if people's emotional, mental, and behavioral problems are related to some medical issue and not to Sin, then there is no need for Jesus.

---

[103] Do not believe the drug companies' commercials as they try to present some issue as if it were an actual medical condition. It's ALL baloney. In fact, listen carefully to what the commercial says, things like: "it may be caused by," or "some research says," etc. The only thing you should believe in these commercials is the long list of side effects their poisons cause!

[104] There is no MRI or brain scan that shows anything in the brain that is causing a person to be schizophrenic. The most recent scientific/medical research has proven, without a doubt, that the so-called "hot spots" in the brains of diagnosed schizophrenics is not evidence of brain damage causing schizophrenia, but rather the brain damage the poisonous chemicals called "medications" caused.

The simple truth is this: When people sow to the flesh they reap the fruit of the flesh. Every issue in which Psychology has invented a "disease," disorder," or "syndrome" the behaviors and feelings can be traced to one or more of the fruits of the flesh Sin-issues.

The acts of the flesh are obvious: sexual immorality, impurity and debauchery; idolatry and witchcraft; hatred, discord, jealousy, fits of rage, selfish ambition, dissensions, factions and envy; drunkenness, orgies, and the like. I warn you, as I did before, that those who live like this will not inherit the Kingdom of God. (Galatians 5:19-21)

Do you not know that the unrighteous will not inherit the Kingdom of God? Do not be deceived. Neither fornicators, nor idolaters, nor adulterers, nor homosexuals, nor sodomites, nor thieves, nor covetous, nor drunkards, nor revilers, nor extortioners will inherit the Kingdom of God. And such were some of you. But you were washed, but you were sanctified, you were justified in the Name of the Lord Jesus and by the Spirit of our God. (1 Corinthians 6:9-11)

But mark this: There will be terrible times in the last days. People will be lovers of themselves, lovers of money, boastful, proud, abusive, disobedient to their parents, ungrateful, unholy, without love, unforgiving, slanderous, without self-control, brutal, not lovers of the good, treacherous, rash, conceited, lovers of pleasure rather than lovers of God – having a form of godliness but denying its power. (2 Timothy 3:1-5a)

Here's what Jesus of Nazareth who created humans said:

What comes out of a person is what defiles them. For it is from within, out of a person's heart, that evil thoughts come – sexual immorality, theft, murder, adultery, greed, malice, deceit, lewdness, envy, slander, arrogance, and folly. All these evils come from inside and defile a person. (Mark 7:20-23)

This is why Jesus' followers are urged because of His Mercy to...

...not conform any longer to the pattern of this world, but be transformed by the renewing of your mind. Then you will be able to test and approve what God's will is – His good, pleasing, and perfect will. (Romans 12:2)[105]

———————

There are of course various experiences that cause people mental and/or emotional pain, such as divorce, loss of a loved one, prolonged illness, abuse, the ravages of combat and war, etc. that did not result from sins they committed. However, people who have experienced traumatic things that did not result from their own Sin do not have a psychological "illness." These people are not sick in the medical sense. There is nothing broken in their bodies. They are in emotional and mental pain, but not because of an actual illness. Thus, taking poisonous chemicals called medicines is not the solution.

It should be good news to hear that a person's "psychological illness" is related to Sin or to trauma and not to some made-up disease, disorder, or syndrome for which a person must take dangerous chemicals pretending to be medicines. And this is because there is an actual and real solution for Sin or trauma – Jesus of Nazareth.

Jesus, the creator of human beings, confronted people with their sins that lead to unhealthy behaviors (e.g. John 5:14). He also bound-up the broken hearts of those who experienced some form of trauma (e.g. Mark 5:24-34). And when necessary, He tossed demons, actual, real evil spirits, out of people's lives (e.g. Mark 5:1-20). He never recognized anything approaching the modern idea of "mental illness" as being a person's problem.[106]

And speaking of demons, several times the writers of the Gospels tell us that Jesus healed the sick and cast out demons, sometimes all night long![107] Why did so many people have so many demons?

Was "having a demon" the ancient, non-scientific way to say the person was "mentally ill"? And if that was just back then when people weren't "scientifically" informed like we Moderns are, why didn't Jesus

———————

[105] See also Ephesians 5:25b-26 and Titus 3:5.
[106] Certainly there can be physiological causes for seizures, such as an extremely high fever, but demons too cause seizures – i.e. Matthew 4:24, 17:15; Mark 9:20.
[107] Matthew 8:16, 14:14, 35-36; Luke 4:40-41

who knows what is ailing human beings correct this wrong "demon view" of "mental illness"? Why didn't He explain that a demonized person didn't have an evil spirit, but rather was merely sick? The answer? Because the person wasn't "mentally ill," but rather they had an actual demonic spirit that was impacting them!

Fact: ALL human beings have complete control over their feelings, thoughts, and will, that is, their soul. Therefore, people can and do chose sinful, unhealthy, and "crazy" feelings, thoughts, and behaviors. Further, some people allow demons, evil spirits to influence their feelings, thoughts, and will. Some have done this for so long that they can't tell the difference between their feelings and thoughts from those of a demon, some even give over control of their will to a demon.

Giving people, the supposed "mentally ill," powerful chemicals to control their feelings, thoughts, and even their wills only makes the connection between the person and the demon(s) stronger, for these filthy spirits love to experience these mind-altering, emotion-suppressing, will-weakening chemicals.[108]

And because every human being has ultimate control over what he or she feels, thinks, and does, demons do not "possess" a person and thus control them by making them do what they want. Even the Holy Spirit does not possess a person and thus control their emotions, will, and thoughts. People ARE able to choose who THEY allow to influence them, whether it's people and/or demons...or Jesus.[109]

Next, here is one of Psychology's most wicked deceptions: Baron von Kraft-Ebing (1840-1902) used Latin and a medical diploma to turn what was considered sinful behavior into a "sickness" in his book, Psychopathia Sexualis. Freud and his associates loved this idea and copied it copiously!

---

[108] As already noted, the root Greek word for "pharmacology" means "sorcery" or "witchcraft." Thus, taking the poisonous chemicals that drug companies falsely call medicine are an attraction to demons.

[109] Adding the word "possessed" to the text when speaking of demons in the English translations of the Bible produces a great misunderstanding. The Greek word for "demon" in pretty much every case in the New Testament is an adjective describing degree of affect. Thus, people are "demonized" to some extent, not possessed or owned by a demon.

It seems all one needs in Psychology is a Latin or Greek lexicon and Presto! one can invent a "mental illness." And as such this HAS become one of Psychology's supremely successful way of selling "mental illness" to all Americans, including Christians, simply by attaching complex and official-sounding names to give an aura of medical and scientific quality to sinful or even normal human feelings, thoughts, and behaviors.[110]

Then, when Psychology joined with the potently powerful drug companies with their poisonous pills that masquerade as medications, Americans took the bait, hook, line, and sinker! For Americans, even Christians love pills. Americans love anything that is quick, easy, and sciency. But these chemicals are no medicines. They fix nothing. Instead, these chemicals produce the very issues they claim to help.[111]

And when Psychology got into bed with her paramour Public Education, she rapidly rose to the lofty place of Supreme Expert![112] Laughably, Psychology is an expert at nothing despite its sciency sounding research, jargon, and approaches to teaching that often borders on stupidity and silliness.

And then, of course, Psychology is one of the areas of study most students are required to take in their college and seminary preparation for the ministry. As a result, Psychology is now one of the "tools" of a minister! What truly insane craziness!

> From a big picture perspective, the harm done in this instance of institutional corruption arises from a very simple fact. Our society, over the past 35 years, has organized itself in response to a narrative told by American Psychiatry that was, in so many of its details, misleading. Our understanding of the biology of mental disorders, our use of psychiatric drugs, our spending on psychiatric services, and even our social policies arise from a story that has been shaped by guild and pharmaceutical interests, as opposed to a narrative told by a medical profession that has shown an adherence to scien-

---

[110] The Diagnostic and Statistical Manuel of Mental Disorders (DSM-MD) has EXPLODED with a flood of "mental illnesses." It seems just about anything can be a "mental illness" today. Really? Do we need the word arachnophobia to say most of us don't like spiders? And is this word suggesting this dislike of spiders is a sickness? And when did the sin of stealing become kleptomania?

[111] WARNING! If you are taking any of these dangerous and poisonous chemicals, DO NOT stop taking them without help. See some of the materials in the bibliography above for advice on this process.

[112] NONE of the labels in Special Education are real medical issues. The ONLY SPED students who have real physiological issues are those few who are labeled as Life Skill Students, such as those with Downes Syndrome, or who are blind and/or deaf, etc.

tific principles and a commitment – at all times – to the best interests of patients. Those may be harsh words, but such is the comprehensive nature of the corruption documented in the previous chapters.[113]

It is one thing for unregenerated people, even the Christianized, to fall for Psychology's lies and deceptions. It's an entirely different thing for those who consider themselves to have the Spirit of Truth, whose assignment is to lead them into Truth, to ignore something as clear as what Paul tells the Christians in Colossae:

> **See to it** (as in it's our responsibility) **that no one takes you captive through hollow and deceptive philosophy, which depends on human tradition and the elemental spiritual forces of this world rather than on Christ.** (2:8)

Answer this: Who knows what's best and what's healthy for human beings? Freud (and his followers) or Jesus of Nazareth? Jesus created human beings. One would think that He knows EXACTLY what is best and what is healthy for them!

There is SO very much more that can be said about the fake field of Psychology and the profoundly destructive impact it has had on people in this country (as well as elsewhere) since its creation, making those involved with it quite rich. The serious followers of Jesus of Nazareth should educate themselves with the facts about this horrific danger.

When each of my children were little, and I would put them to bed, reading the Bible to them, praying with them, maybe telling them a story about what Jerry the Giant, or Ned the Giant, or Erica the Giant did that day and how much their mommy and daddy loved them, sometimes I would also tell them this:

Humpty Dumpty sat on a wall.
Humpty Dumpty had a great fall.
All the king's horses, and all the king's men,
could not put Humpty Dumpty back together again.
So...the Bridegroom-King Himself came,
and HE put Humpty Dumpty back together again,
for He was the ONLY one who could!

---

[113] Psychiatry Under the Influence, page 155.

STONE NUMBER NINE: MUSIC

When I was about eight or nine months old in the Lord, I was having lunch with an older man who had known Jesus for several years. For being together to eat lunch gave me the time to learn more about Jesus from him.

At one point in the conversation I happen to mention that for some reason I was not getting the enjoyment I used to get from the music I listened to.[114] And as I didn't think this was a particularly big deal, I was truly surprised when this older man said he thought that my growing discontentment with the music I listened to was the Holy Spirit's doing.

"The Holy Spirit?!?!? What does He care about the music I listen to?" I said.

"He cares VERY much, for who do you think invented music," responded the man.

I hadn't ever thought about where music came from. Mozart perhaps? Beethoven possibly? The Beatles? Or maybe Elvis. Yeah, definitely Elvis, you know, the King of Rock-n-Roll.

This older man then continued by giving me my very first Bible lesson on the topic of music. He told me about the time when Moses was returning to Israel's camp with the Ten Commandments, met Joshua about half way down, could not see the people but could hear the music coming from the camp, which was clearly not a good thing, for even Joshua said that it was the sound of war (Exodus 32:17).

I was quite impacted by this mini-Bible lesson on music. So I said, "Well, maybe I can give my albums and 45's to someone."

The man responded, "If you were a smoker and decided to quit, would you give your newly opened carton of cigarettes to someone and say, 'Here, you die of lung cancer?'"

This statement really got me! "Of course not," I said. "So what do I do?"

This older man said, "Go home and destroy everything you have. Throw it all away. Get rid of it."

---

[114] I had more than fifty albums and a tall stack of 45's.

As extreme as this may sound...that is exactly what I did without any hesitation. And I didn't just fill up a trash bag and toss everything into the dumpster. Nope. I broke every album and every 45 and tore up all the covers so no one could use any of them. I then put it all in trash bags and tossed everything into the dumpster.

And as I did this, I had this thought going through me: Lord Jesus, I don't want anything to keep me from knowing you as deeply as possible. Whatever I need to purge from my life, tell me what it is, and I will purge it so that I can know you better.

It was much later when I came upon Jesus' words in Matthew, chapter eighteen:

If your hand or your foot causes you to sin cut it off and throw it away. It is better for you to enter life maimed or crippled than to have two hands or two feet and be thrown into eternal fire. And if your eye causes you to sin, gouge it out and throw it away. It is better for you to enter life with one eye than to have two eyes and be thrown into the fire of Hell. (vs. 8-9)

It was also some time later that I read Jesus' words about John the Baptist:

From the days of John the Baptist until now, the Kingdom of Heaven has been forcefully advancing, and <u>forceful men lay hold of it</u>. (Matthew 11:12)

The point is, truly laying hold of the Kingdom and Jesus' ways of living requires radical actions. I didn't realize it at the time, but destroying all my secular music was a radical action! Years later I can point to this, as well as to a few other things, as something that definitely made a HUGE difference in my relationship with Jesus of Nazareth early on.

Now, while music may not seem like something that can seriously impact one's relationship with Jesus for the negative...let's consider some facts about music.

First, Jesus invented music, He enjoys music Himself, He even uses music to minister to His people.

The LORD your God is with you, He is mighty to save. He will take great delight in you, He will quiet you with His Love, He will rejoice over you with singing. (Zephaniah 3:17)

In short, music is a Living God thing and thus a Tree of Life Good thing...when used properly.

Secondly, music does what Jesus designed it to do no matter what. Like with gravity in which what goes up must come down every time, music is a powerful tool that Jesus designed to stir the heart...every time. It stirs Jesus' heart and it stirs Man's heart. This is simply what music was designed to do. However, there is a potential problem.

Satan, the Great Copycat uses music to stir the human heart toward the things he wants, for he knows quite well that music automatically does what it was designed to do – stir the heart. Jesus of course wants human hearts stirred for Him and His Kingdom, which is why He invented music as a tool to do that.

Again, music does what Jesus designed it to do EVERY time, either stirring the heart to love Him or stirring the heart to love the World and its other gods.

So here's an experiment.

Watch some video of a secular concert, but completely turn off the sound. Just watch it. What do you see? What you are seeing is worship. Yes, worship. What you see the people doing is what people do when they worship – they're standing, clapping their hands, raising their hands, swaying to the music, dancing, maybe even shedding tears, etc. In short, their hearts are being stirred.

Next, watch a worship service, say, at the International House of Prayer in Kansas City, but again completely turn off the sound. Just watch it. What do you see? You see people worshiping, for they are doing what people in worship do, namely, they're standing, clapping their hands, raising their hands, swaying to the music, dancing, maybe even shedding tears, etc. Again, hearts are being stirred.

Now, go back and turn up the sound to each of the two worship services. For although the people in both groups are doing the same things, in the sound of and in the words of the music you will discover what and who each group's hearts are being stirred toward. You will hear the first group worshiping the musicians, their music, the philosophies and messages of their songs, and thus the god of this world. Or you will hear the people worshiping Jesus of Nazareth.

Again, ALL music, EVERY concert, EVERY musical event, EVERY song is aimed at stirring the heart toward someone and something – Satan and the ways of the World or Jesus and the ways of His Kingdom.

THERE IS NO NEUTRAL MUSIC. And this is why what music a person listens to DOES have an impact on that person's relationship with Jesus of Nazareth – it either moves a person towards loving Him or it moves a person away from Him.

It is my belief that Jesus gives a gift and a calling to every human being while He is forming them in their mother's womb. And one of these gifts and callings is the anointing/power to lead people to worship. Elvis certainly had it. The Beatles undeniably had it. LOTS of those in secular music have it.

The problem is, who and what they are leading people to worship, for the gifts and callings of God are irrevocable (Romans 11:29), even when the person uses them for himself or for Evil.

Since Satan chose to seek to be worshipped himself, there have been two opposite worship movements on the earth. But since the 1920's these two opposite worship movements have begun to clash, with a very public declaration of war for the hearts of people made by the secular worship movement in the 1960's. This war has escalated to the point that RIGHT NOW there is an intense battle going on between these two worship movements.[115]

STONE NUMBER TEN: AMERICANISMS

What follows is going to be shocking to many readers in this country. The subject is the United States of America and Christianity. And once again here is a brief bibliography that is important to read.

- The Search for Christian America, by Mark Noll, Nathan Hatch, and George Marsden
- Jesus: Made in America, by Stephen Nichols

---

[115] Still not convinced of the power of music? Check out Elisha using it to enhance the prophetic spirit in order to hear from the Living God in 2 Kings 3:15-16a. This also means that music enhances false spirits, which other religions and spiritualists tap into using their music. People who use illegal drugs do so with music.

- <u>America's God</u>, by Mark Noll
- <u>Was America Founded as a Christian Nation?</u>, by John Fea
- <u>Theology in America</u>, by E. Brooks Holifield
- <u>The New Heavens and New Earth</u>, by Cushing Strout
- <u>The Democratization of American Christianity</u>, by Nathan Hatch

Some of these authors are Christians, but most importantly, all of them are professional historians. This is important because how they handle the details of history are not driven by some personal agenda, as is so often the case by history-spinsters who pick pieces and fragments to support what they want to believe. These historians tell the "whole truth," which they are committed to tell by their profession.

In other words, these authors aren't preachers trying to stir-up the faithful to some end; they are professional historians committed to telling the facts of history – clear, simple facts.

The fact is, the colonies were populated mostly by people who were Christianized. For not everyone who came to the New World were actual born-again by the Spirit followers of Jesus of Nazareth.

Thus, establishing a Christianized society in the Colonies is NOT unique. For EVERY European who came to colonize this continent came from Christianized Europe. And living in a Christianized nation, or sitting in a church, no more makes a person a born-again follower of Jesus of Nazareth than sitting in a garage makes one a car.

Further, although the men who founded this nation are portrayed as being brilliantly intelligent, morally outstanding super-heroes, they were nothing of the sort. At their core, they were The-Living-God-less men and political politicians who had been deeply infected by the humanistic influences of The Enlightenment and the Age of Reason.[116]

The facts of history are that the founders of this nation weren't Jews, Hindus, Muslims, or Buddhists, but neither were they born-again by the Spirit followers of Jesus of Nazareth. They wanted to be moral people, even though there is plenty of historical evidence that many of them weren't all that moral.[117]

---

[116] It is a fact that Jefferson wrote his own version of the Bible, which was made up of the moral teachings of Jesus, for Jefferson considered Jesus to simply be a moral man who gave people an example of what it means to have faith.
[117] An online teacher wrote, "Franklin placed great value on self-improvement. He believed

The kindest that can be said about these guys is that SOME of them had a belief in some sort of a vague higher power and some did not, for after all these were "enlightened" men, products of the Enlightenment, and the "enlightened" did not need or really want much of any higher power. And being "enlightened" they certainly did NOT want the Living God, for He was FAR too specific for their tastes.

Since the printing press, everyone read the Bible. Reading the Bible, knowing some parts of it, and even quoting from it was akin to reading Shakespeare, knowing his plays, and quoting from them. The Bible was simply considered by the general population to be one of many pieces of classic literature. For although most of the population "believed" the Bible was "Holy Scripture" or the "Word of God," the practice of their lives was to ignore or rationalize what the Bible said. People went to church, but Church wasn't in the people.

The founding fathers were no different, most of them even less so, for although SOME of them very occasionally attended a church, prayed and read and quoted the Bible, or made references to a higher power, they clearly did not know Jesus of Nazareth personally. They were simply Christianized along with the rest of the society.

And as for some of them alluding to the Bible of a higher power, this is simply what ALL politicians do.[118]

Since one can tell a tree by its fruit, these men's fruit contained in the actual facts of history show that they were either Atheists or Agnostics at the worst and Deists or Universalists at the best.

Paul wrote in Galatians 6:7-8:

Do not be deceived: God cannot be mocked (i.e. fooled). **A man reaps what he sows. The one who sows to please his sinful nature, from that nature will reap destruction; the one who sows to please the Spirit, from the Spirit will reap Eternal Life.**

---

that integrity and moral responsibility" (not Jesus of Nazareth) "were the backbone of a successful life and a strong community. Reading and reflection led him to formulate his own list of 13 personal virtues," (not from Scripture) "which he then attempted to master...."
[118] As an opening to his speech after the tragedy at Sandy Hooks Elementary School, President Obama quoted from 2 Corinthians, combining some snippets from chapters four and five: "To all the families, first responders, to the community of Newton, clergy, guests – Scripture tells us: '...do not lose heart. Though outwardly we are wasting away...inwardly we are being renewed day by day. For our light and momentary troubles are achieving for us an eternal glory that far outweighs them all. So we fix our eyes not on what is seen, but on what is unseen, since what is seen is temporary, but what is unseen is eternal. For we know that if the earthly tent we live in is destroyed, we have a building from God, an eternal house in heaven, not built by human hands.'" Paul is talking about those who are born-again by the Spirit. Mr. Obama applied this to all people.

What a person plants they reap. Plant green beans, and one gets green beans, not corn. Sow to the flesh or to the World and one does NOT get godliness and the Kingdom. Sow to the Tree of Knowledge of Good and Evil and one does not get the Tree of Life.

And this is what the "enlightened" founding fathers did: They sowed into themselves the teachings of the Enlightenment and Age of Reason philosophers. They're not then going to produce a harvest of the Biblical-ness of the Kingdom. And so, once again...

See to it that no one takes you captive through hollow and deceptive philosophy, which depends on human tradition and the elemental spiritual forces of this world rather than on Christ. (Colossians 2:8)

The founders of this nation absolutely LOVED the world and the world's philosophies. As men of the Enlightenment and the Age of Reason, they believed utterly in Man's knowledge and Man's wisdom and Man's abilities and Man's moral goodness. These men considered Evil as being good and This God's Good as being evil. And they came to this because while a FEW of them MAY have read the Bible occasionally, their TRUE nourishment came wholly from the Tree of Knowledge of Good and Evil and NOT from the Tree of Life Himself.

How do I know this? Because one can tell a tree by its fruit, and the fruit these men produced in their personal and professional lives is clearly the fruit of the Tree of Knowledge and Good and Evil.

For example, Democracy is NOT some jewel that dropped out of Heaven. The God of Abraham, Isaac, and Jacob, the God of Israel, the One, True, Living God did NOT invent Democracy. He also did NOT create Man to govern himself by majority vote.[119] He created Man to be in subjection to a king. He invented Monarchy. The religiously pagan, the sexually perverted, and the arrogantly pompous Greeks invented Democracy. Does The Church in this country actually think that something godly can come from such a filthy source as the Greeks?!?!?[120] Philip Schaff, a nineteenth-century Church historian wrote:

---

[119] A majority can often be wrong, as in Numbers 14:2.

"The Church, embracing the mass of the population of the [Roman] Empire, from Caesar to the meanest slave, and living amidst all its institutions, received into her bosom vast deposits of foreign material from the world and from heathenism.... Although ancient Greece and Rome have fallen forever, the spirit of Graeco-Roman paganism is not extinct. It still lives in the natural heart of man, which at this day as much as ever needs regeneration by the Spirit of God. It lives also in many idolatrous and superstitious usages of the Greek and Roman churches, against which the pure spirit of Christianity has instinctively protested from the beginning, and will protest till all remains of gross and refined idolatry shall be outwardly as well as inwardly overcome, and baptized and sanctified not only with water, but also with the spirit and fire of the Gospel."

What is best for human beings is NOT determined by other human beings. What is best for human beings are the things Jesus of Nazareth says are best for human beings. For although it may seem that there are so-called creator-endowed truths that are self-evident in which all people are created equal, having certain unalienable Rights, such rights are nowhere stated in the Word of God. The Living God did not endow people with Rights, He stresses human Responsibilities.

What is best for people is what Jesus of Nazareth says is best for people. And governmentally people were designed to be in subjection to the Bridegroom-King. Human beings simply were not designed to govern their own lives, doing what they think is best. They were designed by the Son to crave His leadership...which is available no matter what kind of earthly government they live under – a monarchy, democracy, communistic, or totalitarian.

Again, it was the pagan, perverted, pompous Greeks who believed themselves to be SO smart who came up with the demonic idea of Democracy. And it was the worldly philosophers of the Renaissance, the Enlightenment, and the Age of Reason who promoted such unbiblical ideas. American followers of the Real Jesus should be ashamed to celebrate the Rebellion on the Fourth of July.

---

[120] Paul called the philosophers in Athens ignorant (Acts 17:22-23) and demeaned Greek culture in general in what he told the Christians at Corinth (1 Corinthians 1:18-25).

Freedom of Religion also is NOT a divine concept and thus it is NOT a blessing from the Living God. It's an antichrist concept. For just this one thing alone has done HUGE damage to The Church in this country.

Why is this a fact? Because we know from history that by about the third generation of Church leaders there began to be compromise with the Roman world in order to avoid persecution. And when a worldly form of Christianity was made the official religion of Rome creating a form of religious freedom which stopped the persecution, The Church (and European society) plummeted into a great darkness called the Dark Ages. Thus, for hundreds of years VAST numbers of people in the Christianized nations of Europe were shoveled into Hell due a compromised-with-the-World version of Christianity.

Satan was the instigator of this, and he did it again with the worldly minds of the founding fathers.

The truth is that The Church was never intended to be acceptable to the surrounding culture and society. Jesus prophesied and promised that those who were faithful to Him WOULD suffer for being faithful to Him (e.g. Matthew 10:18-39; John 15:18-25). Even more, suffering for the sake of righteousness, for Jesus Himself, and for His Kingdom is one of the eight foundational principles of the constitution of Jesus' Kingdom (Matthew 5:10-12).

Fact: the lack of real suffering in the lives of those who claim to belong to Jesus of Nazareth in this country due to Freedom of Religion has absolutely debilitated and enfeebled The Church in this country. Truth: Persecution ALWAYS purifies The Church; lack of persecution ALWAYS makes The Church pitiful and powerless.

———

Now, as for the founding of this nation, here are just a few history-ical FACTS which seem to get left out when telling this nation's history.

The king of England fought a very expensive war called the French and Indian War. One of the points of this war was to stop Catholic France from taking control of the Protestant colonies. Thus, this was a war which benefitted most of the colonists. All the king of England asked of the colonists after winning this war was to repay some of what it cost him to fight this war. Frankly, that doesn't seem unreasonable, much less enslaving.

But the colonists were quite spoiled, having lots of freedom already due to living in the colonies. Why, they paid fewer taxes than people living in England! And yet, the colonists got all uppity about being asked to pay some of the costs of a war from which THEY benefitted.

Then, to justify their arrogance and spoiled attitude, as well as being infected with the worldly yeast of philosophers, the rhetoric began. Rhetoric such as the king of England and the Pope were the Antichrist. Rhetoric such as the king's taxing of the colonists was his attempt to enslave them. Rhetoric such as political freedom replacing freedom from Sin and manipulating the Bible to support this.

Patrick Henry is just one obvious example.

In Henry's "give me liberty or give me death" speech before the Virginia legislature in which he sought to convince these men to join the Rebellion, he changed clear biblical concepts to support what he believed and wanted, for he clearly twisted the Bible to say what he wanted it to say. In this famous speech, Henry changed the meaning of freedom in the Bible from freedom from Sin to political freedom. And yet, as far as Jesus is concerned one can be free from Sin while not being free politically.[121] In fact, to Jesus, what good is being free politically if one isn't free from Sin?!?

Here are a couple of passages of Scripture most people, including these famous (or infamous) leaders utterly ignored because what these passages say did not fit with their worldly wants.

Let everyone be subject to the governing authorities, for there is no authority except that which God has established. The authorities that exist have been established by God. Consequently, <u>whoever rebels against the authority is rebelling against what God has instituted, and those who do so will bring judgment on themselves</u>. For rulers hold no terror for those who do right, but for those who do wrong. Do you want to be free from fear of the one in authority? Then do what is right and you will be commended. For the one in authority is God's servant for your good. But if you do wrong, be afraid, for rulers do not bear the sword for no reason. They are God's servants, agents of wrath to

---

[121] E.g. "...if the Son sets you free, you will be free indeed!" (John 8:36)

bring punishment on the wrongdoer. Therefore, it is necessary to submit to the authorities, not only because of possible punishment but also as a matter of conscience. This is also why you pay taxes, for the authorities are God's servants, who give their full time to governing. Give to everyone what you owe them: If you owe taxes, pay taxes; if revenue, then revenue; if respect, then respect; if honor, then honor. (Romans 13:1-7)

Submit yourselves for the Lord's sake to every human authority: whether to the emperor, as the supreme authority, or to governors, who are sent by him to punish those who do wrong and to commend those who do right. For it is God's will that by doing good you should silence the ignorant talk of foolish people. Live as free people, but do not use your freedom as a cover-up for evil; live as God's slaves. Show proper respect to everyone, love the family of believers, fear God, honor the emperor. (1 Peter 2:13-17)

The emperor at the time of Peter's writing was Nero, the ruler who conducted an empire-wide persecution of Jesus' followers. Surely the king of England was doing nothing as bad as that!

And yet, the people of the colonies who were spoiled and stirred-up with unbiblical ideas, easily ignored passages such as these...in the same way as those in this country who claim to belong to Jesus ignore what Jesus and the Bible say about the god of Money and Materialism or Psychology and Self-Esteem.

There were of course people who opposed the Rebellion, for they rightly saw the Real Issue: the demonic spirit of rebellion. And thus they knew that...

...rebellion is like the sin of divination, and arrogance like the evil of idolatry. (1 Samuel 15:23a)

Next, and of CRITICAL importance to grasping the falsehood that the United States is in some way special before the Living God is the fact that there are only five covenants in the Bible. And there is plenty of confusion about these, some even teaching a blending of the Mosaic and the Messianic Covenants, something Paul fought hard against.[122]

And the MOST foundational fact about ALL the covenants the Living God is in is that when it comes to being in covenant with the Living God, Man cannot – as in being unable – initiate a covenant with Him. And this is because there is nothing the Living God needs from Man. Man has needs that only This God can do for him, but there is nothing Man has that This God needs (e.g. Psalm 50:7-13).

And since this is a fact, the fact is that the God of Abraham, Isaac, and Jacob, the God of Israel, the One, True, Living God did NOT cut a covenant with the early settlers on this continent. Those settlers may have tried (i.e. Jonathan Winthrop) to establish a covenant with Him, but He did NOT respond. Again, ALL the covenants the Living God is involved in HE initiated, not men. Thus, the colonies, and later the United States of America, is NOT a "city upon a hill." This country does NOT have some special calling or purpose, such as spreading political freedom in the form of Democracy around the world.[123]

Think: Why would Jesus want to spread something as demonic and as contrary to His ways as Democracy? While He is not in favor of physical or political slavery, HIS concern is not physical or political freedom. His concern is the freedom not to Sin no matter what political situation one lives under.

Bottom-line biblical truth: The United States of America is not a Christian nation, it is not special with a special calling, it has no covenant with the Living God, and it is definitely not a new Israel! At the best this country was initially Christianized, but from its very beginning most of the people who lived here have given themselves to various versions of a god (i.e. Polytheistic-Monotheism) and thus mostly to Churchianity, NOT Apostolic Christianity.

Jesus of Nazareth did NOT tell His followers to go and to make "Christian" nations. Neither did He tell them to make "Christian" cities.[124] Just as there will NEVER be World Peace until the Prince of Peace returns and establishes it, so there will NEVER be a Christian na-tion until the Bridegroom-King returns and establishes HIS nation, the Kingdom of Heaven on Earth. If there is anything The Church in this country should learn from the failures of "Christian" Rome, Calvin's

---

[122] See Appendix F
[123] See Appendix G
[124] I.e. John Calvin's Geneva.

Geneva, and the Puritan's "New Israel" is that these do NOT work... AND...are utterly unbiblical!

Therefore, the Living God is not concerned about the nation of the United States of America, not that Jesus doesn't care about the people living within every nation, but the nation itself is of no concern to Him. The Living God isn't trying to rescue nations, for every nation is going to go away and be replaced by His Kingdom (Revelation 11:15).

This God would like for all Americans to repent of their sins and to become a part of His Bride (2 Peter 3:9). But This God is not on some crusade to save America and Democracy as if America is the same thing as the Kingdom. It seems to me that most Christians do not realize that Jesus is not an American, and that He does NOT support the vast majority of what goes on here and what this country is all about.

Further, Jesus of Nazareth is a Jew, and He's a king, not a president. Most especially, the United States is ALREADY full of the Harlot-Babylon (a spiritual/moral and economic system) as well as the spirit of antichrist. Thus this nation is ALREADY leading the world to accept the Harlot-Babylon by putting people's rights, freedoms, and finances over godly standards which results in Sin no longer being considered Sin.

So...as for this country...it is NOT the greatest nation on the earth, at least not by Jesus of Nazareth's measurement of greatness.[125]

STONE NUMBER ELEVEN: MARRIAGE

The only people who stand before Jesus of Nazareth in judgment are those whose names are written in the Lamb's Book of Life.[126] Those whose names are not listed there are taken from Hell (a holding prison for the Lost who have died, just as Heaven is a holding place for the Saints who have died) to the Lake of Fire. There is no discussion. No

---

[125] Politicians are politicians. And one of the critical tactics of politicians is to know their audience, and thus use things they know their audience likes, such as what Obama did above. Another example is what senator Tom Daschle did in his speech the day after 9/11 in which he quoted Isaiah 9:10 to make a motivational pronouncement. Sadly, he or someone on his staff who came up with this verse did not keep it in its context, not even reading the very two verses before it – 9:8-9.
[126] 2 Corinthians 5:10; Revelation 21:27

opportunity to explain oneself or to plead for Mercy. In short, no audience with Jesus of Nazareth.

Again, only those whose names are in the Lamb's Book of Life get a conversation with Jesus when He judges them, for this is when they receive either rewards or suffer losses (e.g. 1 Corinthians 3:12-15).

Further, I believe biblically that for those who stand before Jesus in judgment, the very first issue He will judge, if a person was married, will be what he or she did as a husband or wife.

Why? Because marriage is THE most important human-to-human relationship. Then, if the person had children, Jesus will judge what he or she did as a parent. Then He will judge what one did with their parents, then what one did with one's siblings, then what one did with the "family of Believers," then what one did with all other people. And in judging through these levels of relationships, this process will reveal quite clearly one's relationship with Jesus, for what one does with others says much about where one is with Him (e.g. Matthew 25:37-45).

But again, THE relationship that says the MOST about a person's true relationship with Jesus is the marriage relationship.

So, sadly, this is one of the not-so-talked-about issues in The Church: The enormous numbers of failed marriages, both kinds, those that end in divorce as well as those that are un-divorced yet pathetic at the worst and mediocre at the best...and the impact these have on The Church! And one of the major reasons for this disgraceful condition of the vast majority of marriages between Christians (and the impact this is having on The Church) concerns the fact that the husbands and the wives are NOT growing and are NOT maturing in the First and the Greatest Commandment.

> **Whoever claims to love God yet hates a brother or sister** (i.e. one's spouse) **is a liar. For whoever does not love their brother and sister, whom they have seen, <u>cannot</u> love God, whom they have not seen.** (1 John 4:20)

When a person does not love his or her spouse...truly, it does not matter what else that person is doing.

This prolific failure of marriages (divorced or un-divorced but pathetic or mediocre) between two followers of Jesus of Nazareth is probably one of the most revealing evidences of the pitiful compromise-ing condition of The Bride in this country. Don't be fooled, there IS a spiritual connection between what is happening in The Bride in this country and what is going on in marriages between Christians.

In 1 Corinthians 15:46 Paul asserts a spiritual principle that occurs whether one realizes it or not.

The spiritual did not come first, but the natural, and after that the spiritual.

In other words, sometimes what is going on in the natural realm tells us something about what is going on in the spiritual realm.

Women and wives, it does not appear that you grasp the incredible importance you have as a woman and/or a wife, thus neither do you appear to comprehend the PROFOUND impact your actions have in the spiritual realm. Submitting, honoring, and following your husband, fitting yourself into his life has far more bearing than you can imagine.

Women want to be considered important. Well...they ARE! They ABSOLUTELY are! Just not as our culture says they are, but rather how Jesus says they are. Feminism and the Americanisms say that Jesus' assignment to wives is wrong, demeaning even. But these are demonic liars! For there is no Democracy in a godly marriage.[127]

It is true, women ARE the HIGHEST creature of Creation! For Creation moves from the most simple to the most complicated. Truly, women ARE the BEST of all that the Son made! Of course what is ALSO true is that to whom much is given...much is expected.

So it is a GREAT honor and an AWESOME privilege, as well as a HUGE responsibility to be the creature who represents Jesus' Bride in the natural. And not only is this a great honor and an awesome privilege and a huge responsibility to women, but there is also an EXECELLENT wisdom in one's assignment as a woman!

Think. As I just said, women ARE the highest and the best of all of Creation. But, as with the apostle Paul (2 Corinthians 12:7a), to keep women from becoming conceited about being the highest and the best of all of Creation, Jesus put them under a lesser creature, namely, their husband and/or male leadership in general. This is the place where wo-

---

[127] A wise husband wants and needs his wife's input, her perspective. However, the husband has the responsibility to make the final decision...which is not up for debate and a vote. This is because Jesus puts the husband in charge.

men can excel and shine, revealing the indescribable, breathe-taking beauty of being a woman! Remember, going down is going up in the Kingdom, and being the least and the last is to be first and great in the same way that This God's Grace is made perfect in weakness.

So, it is actually true, men ARE below woman. I'm not joking here. This is a biblical fact. However, in Jesus' wisdom He put women under male authority and male leadership, for better or for worse.

Now, do men screw up? YES and ABSOLUTELY!!! But that is not to be women's concern. Women get to trust Jesus to deal with the men and/or a husband when, not if, they're stupid (1 Peter 3:5-6). And in doing this, women get the PRIVILEGE of being an example to the world of Jesus' Bride who submits to HIM in ALL things.

Granted, Jesus is a perfect Husband and human husbands (or male leaders) are nothing of the sort, not even on a good day. But in this women get to acquire **"the unfading beauty of a gentle and quiet spirit"** (i.e. humility), something that is of **"great worth"** – GREAT WORTH! – to Jesus of Nazareth (1 Peter 3:4). So, do NOT minimize one's assignment as a woman, for if a woman demeans this, she is telling Jesus He is an idiot and doesn't know what He's doing!

———

Further, and this is a critically critical point: A wife is to serve the purpose of her husband.[128] For Woman was made FOR Man, not the other way around. Wives are their husbands' helpmeet, not the other way around.

And this is the SAME for The Church. The Church was made for Jesus, she is to be His helpmeet, not the other way around. Certainly Jesus serves His Wife, but NOT in the sense of giving over His place as the Head and the Leader. And so it is with husbands and wives, or male leaders and women, for there is no such thing as mutual submission.[129]

---

[128] This is a VERY important thing to consider when considering a husband, for if the man loves bowling, you're going to be doing a lot of bowling.

[129] Paul's statement **"Submit to one another out of reverence for Christ"** in Ephesians 5:21 is referring to what he had just said about Christian relationships in general. Then, he addresses husbands and wives separately, telling the wife specifically to submit to her husband. Paul does not tell the husbands to submit to their wives. Therefore, there is NO mutual submission in marriage. The husband is the head and the leader, for human marriage is a reflection of the Bridegroom-King's marriage with The Church in which He does not submit to His Wife, she submits to Him.

This is the Son's design. When Paul addressed this issue of wives and/or women usurping their husbands and/or male leadership, he pointed to Creation to support what he was saying (1 Corinthians 11:8).

And note this: When a wife agrees with her husband that's NOT submission. The-Living-God-less wives can do that! Submission BEGINS when the wife disagrees with her husband.

Wives, Jesus put your husband in charge. Even if he isn't doing a good job, that is between him and Jesus, not you and him. Jesus WILL hold him accountable at some point. In the meantime, as long as your husband doesn't ask you to deny Jesus or to do something immoral, you are to submit to him in ALL things. And you're to do so in the same way Jesus expects His Wife to do it to Him...BECAUSE you LOVE your Husband, and thus you LOVE your husband!

Feminism would disagree. So are you a Feminist-Christian, or are you an obedient follower of Jesus of Nazareth who does what He says to do? More, various Americanisms – Democracy, Personal Rights, Independence – would also disagree. So are you an American-Christian, someone who puts these unbiblical, pagan, humanistic beliefs over the qualities of the Kingdom, or are you someone who obeys the clear commands (not suggestions) of Jesus of Nazareth to women and wives?

The bottom-line wives is this: You are not only modeling what a godly wife is to other women (Titus 2:3-5[130]), but you also have the TREMENDOUS honor of modeling in miniature for all to see how The Church, the Wife of the Bridegroom-King relates to Him. Do not take either of these lightly!

If, women, you want some help from a woman, I suggest the book Created to Be His Help Meet, by Debi Pearl. It is excellent!

———————

Husbands. You have a gargantuan responsibility: loving and leading your wife (and your children) to know Jesus of Nazareth deeply! And while wives only have to submit, which to them may seem impossible but is doable, you are commanded to love and to lead like Jesus loves and leads...something that really IS impossible. For what human – male or female – can do that?!? What Jesus expects of husbands will take all their lives to try to get to, and even then they still won't have matched-up with Him![131]

---

[130] Note especially the reason: **"...so that no one will malign the Word of God."**

128

Certainly Jesus understands that you are nowhere near Perfect. He also knows no husband will ever love and lead his wife exactly like He does His. BUT...He does expect you to grow in the First and the Greatest Commandment, which is your only hope of developing His Love and His Wisdom in you with which to love and to lead your wife even somewhat like He loves and leads His Wife.

I don't have adequate words to describe the giganticness of this lifelong goal and purpose. And yet, just because it is insurmountable, even impossible, it is not optional. The good news is that men were designed to do it – to love and to lead. Therefore, as the husband you get to not only model to others what a godly husband is, but you also get to model in miniature what Jesus is like with His Bride.

So, human marriage is not merely about companionship and having children, as good as those are. Human marriage is about one man and one woman having the opportunity and the privilege of tasting a little something of why Jesus created Creation and to model that before others. And this is why divorce and un-divorced but pathetic or mediocre marriages are simply NOT acceptable. For more information and motivation, I suggest the following.

- Recovering Biblical Manhood and Womanhood, by John Piper and Wayne Grudem
- Countering the Claims of Evangelical Feminism, by Wayne Grudem
- No More Christian Nice Guy, by Paul Coughlin

One last issue about marriage.

A marriage between one man and one woman (only!) is established with a covenant. It is the only human-to-human relationship that is based upon a covenant. Neither partner has a covenant with their parents. They have no covenant with their siblings or friends. And they absolutely have no covenant with their own children. But the man and the woman do have a covenant with each other.

Therefore, NO ONE is to come between a husband and his wife. NO ONE is to seek to have a place with either one of them that is equal to what the person has with their partner, much less to have something

---

[131] This is like Paul's statement in Philippians 3:12-14.

greater than they have with their partner. Not the couple's parents. Not the couple's siblings. Not the couple's friends. Not the couple's own children even. A married couple is to keep their relationship high and above, foremost and before ALL other relationships.

And along this line of a couple protecting the sanctity and the pre-eminence of their covenantal relationship, the VERY BEST way to teach children, young and older, about Love is how a husband and wife express Love to each other that the children see them doing. When children are young and Daddy and Mommy, and later when they're older and Dad and Mom, are loving each other...this has a HUGE impact on the couple's children. HUGE!!!

STONE NUMBER TWELVE: LEADERS

All grocery stores sell food. And yet, as we all know, not much of what is sold is healthy for us, what with all the additives, preservatives, fructose, bad oils, processing, etc., etc., etc. I know a person who has been a nutritionist for some forty years, and she told me, "If there are more than about two lines of ingredients, put it back!"

I would give some similar advice concerning the "food" produced by various Christian leaders that is sold through various outlets.

For example, if the person's photo is prominent, or if the person has titles before his or her name and/or letters following their name, put it back. If the person is a popular leader of some mega-ministry, put it back. If the person openly lives the American Dream lifestyle, put it back. If there's a lot of fanfare and advertising about the person, put it back. If the person is making money from the sale of his or her materials, put it back quickly...and go wash your hands!

There are probably some more issues to consider when ingesting something considered to be Christian, but hopefully you get the point. Popularity, titles, bigness, charisma, accolades, the American version of success, etc., such things are good American advertising techniques for helping to push sales, but they are NOT what Jesus of Nazareth is about. And since one of the issues He addressed in "The Shaking Dream" concerns leaders, Jesus knows most people don't know how to measure whether a man is a godly leader or not.[132]

For Jesus and the apostles one of the major measurements of a godly leader has to do with suffering and lowliness, NOT seminary degrees, or personality, or leadership and/or administrative abilities, or any of the American versions of success, or even preaching/teaching skills. Here is something Paul says about himself that he says qualified him to be a leader:

> God chose the foolish things of the world to shame the wise; God chose the weak things of the world to shame the strong. God chose the lowly things of this world and the despised things – and the things that are not – to nullify the things that are, so that no one may boast before Him. It is because of Him that you are in Christ Jesus, who has become for us wisdom from God – that is, our righteousness, holiness and redemption. Therefore, as it is written: "Let the one who boasts boast in the Lord." <u>And so it was with me</u>, brothers and sisters. When I came to you, <u>I did not come</u> with eloquence or human wisdom as I proclaimed to you the testimony about God. For I resolved to know nothing while I was with you except Jesus Christ and Him crucified. <u>I came</u> to you in weakness with great fear and trembling. My message and my preaching <u>were not with</u> wise and persuasive words, <u>but with</u> a demonstration of the Spirit's power, <u>so that</u> your faith might not rest on human wisdom, but on God's power. (1 Corinthians 1:27 – 2:5)

Reread this. Carefully take in each thing Paul is saying about himself – he did not do ministry with eloquence or human wisdom; he knew nothing but Jesus crucified; he ministered in weakness, great fear, and trembling; his preaching was not with wise and persuasive words; he focused on having demonstrations of the Spirit's power; and he did all of this "so that" at the end of the day the people knew that whatever good may have happened it was NOT because of Paul and his human abilities, but rather because the Living God was working powerfully

---

[132] That's right, I said, "man." All leadership, especially upper levels of leadership and the teaching/ preaching ministry within The Church are to be done by men. This isn't Chauvinism; this is simply Jesus' design If you need more information, read <u>Leadership Is Male</u> by David Pawson.

among them. In short, if there was going to be any boasting, it would be boasting in the actions of the Almighty...NOT the person.

Biblically, as oppose to American thinking, the way up in Jesus' Kingdom is down. And a godly leader is to exemplify this. John the Baptist said it clearly:

> **The Bride belongs to the Bridegroom** (most leaders have forgotten this, or simply ignore it). **The friend who attends the Bridegroom waits and listens for Him, and is full of joy when he hears the Bridegroom's voice** (godly leaders don't do what they think; they do what Jesus tells them to do). **That joy is mine, and it is now complete. He must become greater; I must become less.** (John 3:29-30)

As long as The Church's leaders in this country can do "it" without the Holy Spirit, the Holy Spirit won't do anything! The days in which He allowed for some Ishmael-stuff are over!

True godly leaders "must" be people who have become less and not more, losers and not winners, poor in spirit and not superstars, persecuted and not glorified, etc. This is a "must" because as long as the leader has not gone down, Jesus cannot – as in being unable – go up. Only one person can be on top: either a leader or Jesus.

———————

Thus, one of the issues in The Church in this country are leaders who are building THEIR little kingdoms while claiming they're building Jesus' Kingdom. In case you didn't know this, Jesus does not need help doing what He wants to do. He does enjoy doing things with those who will follow Him and do it HIS way, but He is not dependent on people. He can make His own church service with rocks worshiping Him and donkeys preaching.[133]

(I'll restrain a sarcastic comment about what happens in SO many church services and flows from SO many pulpits in this country.)

When Paul defended his ministry before the Christians in Corinth in his second letter to them, he contrasted himself with the "super-apos-tles." Just think of this title of ridicule and derision. And yet, SO many

---

[133] Luke 19:40 and Numbers 22:28-30

of the leaders in this country have MUCH more in common with the "super-apostles" than with Paul!

For example, Paul listed all his persecution and failures as proof and evidence of his true calling and true anointing to be a true apostle:

> Whatever anyone else dares to boast about – I am speaking as a fool – I also dare to boast about. Are they Hebrews? So am I. Are they Israelites? So am I. Are they Abraham's descendants? So am I. Are they servants of Christ? (I am out of my mind to talk like this.) I am more. I have worked much harder, been in prison more frequently, been flogged more severely, and been exposed to death again and again. Five times I received from the Jews the forty lashes minus one. Three times I was beaten with rods, once I was pelted with stones, three times I was shipwrecked, I spent a night and a day in the open sea, I have been constantly on the move. I have been in danger from rivers, in danger from bandits, in danger from my fellow Jews, in danger from Gentiles; in danger in the city, in danger in the country, in danger at sea; and in danger from false believers. I have labored and toiled and have often gone without sleep; I have known hunger and thirst and have often gone without food; I have been cold and naked. Besides everything else, I face daily the pressure of my concern for all the churches. Who is weak, and I do not feel weak? Who is led into Sin, and I do not inwardly burn? If I must boast, I will boast of the things that show my weakness. The God and Father of the Lord Jesus, who is to be praised forever, knows that I am not lying. (2 Corinthians 11:21b-31)

Paul continues with one of his most vivid defenses AND stated differences between himself and the "super-apostles" in chapter twelve of 2 Corinthians:

> I must go on boasting. Although there is nothing to be gained, I will go on to visions and revelations from the Lord. I know a man (he's talking about himself) in Christ who fourteen years ago was caught up to the third Heaven. Whether it was in the body or out of the body I do not know – God knows. And I know that this man – whether in the body or apart from the body I do not know, but God knows – was caught up to paradise and heard inexpressible things, things that no one is permitted to tell. I will

boast about a man like that, but I will not boast about myself, except about my weaknesses. Even if I should choose to boast, I would not be a fool, because I would be speaking the truth. But I refrain, so no one will think more of me than is warranted by what I do or say, or because of these surpassingly great revelations (which is how we know Paul is talking about himself). Therefore, in order to keep me from becoming conceited (due to these incredible revelations Jesus gave him), I was given a thorn in my flesh, a messenger of Satan, to torment me. Three times I pleaded with the Lord to take it away from me. But He said to me, "My grace is sufficient for you, for my power is made perfect in weakness." Therefore I will boast all the more gladly about my weaknesses, so that Christ's power may rest on me. That is why, for Christ's sake, I delight in weaknesses, in insults, in hardships, in persecutions, in difficulties. For when I am weak, then I am strong. (vs. 1-10)

So, how does the person you're following measure up? Is he like Paul or is he like the super-apostles?

Americans hate this! To Americans, even Christian Americans, success is up into greater and bigger and better things...NOT downhill into weakness, insults, hardships, persecution, and difficulties. Such things are for those with "issues," and The Church prefers leaders who are winners who have their act put together quite well.

Well, Real Christians ARE to lose as far as the things and the philosophies of this world are concerned. And yet, SO many of The Church's leaders in this country live lives which reveal the American standards for success rather than Jesus' standards of success.

Paul continues his "crazy" talk:

Further, my brothers and sisters, rejoice in the Lord! It is no trouble for me to write the same things to you again, and it is a safeguard for you. Watch out for those dogs, those evildoers, those mutilators of the flesh. For it is we who are the circumcision, we who serve God by His Spirit, who boast in Christ Jesus, and who put no confidence in the flesh (or worldliness) – though I myself have reasons for such confidence. If someone else thinks they have reasons to put confidence in the flesh, I have more: circumcised on the eighth day, of the people of Israel, of the tribe of Benjamin, a Hebrew of Hebrews; in regard to the Law, a Pharisee; as for zeal, persecuting The Church; as for righteousness based on the Law, faultless. But <u>whatever were gains to me I now consider loss for the sake of Christ</u>. What is more, I consider everything a loss because of the surpassing worth of knowing Christ Jesus my Lord, for whose sake <u>I have lost all things</u>. I consider them dung that I may gain Christ and be found in Him, not having a righteousness of my own that comes from the Law, but that which is through faith in Christ – the righteousness that comes from God on the basis of faith. <u>I want to know Christ – yes, to know the power of His resurrection and participation in His sufferings, becoming like Him in His death, and so, somehow, attaining to the resurrection from the dead</u>. Not that I have already obtained all this, or have already arrived at my goal, but I press on to take hold of that for which Christ Jesus took hold of me. Brothers and sisters, I do not consider myself yet to have taken hold of it. But one thing I do: Forgetting what is behind and straining toward what is ahead, I press on toward the goal to win the prize for which God has called me heavenward in Christ Jesus. All of us, then, <u>who are mature</u> should take such a view of things. And if on some point you think differently, that too God will make clear to you. Only let us live up to what we have already attained. Join together in following my example, brothers and sisters, and just as you have us as a model, <u>keep your eyes on those who live as we do</u>. For, as I have often told you before and now tell you again even with tears, <u>many live as enemies of The Cross of Christ</u>. Their destiny is destruction, their god is their stomach, and their glory is in their shame. <u>Their mind is set on earthly things</u>. But our citizenship is in Heaven. And we eagerly await a Savior from there, the Lord Jesus Christ, who, by the power that enables Him to bring everything under His control, will transform our lowly bodies so that they will be like His glorious body. (Philippians 3).

Without suffering, without going down, without there being some sort of dying to Self, NO leader can truly know Jesus of Nazareth. In fact – IN FACT! – the exact opposite is true. The more "successful" by the world's standards a leader is the LESS he knows the Real Jesus and the less of the power of the Holy Spirit is expressed through him. This is a FACT! Like 2 + 2 is 4.

While some may question what I just said, remember Jesus' warnings about false expressions of power (e.g. Matthew 24:24). The Living God's power is made perfect in weakness, NOT in any sort of strength, and definitely NOT in American versions of strength.

Shouldn't every godly leader of Jesus' Bride in this country say in relation to how they're living life (not just in relation to doing ministry) what Paul said: **"Follow my example, as I follow the example of Christ"** (1 Corinthians 11:1)? The honest truth, the blatantly obvious actualities are that the VAST majority of leaders in this country are living NOTHING like the way Paul lived! Need just one example? How about the following standard for a measurement of a leader?

> **Now the overseer is to be above reproach, faithful to his wife, temperate, self-controlled, respectable, hospitable, able to teach, not given to drunkenness, not violent but gentle, not quarrelsome, <u>not a lover of money</u>.** (1 Timothy 3:2-3)

When a leader's lifestyle has more in common with the American Dream than with the fasted, self-denying lifestyle of the Kingdom, he is NOT a godly man or leader no matter how "good" his teaching, how many books he's written, how sharp his physical appearance, or how wonderful his personality and demeanor may be. And not only is a leader to live the fasted, self-denying lifestyle of the Kingdom, but he is also to call those under his care to do the same! The Church in this country MUST stop rationalizing this biblical standard for her leaders.

I need to say something about how Jesus of Nazareth trains the people HE calls to perform some leadership with HIS people.

First, not everyone who enters the ministry in this country did Jesus choose for that endeavor (Matthew 20:1-16, especially 16b). Attending a Bible college or a seminary means nothing to Jesus. Having degrees and letters and titles before or after one's name means even less to Him. He's not impressed with such things.[134] And it's not that learning some theology or even some practicum is wrong, but having

---

[134] The Pharisees loved having titles (Matthew 23:1-12).

lots of theology and experienced practicum is not evidence that Jesus of Nazareth called the person to the assignment of leadership. Thus, this is clearly one of the many problems among those in leadership in The Church in this country – very few were chosen by Jesus of Nazareth.

Secondly, the training Jesus puts those He has chosen through is very different than what The Church in this country says such a person needs. Again, it's not that learning is bad, it's not. It's even helpful. BUT, having knowledge without the anointing and purpose of the Holy Spirit only results in more religion and not the evidences and the realities of the Kingdom.

Therefore, one of the most important trainings Jesus puts those HE chose through is time in "the desert." Remember, pretty much everything Jesus does "comes in from the desert." If you're following a leader who has not come in from some sort of "the desert"...good luck!

If you are currently a leader, and you are not living the way Jesus of Nazareth expects of those in leadership, and I don't just mean morally, but also concerning the American Dream and the ways of weakness Paul wrote about, as well as per the all of the "stones" I've listed, and most importantly, there is no evidence of the Holy Spirit's anointing in your life, shouldn't the following concern you?

Watch out for false prophets (i.e. leaders). **They come to you in sheep's clothing, but inwardly they are ferocious wolves. <u>By their fruit you will recognize them</u>. Do people pick grapes from thornbushes, or figs from thistles? Likewise every good tree bears good fruit, but a bad tree bears bad fruit. A good tree cannot bear bad fruit, and a bad tree cannot bear good fruit. Every tree that does not bear good fruit is cut down and thrown into the fire. Thus, <u>by their fruit you will recognize them</u>. Not everyone who says to me, "Lord, Lord," will enter the Kingdom of Heaven, but only he who does the will of my Father who is in Heaven. Many will say to me on that Day, "Lord, Lord, did we not prophesy in your Name, and in your Name drive out demons and perform many miracles?" Then I will tell them plainly, "I never knew you. Away from me, you evildoers!"** (Matthew 7:15-23)

Not many of you should presume to be teachers, my brothers, because you know that we who teach <u>will be judged more strictly</u>. (James 3:1)

A true godly leader is someone who keeps on being filled (i.e. drenched, saturated) with the Holy Spirit and thus follows the Holy Spirit, manifesting the power/anointing of the Holy Spirit. Whether he has degrees from professional schools or not, matters not. If he is a morally good guy, looks good in a suit, is charismatic in his preaching, has an outgoing personality, or has any other worldly measurements or qualifications, absolutely matters not.

Which kind of a leader a person is – like Paul or like the "super-apostles" – is not too difficult to see. Sadly, it is extremely difficult to find those today in this country who are in fact consistently manifesting the character and the power of the Holy Spirit as a lovesick, humble, obedient follower of the Bridegroom-King who serves HIS purposes instead of their own.

Israel's watchmen are blind, they all lack knowledge; they are all mute dogs, they cannot bark; they lie around and dream, they love to sleep. They are dogs with mighty appetites; they never have enough. They are shepherds who lack understanding; they all turn to their own way, each seeks his own gain. "Come," each one cries, "let me get wine! Let us drink our fill of beer! And tomorrow will be like today, or even far better." (Isaiah 56:10-12)

Truly, as bad as it was in Isaiah's day, it's worse today among the vast majority of those in Christian leadership in this country! For not only do so very many of the leaders today have no shame in what they are doing, but they boast and claim biblical grounds for their lifestyles and their worldly teachings.

If you would like to see something more of the brokenness of Churchianity, I suggest Frank Viola's book Pagan Christianity?.

O come let us adore Him
O come let us adore Him
O come let us adore Him
Christ the Lord

For You alone are worthy
For You alone are worthy
For You alone are worthy
Christ the Lord

We'll give You all the glory
We'll give You all the glory
We'll give You all the glory
Christ the Lord[135]

---

[135] By Matt Redman

THE SOLUTION

The Solution

In those days John the Baptist came, preaching in the Desert of Judea and saying, "Repent, for the Kingdom of Heaven is near." This is he who was spoken of through the prophet Isaiah: "A voice of one calling in the desert, 'Prepare the way for the Lord, and make straight paths for Him.'" John's clothes were made of camel's hair, and he had a leather belt around his waist. His food was locusts and wild honey. People went out to him from Jerusalem and all Judea and the whole region of the Jordan. <u>Confessing their sins,</u> they were baptized by him in the Jordan River. But when he saw many of the Pharisees and Sadducees coming to where he was baptizing, he said to them: "You brood of vipers! Who warned you to flee from the coming wrath? <u>Produce fruit in keeping with repentance.</u> And do not think you can say to yourselves, '<u>We have Abraham as our father.</u>' I tell you that out of these stones God can raise up children for Abraham. The ax is already at the root of the trees, and <u>every tree that does not produce good fruit will be cut down and thrown into the fire.</u> I baptize you with water for repentance. But after me will come One who is more powerful than I, whose sandals I am not fit to carry. He will baptize you with the Holy Spirit [power] and with fire [purity]. His winnowing fork is in His hand, and He will clear His threshing floor, <u>gathering His wheat into the barn and burning up the chaff with unquenchable fire.</u> (Matthew 3:1-12)

I just wanted to remind you of the difficult and personally unpleasant assignment forerunners have, that, in the words of my older half-brother the surgeon, we cut people in order to heal them. Then, we hope that there will be some response to the "cutting" in the form of serious and deep conviction that ignites repentance.

Here's reality: Forerunners are terribly DIS-liked by MOST people, even those who consider themselves, and may even actually be, real followers of the Real Jesus. And such forerunners are disliked because of the Truth and the Reality with which the forerunner is confronting them. The simple fact is, what the forerunner is saying is considered harsh, and it IS harsh. But it's harsh BECAUSE the situation and the people are in VERY BAD condition and NEED to repent.

Thus, most forerunners are treated like Elijah who was considered the "troubler of Israel" (1 Kings 18:17) despite the fact that his intensions were godly, and his message was right.

For centuries Jesus has somewhat allowed some things that He really does not like. I call these things "Ishmaels," things men come up with that Jesus had no part in doing. Those days are OVER. Jesus will NOT have ANYTHING to do with "Ishmaels" any longer. The Church will do things His way or He will walk away.

So, here is The Solution: Repent: Turn FROM the evil AND turn TOWARD loving Jesus and showing that love by obeying Him.

No, really. Stop doing what you're doing with the "stones" (Two Trees, Which God, the Actual Presence, the Fear of the Lord, the True Gospel, Materialism, Psychology, the First and the Greatest Commandment, Music, Americanisms, Marriage, and Leaders), turn around, and go the completely opposite direction.

The Church in this country has got to stop putting Band-Aids on broken-bone-issues. She has got to stop covering up, or explaining away, or simply ignoring all the MANY warning signs that she is incredibly wrecked and in critical need of major repairs.

For those who put away their stupid, shallow, and worldly solutions, for those who wake up, see the warning signs, pull over, and cry out to the Chief Mechanic for REAL help...for to those who do this there may be some possibility that Jesus will respond with Real Help. For those who keep on ignoring the Check Engine lights while continuing to put on a charade...they and those who agree with them are headed off a cliff to their destruction.

Jesus answered: "Watch out that no one deceives you...many false prophets/leaders will appear and deceive most people." (Matthew 24:4 &11)

Further, whatever solution SOME of those who make up The Church in this country chose, it MUST be focused on what pleases Jesus of Nazareth, NOT what pleases people.

I am not knowledgeable in subjects like Math and Science. However, I did learn something from Algebra: Make one tiny, little mistake at the beginning, and one's final answer is WAY off! This is what I call the "Algebraic Conundrum." Here's what I mean.

A	B
$2 + 3 \times 4 - 1 + 3^2$	$2 + 3 \times 4 - 1 + 3^2$
$5 \times 4 - 1 + 3^2$	$2 + 3 \times 4 - 1 + 9$
$20 - 1 + 3^2$	$2 + 12 - 1 + 9$
$19 + 3^2$	$14 - 1 + 9$
$22^2 = 484$	$13 + 9 = 22$

Whether you know which equation is correct or not, note the HUGE difference between the two answers. As I said, in Algebra one doesn't miss the right answer by just a few digits. One small error at the beginning causes one to be WAY off in the final result.

Another example.

Two men walk into a bar. The barkeep asks, "What'll you have?"

The first man says, "A tall glass of H-two-O." The barkeep serves him his drink, the man guzzles it down, and says, "Thanks!"

The barkeep then asks the second man, "What will you have?"

This man says, "I'll have some H-two-O too."

The barkeep serves the man his drink, he also guzzles it down...and then drops dead.

Why? Well, H_2O is of course water. H_2O_2 is hydrogen peroxide. Just one additional atom makes water into a poison!

———

For millennia the God of Abraham, Isaac, and Jacob, the God of Israel, the One, True, Living God focused His attention on a very specific spot on the earth: Palestine. He did some things in some other areas around Palestine (i.e. Egypt, Assyria, Babylon, etc.), but always relating His actions to Palestine and to His people who lived there.

And Yahweh didn't just focus His attention on this part of the world, He actually dwelled there. For He promised to always be upon the Ark of the Covenant that was supposed to be placed in the Holy of Hollies in the Tabernacle of Moses.

Yahweh, because He is Holy and cannot turn down His Holiness, commanded that only the high priest, after he had been sanctified, and only one time a year, could enter this holiest of all places, made holy by His actual Presence. This was supposed to be an awesome thing. The actual Presence of the Son right there! Not far away. But in Person. Among His people.

And yet, it wasn't very long before this incredible blessing was taken for granted, and the Ark became something of a "lucky charm." Ignored even!

Here's a little of that story.

The Philistines were giving Israel problems. Having had enough, Israel decided to go to war against the Philistines. Unfortunately, this was at a time when Yahweh was not happy with His people. Why? Simple. The usual stuff. Israel was living a compromised life.[136]

So when Israel went out to battle the Philistines, with their "lucky charm" the Ark, Yahweh did not go with them. As a result, they got their butts kicked. The butt kicking was so bad that the Philistines even captured the Ark! Israel went home with their tail between their legs and the Philistines went home parading the Ark to show their victory.

However, it wasn't long before the Ark began to cause problems for the Philistines. Their butts began to blister and bleed. And it didn't take long for even these dull pagan Philistines to realized that it was the presence of the Ark that was causing their affliction.

So the Philistines had a meeting and decided to send the Ark back to Israel. But since nobody wanted to volunteer to take it back they decided to put the Ark on a cart hitched to two cows and to send the animals off in the direction of Israel, figuring that at some point some Israelites would see it and take it back.

Well, some Israelites did see it.

"Hey Moshe. Is that the Ark coming down the road?" wonders Eliezer.

"Naw, it can't be," says Moshe.

Squinting to get a better look, "I think it is! It sure looks like it," says Eliezer.

Eliezer and Moshe stop the cows and see that it IS the Ark on a cart.

"Whatever you do...DO NOT touch that thing!" cautions Eliezer. "It'll kill you quick as lightning."

"What should we do with it?" asks Moshe.

---

[136] There IS a lesson here to The Church in this country that explains SO much as to why she's SO pathetically powerless.

"Uh, I don't know. Maybe we should ask Abinadab if we can put it in his garage. He's got a nice big garage," suggests Eliezer.

"But isn't the Ark supposed to be in the Holy of Hollies in the Tabernacle of Moses?" queries Moshe.

"Yeah, I think so," says Eliezer.

"Well, shouldn't we take it there?" says Moshe.

"We're too busy. Let's just take it to Abinadab and be done with it," advises Eliezer.

This is the Ark of the Covenant with the ACTUAL Presence of the Living God...and Israel decides to put it in this guy's barn, throw a tarp over it, and essentially forget about it, going about their lives without it...without Him.

Sound familiar? It should. And if it doesn't...you're in a very, very bad place.

Quite a long time later, when David becomes king of Israel, he is quite "OCD" about having the Presence of the Living God with HIM.

[David] **swore an oath to the LORD, he made a vow to the Mighty One of Jacob: "I will not enter my house or go to my bed, I will allow no sleep to my eyes or slumber to my eyelids, till I find a place for the LORD, a dwelling for the Mighty One of Jacob."** (Psalm 132:1-5)

And after an initial attempt to bring the Ark into Jerusalem that failed rather badly, David finally succeeded in bringing the Ark into his city and putting it in a big tent he had set up on some property he had purchased (i.e. David's backyard).

David then threw open the flaps of this tent and said, "Who's with me? Let's go in and worship Yahweh in His Presence!" His buddies, guys like Asaph and the sons of Korah, must have just stood there frozen in fear and wondering if David was crazy.

David says, "Hey! Guys! Let's go in and worship Yahweh!" Pausing, seeing no intention to respond, "What are you waiting for? We've got the actual Presence of the Living God in there! Come on, let's do this!"

Asaph may have said, "Uh, David, it's the Ark. You know, only the high priest and only one time a year. We'll all die in there!"

Maybe that's when David said, "If I die, I die, I've GOT to have the Living God!!! Again, who's with me? Let's go for it!"

Maybe David's buddies looked at each other, shrugged their shoulders, and said, "What the heck. If we die, we die, for we too HAVE to have the Living God!"

And what about the Tabernacle of Moses? Oh, it was up and operational just a few miles down the road from Jerusalem and David's Tent ...WITHOUT...the Presence of the Living God! There are the priests in their rotating shifts doing religion while David and his group had Yahweh Himself.

This is DEFINITELY a lesson to The Church in this country!

At Pentecost the Presence of the Spirit was poured out.

This was PROFOUND. People were undone and overwhelmed by it. There were all sorts of manifestations of the Holy Spirit's Presence too, Fear of the Lord producing manifestations.

But in time, people once again seemed to take for granted this awesome Gift – the gift of the actual Presence of Jesus of Nazareth.

So, the Spirit moved out of Palestine and moved on to Asia Minor. Asia Minor then became the center of His Presence and what He was doing. But, again, the people forgot this Blessing and He withdrew, moving into Europe. It wasn't long before things repeated themselves yet again, and yet again Jesus turned His back and moved out of Europe and on to this country.[137]

When people take His Presence for granted, when they don't respond to Him, when they make the sacred and the holy secular and common, when they compromise with the world, He moves on. Oh, He will try to reach them, to convict them of what they're doing. But at some point, if at least some of the people fail to respond in the way He expects, He WILL move on.

So what I'm now going to say is beyond sad to me.

There is NO location on earth, NO group of people in which Jesus has done more for and given more to than to The Church in the United States of America. Again, the Holy Spirit has given and done more to The Church in this country than to ANY other people in ANY other place at ANY other time since Pentecost. That's a good thing...except that it comes with expectations.

---

[137] This is not only the facts of history since Pentecost, but it is also biblical. Chorazin and Bethsaida, two communities Jesus cursed and do not exist today (Matthew 11:21).

From everyone who has been <u>given much</u>, <u>much will be demand-</u><u>ed</u>; and from the one who has been <u>entrusted with much</u>, <u>much</u><u>more will be asked</u>. (Luke 12:48)

The Living God did incredible things for Israel, thus He had expectations of them. And when they failed severely, crucifying the Son, He has cut them off for nearly 2,000 years now. And these are people with whom He has a permanent covenant! Paul warned the Gentiles in Rome not to take the Living God for granted as Israel did, for He could cut them off just as He did Israel (Romans 11:21-23).

Since what I just said is true, has Jesus' standard changed for His Bride in this country? Is the Bride here SO arrogant as to think herself to be SO special that Jesus would never cut her off as He did Israel and as Paul warned the Gentiles in Rome?

Yes, this IS exactly the attitude of The Church in this country!

Well…I have some news for you.

Jesus of Nazareth has left this country.

He is no longer here.

And neither is He coming back.

He's moved on, something He has done several times down through history.

Mercifully, He has left a remnant. There are a few people and a few places, a VERY few, in this country where He is still involved. But not many.

For as much as He has given to His Wife here, and as much as He has done for His Wife here, just in the number of revivals and renewals and outpourings and resources, etc. etc., etc., the majority of His Bride in this country is NOT responding and is NOT doing what He expects. Again, to whom much is given…much is required.

So Jesus of Nazareth is done here.

He's moved on to a people who really do want him, people who live in countries the people of this country look down upon, thinking we're better than they are. The first will be last and the last will be first.

There is one last great harvest that will happen in the Last Days. However, little of it will happen in this country. Tellingly, many of those who know about this last great move of the Holy Spirit have assumed most of it will happen here in this country. This assumption flows from American arrogance! The truth is, most of the harvest will come from other nations, leaving this one out for the most part.

In short, Jesus' Wife (not the general The-God-less population) in this country, upon whom He has lavished more wonderful things than ANY other people, at ANY other time in history, in ANY other location on earth, has been unfaithful to Him. Jesus' Wife (not the general The-God-less population) in this country has loved herself, as well as other gods, instead of loving and thus obeying her Husband. And she is now suffering the consequences of her choices – the loss of His Presence.

Sadly, multitudes don't even recognize or sense His absence. Like the priests of the Tabernacle of Moses, they merely go through the Life-less-ness of Churchianity.

I am the true vine, and my Father is the gardener. He cuts off every branch in me that bears no fruit, while every branch that does bear fruit He prunes so that it will be even more fruitful. If anyone does not remain in me, he is like a branch that is thrown away and withers; such branches are picked up, thrown into the fire and burned. (John 15:1-2, 6)

Having said this, there MAY be SOME possibility that Jesus will have SOME response to SOME people who rend their hearts. Do you remember the prophetic dream I wrote about earlier in which a large group of Christians were praying based on Isaiah 64:1-3? Do you remember in this same prophetic dream that there were thousands of angels standing behind these praying Christians? And do you remember that every time these Christians cried out for the Lord to come and do incredible things, the angels pointed at these Christians and said:

Rend your heart and not your garments! (Joel 2:13a)

So the following provides some detail as to what this rending/tearing means.

As the research and data from Barna and Rainer show, MOST people who consider themselves to be Christians are into Churchianity, not Apostolic Christianity, the version of Christianity the apostles lived and preached. And these two things do NOT mix. Use whatever metaphor you like, new wine in old wine skins, darkness and light, the Living God and idols, etc., the bottom-line is that if you want the Real Jesus you will have to COME OUT of Churchianity.

I'm talking to the person who is not satisfied with what satisfies most. For it is right to want Jesus of Nazareth over Churchianity, or the Tent of David over the Tabernacle of Moses. So when I say, "come out," I mean literally. If you want Jesus of Nazareth you will NOT find Him among those doing Churchianity.

It truly is true that those who have been enlightened, those who have tasted the heavenly gift, those who have shared in the Holy Spirit, and those who have tasted the goodness of the Word of God and the powers of the coming Age (Hebrews 6:4-5) simply do not fit in with those who have not experienced Jesus of Nazareth and thus prefer the ritual of religion, the flamboyancy of theatrics, the emptiness of Churchianity, and the poisons of Worldliness.

Most Christians in this country will choose the Wide Road and will build their lives on sand. Only a few will find the Narrow Way and earnestly seek to build their lives on the Rock. This is what Jesus said would be the case. This is just the way it is.

And this is why Jesus and Paul could no longer or would no longer enter the synagogues. What they had was not wanted by the majority of the people. This is still true today. Most people prefer Churchianity over the Presence of Jesus of Nazareth. Don't try to change this. It will not change. Jesus said so:

The Kingdom of Heaven is like a man who sowed good seed in his field. But while everyone was sleeping, his enemy came and sowed weeds among the wheat, and went away. When the wheat sprouted and formed heads, then the weeds also appeared. The owner's servants came to him and said, "Sir, didn't you sow good seed in your field? Where then did the weeds come from?" "An enemy did this," he replied. The servants asked him, "Do you want us to go and pull them up?" "No," he answered, "because while you are pulling the weeds, you may uproot the wheat with them. Let both grow together until the harvest. At that time I will tell the harvesters: First collect the weeds and tie them in bundles to be burned; then gather the wheat and bring it into my barn." (Matthew 13:24-39)

Jesus of Nazareth is not going to purge Churchianity. He's going to allow it. Thus, those who want the Presence of Jesus need to connect themselves with others who are in pursuit of the Bridegroom-King.

Do not be yoked together with unbelievers. (Those in Laodicea were a form of unbelievers.) **For what do righteousness and wickedness have in common? Or what fellowship can light have with darkness? What harmony is there between Christ and Belial? Or what does a Believer have in common with an unbeliever? What agreement is there between the Temple of God and idols? For we are the Temple of the Living God. As God has said: "I will live with them and walk among them, and I will be their God, and they will be my people." Therefore, "Come out from them and be separate, says the Lord. Touch no unclean thing, and I will receive you." And, "I will be a Father to you, and you will be my sons and daughters, says the Lord Almighty."** (2 Corinthians 6:14-18)

For the person who wants to pursue Jesus of Nazareth this pursuit is impossible to do among people who are lost Unbelievers or worldly, compromised, name-it-claim-it, health-and-wealth, lukewarm Believers. To "spur one another" one needs to be with others of like heart, other-wise one's spurring will be viewed as offensive, bothersome, a problem, making waves.[138] Fact: People who do not want Jesus of Nazareth do not like being around those who do.

Another reason to come out of Churchianity and to connect with even a few of like desire – to deeply know, love, and follow Jesus of Nazareth – is expressed in a little psalm, Psalm 133.

How good and pleasant it is when brothers live together in unity![139] It is like precious oil poured on the head, running down on the beard, running down on Aaron's beard, down the collar of his robes. It is as if the dew of Hermon were falling on Mount Zion. For there the LORD commands His blessing, **even life forevermore.**

The psalmist says that when there is a people who are of like pas-sion for the Presence of the Living God, when there is a people who will

---

[138] In Hebrews 10:25 the author is NOT telling these Hebrew followers of Jesus of Nazareth who were being persecuted to "attend church." The author is talking about finding a way, even in persecution, to occasionally hangout with a few other faithful followers of Jesus.
[139] This is not ecumenical unity. This is unity like those in the upper room who were all in one accord as they sought and waited for the Holy Spirit, the Presence of Jesus. Check out the song, "Hinei Ma Tovu."

not settle for anything but being drenched and soaked in His power and His anointing (e.g. the "precious oil"), when there is a people who hunger and thirst for the High Priest Himself, that there, among THOSE people, the Living God will command His blessing to also be.

In other words, when a group of people are like David, wanting the Presence of the Living God no matter the cost, for they are sick of being in the Tabernacle of Moses (i.e. Churchianity) with its empty ritual and lack of the Presence of the Almighty, THOSE are the people the Living God blesses with Himself.

So once again, come out from among those who are settling for Churchianity and join with those, even those few, who are in hot pursuit of Jesus of Nazareth Himself. Don't settle. Don't compromise. Don't drink from a cistern. Demand that Jesus give you the Real Thing, for it is better to "die" of thirst than to drink from a cistern or a sewer, for "death" by dysentery is far worse.

Besides coming out of Churchianity and connecting with even a few who want Jesus of Nazareth (e.g. in someone's living room), another thing that is critical to pay close attention to are the things this Jesus says TO do and the things He says NOT to do in the seven letters He dictated in the Revelation, chapters two and three.[140]

———

Lastly, remember Who you are pursuing.

These are rebellious people, deceitful children, children unwilling to listen to the LORD's instruction. They say to the seers, "See no more visions!" and to the prophets, "Give us no more visions of what is right (straight)! Tell us pleasant (smooth) things, prophesy illusions (deceptions). Leave this way, get off this path, and stop confronting (presenting) us with the Holy One of Israel!" (vs. 9-11)

Not the loving one, or the merciful one, or the grandfatherly one. Not that the Living God isn't loving and merciful. He is. But even in His Love and Mercy, and before His Love and Mercy, He is Holy. Sadly, The Church in this country does not seem to know this, and most do not want to be confronted with this Holy One.

---

[140] See Appendix H

This is what the LORD says: "Let not the wise man boast of his wisdom or the strong man boast of his strength or the rich man boast of his riches, but let him who boasts boast about this: that he (intimately) **understands and** (personally) **knows ME** (who He actually is)**, that I am the LORD, who exercises kindness, justice, and righteousness on Earth, for in these I delight," declares the LORD.** (Jeremiah 9:23-24)

My point? Don't be among those who reject prophetic words of what is "right" (i.e. straight). Don't be among those who prefer "pleasant things" (i.e. smooth) and "illusions" (i.e. deceptions). And MOST importantly, be sure you actually and intimately know the Holy One of Israel who exercises kindness, justice, and righteousness – The Jesus.

In fact, being forceful and violent, hungry and thirsty to have this Jesus is Step One, for anything less than this quality is either being Cold, which is bad, or being Religious, which is worse, or being Lukewarm, which is significantly worse.

Those who know Jesus intimately and deeply are people who have an insatiable hunger and a driving thirst to have Him intimately and deeply. So if you do not have this characteristic...then ask the Holy Spirit for it. For one of His job assignments is to reveal the glory and the magnificence of Jesus of Nazareth to those who MUST have Him.

If all of this sounds too hard, that is probably evidence that you need to repent, for no one should say that following Jesus is easy. IT IS NOT. Following the Real Jesus, Jesus of Nazareth requires hard choices:

Large crowds were traveling with Jesus, and turning to them He said: "If anyone comes to me and does not hate (Greek: "treat as secondary") **father and mother, wife and children, brothers and sisters – yes, even their own life – such a person cannot be my disciple. And whoever does not carry their cross and follow me cannot be my disciple. Suppose one of you wants to build a tower. Won't you first sit down and estimate the cost to see if you have enough money to complete it? For if you lay the foundation and are not able to finish it, everyone who sees it will ridicule you, saying, "This person began to build and wasn't able to finish." Or suppose a king is about to go to war against another king. Won't he first sit down and consider whether he is able with ten thousand men to oppose the one coming against him with twenty thousand? If he is not able, he will send a**

delegation while the other is still a long way off and will ask for terms of peace. <u>In the same way</u>, those of you who <u>do not give up everything</u> you have <u>cannot</u> be my disciples. Salt is good, but if it loses its saltiness, how can it be made salty again? It is fit neither for the soil nor for the manure pile; <u>it is thrown out</u>. <u>Whoever has ears to hear, let them hear</u>.[141] (Luke 14:25-35)

I will worship
With all of my heart
I will praise you
With all of my strength
I will seek you
All of my days
I will follow
All of your ways

I will give you all my worship
I will give you all my praise
You alone I long to worship
You alone are worthy of my praise

I will bow down
Hail you as King
I will serve You
Give you everything
I will lift up
My eyes to your throne
I will trust you
Trust you alone

I will give you all my worship
I will give you all my praise
You alone I long to worship
You alone are worthy of my praise[142]

---

[141] Jesus is referencing Isaiah 6:9-10, which He also quoted in Matthew 13:13-17.
[142] Song by David Ruis.

THE RETURN

The Return

Okay, here's the last thing I believe Jesus of Nazareth put in me to deliver...and **WHY** all I've express above matters.

Do you remember the book, <u>88 Reasons Why The Rapture Will Be In 1988</u>, by Edgar Whisenant? I'm not trying to be funny (although there is something funny about this, c'mon, admit it), but if my memory serves me correctly, I believe this book was followed by Mr. Whisenant's attempt to save his reputation with another book titled something like, <u>89 Reasons Why Jesus Is Returning In 1989</u>.

Also, are you aware of how MANY times people thought, "This is it; this is the Big One; Jesus is returning any minute now!"?

Let's see, just since the 1700's, there was the Revolutionary War in which most of the pastors in the Colonies taught that the King of England and the Catholic Pope were the Antichrist and that the Colonies were the New Israel and that Jesus was returning to establish His Kingdom on this continent among the Colonies.[143]

Then there was the Civil War, with some on both sides claiming the other was the Antichrist and Babylon.

Then there was World War I. Approximately 20 million people lost their lives in this war, a sum NEVER before even imagined in the annals of war, making it seem like Armageddon. But it wasn't Armageddon.

In the next war, WWII, approximately 60 million people perished, which really made this war seem like The End.[144] Ironically WWII was something of the End Times in miniature, for EVERY issue in WWII is going to make a comeback, only this last time on a MUCH greater scale. But, WWII was not the End Times, Hitler was not the Antichrist, and Germany was not Babylon.

And today there seems to be an explosion of this-and-that End Times scenario.

Here's some good news: The United States of America is NOT the Harlot-Babylon. However, the people in this country, as well as people all over the world, ARE AT THIS MOMENT being set up to receive the Harlot-Babylon's influence as she acts as the interim step between

---

[143] In those days no one spoke of a Pre-Tribulation Rapture.
[144] Look at the percentages John gives in the Revelation of the death toll in the war in which Jesus of Nazareth drives Evil off the planet. These numbers will be in the billions!

where people are now and where the Antichrist will want them to be. Although the Harlot-Babylon will one day be located in the area of ancient Babylon, it is important to keep in mind that at its core this prostitute is a moral and economic entity more than a location.[145]

For example, most people are not going to make the leap from being Catholic, Methodist, Presbyterian, Baptist, Evangelical, Pentecostal, Charismatic, Hindu, Buddhist, Muslim, New Age, or whatever to...worshiping Satan! Most people need an in-between step. This is what the Harlot-Babylon is. Its purpose is to move people from where they are now in some religious/moral view toward worshiping the Antichrist. Thus, all the talk about tolerance, acceptance, Democracy and personal freedoms and individual rights, save the planet, etc....THAT'S the essence and the message of the Harlot-Babylon.

And by the way, it is NOT the assignment of The Church to stop this movement toward the Harlot-Babylon, and then the Antichrist. The Church is ABSOLUTELY NOT to use human tools such as legislation to attempt to reverse this trend. Laws do not make people righteous, for the problem is internal (i.e. one's heart) and not external.

Just as Jesus told the Disciples that His being tortured and killed MUST happen, and thus Peter's sword and his desire to save Jesus were of no use (Matthew 26:52-54), SO IS THIS downward deprivation supposed to happen. Again, the Church isn't to try to stop the direction American society and the world is going, she's to prepare to stand in the midst of it and to declare The Truth no matter the results.

Now of course, when the real followers of Jesus stand up and say things like, "Homosexuality is not normal, it's Sin, just like adultery, incest, pedophilia, necrophilia, or zoophilia," they're going to catch Hell... literally. And this too is supposed to happen, for Jesus said so (e.g. Matthew 10:17-39; John 15:18-25).

And as for getting End Time teachings from the news media, this is very foolish! So what if the United States is attacked by some electromagnetic pulse (an EMP) that wipes out much of our communications. So? What does that concern The Church? It may make life in this country difficult, but again, so what? How is that some sign that Jesus is about to return? Because the cable TV went out? Because cell phones don't work? Because one can't get cash from the ATM? Really?

---

[145] For more information I suggest: Babylon: The Resurgence of History's Most Infamous City, by Peter Herder.

More to the point: Do we actually think that Jesus is returning to save America, as if America is His Kingdom? Are the issues of the End Times about some sort of battle for the American lifestyle of personal freedom and rights, wealth and materialism? Jesus isn't "saving" nations. He's inviting individual people of any nation, the whosoever's, to be a part of His Bride. So He's not "saving" nations (except the nation of Israel) because He's going to establish His own nation – the Kingdom.

And the thing is, Jesus told us point-blank NOT to look at the news and the current events to discover ANYTHING about the End Times, other than the obvious fact that the world is crumbling and thus moving toward the time when He will return.

> **You will hear** (e.g. from the media) **of wars and rumors of wars, but see to it that you are not alarmed. Such things must happen, but the End is still to come.**   (And it will get even worse.) **Nation will rise against nation, and kingdom against kingdom. There will be famines and earthquakes in various places. All these are the beginning of birth pains.** (Matthew 24:6-8)

Now I'm going to say some things I believe are critically important for The Church in this country to know concerning what is about to unfold. Obviously, I think Jesus of Nazareth showed me these things, which I'm sure every person who has expressed some sort of End Time scenario believes about what they are saying about the End Times.

BUT...here's the difference: I'm going to simply go through what Jesus SAID. This is NOT my opinion based on doing some twisting or pasting together of snippets of scriptures or listening to the news media or researching the Internet. What I'm about to show you is simply what Jesus of Nazareth said about the End Times.

But first...

———————

The Living God has provided general timeframes concerning His actions on several occasions. Thus, this is not unusual for Him.

For example, the very first timeframe He gave had to do with the timing of The Flood. This began when Yahweh decided to judge the people of the earth. Being patient, He called Enoch to be a preacher of righteousness, to tell the human race that the Living God was going to deal with all ungodliness unless there was massive repentance.

Enoch, the seventh from Adam, prophesied about these men: "See, the Lord is coming with thousands upon thousands of His holy ones to judge everyone, and to convict all the ungodly of all the ungodly acts they have done in the ungodly way, and of all the harsh words ungodly sinners have spoken against Him." (Jude 14-15)

When Enoch was in his sixties he had a son who Yahweh told him to name Methuselah, which means, "when he dies it will happen." Enoch was a prophetic person who named his son a prophetic name in order to prophesy the timing of This God's judgment of the entire human race. So both Enoch and Methuselah knew that when Methuselah died Yahweh would judge the earth.[146]

And Methuselah lived longer than any other human being, nine hundred, sixty-nine years, which is a testimony to Yahweh's patience with mankind. But when Methuselah died it began to rain, really, really rain! Noah was Methuselah's grandson; thus he knew the propheticness of his grandfather's name, believed it was true, and acted upon it by building an ark.

Another time Yahweh provided a timeframe was when He told Abraham that his descendants would be slaves for four hundred years.

Then the LORD said to him, "Know for certain that for four hundred years your descendants will be strangers in a country not their own and that they will be enslaved and mistreated there. In the fourth generation your descendants will come back here, for the Sin of the Amorites has not yet reached its full measure." (Genesis 15:13, 16)

He didn't tell Abraham the day and hour his descendants would be released, but He did give Abraham a timeframe of four hundred years.

Yet another occasion in which the Living God provided a timeframe was when He told Judah that they would be in captivity in Babylon for seventy years. Again, He didn't tell them the day and the hour of their release, but He did give them a timeframe of it.

---

[146] This is not unusual, for others have prophetic names, such as Hosea's three children, as well as Jesus Himself, whose name means "Yahweh saves."

This is what the LORD says: "When seventy years are completed, I will come to you and fulfill my good promise to bring you back to this place. (Jeremiah 29:10)

Another example.

Surely you know that Jesus was not born on December 25th. December 25th was a pagan holiday that the Catholic Church adopted when it did its usual thing of trying to blend the World with The Church (ignoring Colossians 2:8). Sadly, Catholic leaders, and later Protestant and Evangelical leaders, failed to check the Bible, for the Bible tells us the timeframe – not the day and the hour – in which Jesus of Nazareth entered this world born of a virgin.

At the beginning of Luke's account of Jesus' life and ministry he tells us that Zechariah, John the Baptist's father, belonged to the priestly tribe of Abijah (1:5-25). And we know from 1 Chronicles 23:24-32 which month this tribe was assigned to serve in the Temple – the fourth month of the Jewish calendar which is Tammuz, or by our calendar, late June and early July. Luke also tells us that after Zechariah's encounter with the angel Gabriel that when he had finished his assigned service time he went home to his wife Elizabeth, who had been unable to get pregnant, and he got her pregnant.

Let's consider what happened to Zachariah with the angel Gabriel.

First, ole Zach had a face-to-face encounter with an angel! And not just some angel, but Gabriel, one of the high-ranking angels! This alone was incredible!!!

But, why did Zach have this angelic encounter? Well, the Living God sent Gabriel to tell Zach that He had heard his years and years and years of pleading to give him and his wife at least one child...and now... Zachariah and Elizabeth are going to have a child, a baby. Finally!!!

Surely Zach must have sensed that there was more to what Gabriel was doing than merely informing him that he was finally going to have a child. Well, there was more.

The angel tells Zach that the child is going to be a boy! Now, to a Jewish man having a son is important, not that having daughters is bad. It's just that having a son is considered a great honor, and having a first-born son is a very great honor.

But it gets better.

Gabriel tells Zachariah that this boy is going to be a godly man. To Zachariah this is REALLY wonderful news, for what godly father doesn't hope for children who will deeply know and love Yahweh? But again, why send Gabriel to tell Zach these two things: it's a boy and he's going to know This God.

So it gets even better.

The angel tells Zach that this boy isn't going to be a common laborer or a businessman, but a person who does ministry. And not just the ministry of a lowly, unknown priest like Zachariah. Instead, many people are going to be impacted in some way by this kid's ministry. "Cool," Zach must have thought.

But it still gets much better.

Gabriel tells Zach that this boy's ministry will be that of being the forerunner to the Messiah.

"Whoa, whoa, whoa," Zach must have said! "My son is going to be the forerunner to the Messiah with the anointing of Elijah on him as prophesied in Scripture???"

Then, as what Gabriel is telling him sinks in, Zach must have suddenly burst out, "The Messiah is coming?!?!? Are you kidding me?!?!? The One my people have been praying, hoping, and longing for is going to actually be here?!?!? And MY son is going to prepare the way for Him?!?!? I don't believe it!!!"

Wouldn't it have been hard for you to hear all this incredible news? That you are finally going to have a child, a male-child, and that he will be a godly man with a vital ministry – that of being the forerunner to the actual Messiah? And wouldn't you have been blown away to hear the timeframe (not the day and the hour) of the Messiah's coming as it relates to your son's life? Wouldn't you have doubted all of this?

I would have.

So, when Zach's time of service was over, do you think he nonchalantly made his way home? Maybe stopping by Home Depot to check out a new something or other. I don't. I think he RAN home, burst into his house, rushed up to Elizabeth, who was probably busy doing something, and gave her "the look." Women know "the look." The look that says, "I want you and I want you NOW!" And being unable to speak, Zach probably started pulling on her out of sheer intensity to see all Gabriel told him begin to come to pass. Further, I believe Zach got Elizabeth pregnant on the first try!

Luke also tells us that Elizabeth was in her sixth month of her pregnancy when Mary shows up to tell her that she had just been impregnated by the Holy Spirit (1:26-38). Thus, we can calculate that Jesus was born fifteen months after John was conceived by Zechariah and Elizabeth. This puts Jesus' birth sometime in the seventh month of the Jewish calendar – Tishri, which is our late September and early October. And it is at this time of the year that the Feast of Trumpets occurs.

The rabbis had taught for centuries that this would be the season when the Messiah would come, for the whole point of the Feast of Trumpets is to announce a new beginning. This feast is made up of three events: Rosh Hashanah which is the New Year, Yom Kippur which is the Day of Atonement, and the Feast of Tabernacles which remembers the wandering in the desert and the final harvest and ingathering.

Again, we don't know the day and the hour of Jesus' birth, His first coming, but we DO know FROM the Bible the timeframe.

One more example.

Jesus told the disciples the following several times:

From that time on Jesus began to explain to His disciples that He must go to Jerusalem and suffer many things at the hands of the elders, the chief priests, and the teachers of the Law, and that He must be killed and on <u>the third day</u> be raised to life. (Matthew 16:21)[147]

Jesus gave the Twelve a timeframe of what He was about to do – He would be killed and on the third day after His death He would come back to life. How this wildly incredible thing Jesus is telling them must have struck the Disciples!

"You're going to die…and then you're going to come back to life?!?!? Wow!"

When Jesus told them this they didn't really grasp what He was saying. However, later they would understand why He had to do this. So when Jesus tells them this three-day plan He is helping them by telling them the timeframe of this plan. All they have to wait is just three days, in fact, not even three twenty-four-hour periods, but just from Friday at about 6:00 pm to Sunday very early in the morning. Surely, despite their confusion, remembering that Jesus had told them this timeframe helped the Disciples to some degree.

And so, Jesus is also helping His followers concerning His return to this planet by giving the timeframe of that process. Jesus said no one knows the day and the hour of it (Matthew 24:36), but He DID give the Disciples, and The Church today who has ears to hear, the timeframe of

---

[147] Matthew 17:23, 20:19b

His return to this planet. This is not unusual, for as you can see He has given timeframes many times.

———————

I'm going to use Matthew's account of Jesus' teachings on the End Times as the main text, for Matthew tells us the most. And to get this complete picture from Jesus in Matthew's gospel one needs to keep what He says in the context of chapters twenty-one through twenty-five, for most of what is contained in these chapters happened on a single day.

Here's the scene.

It's the Passion Week. It is the first day of that week, Sunday. Jesus had been telling His disciples that He would be killed, that He MUST be killed, but that He would come back to life three days later (i.e. Matthew 20:17-19). So on this Sunday, as per the Scriptures (Zechariah 9:9), Jesus enters Jerusalem on a little donkey, a symbol of peace (as opposed to coming on a warhorse – Revelation 19:11).

Mark gives us the detail that after entering the city Jesus went to the Temple to see what was going on. But because the day was getting late, all Jesus did was to take note of the activities there, turn around, and leave.

Pause for just a moment.

I need to back up the story to about three years earlier.

The very first thing Jesus did on His very first official day as The Messiah was NOT to go by the Sanhedrin with Starbucks and Krispy Kreme donuts for everyone, cordially introduce Himself, and inform the leaders that, golly-gee, He was the actual Messiah. You know, approaching them in a friendly, non-offensive, non-threatening way...and definitely doing some personal miracles to butter them up, maybe even making some promises to some of them of some lofty position they will have in His Kingdom.

Nope, instead, deliberately and with resolute purpose, Jesus makes a whip out of some pieces of rope. Then, suddenly and without any warning, He begins violently and indiscriminately striking people, throwing over furniture even, raging angrily and shouting at the top of His lungs, "What are you doing?!?!? You have turned my Father's House, which is supposed to be a place of intercession for all ethnic groups, into a Wal-Mart!!!" Not exactly a polite and dignified way to start His public ministry.

Now back to Monday of the Passion Week.

It's Monday morning and Jesus is on His way back to Jerusalem, having spent the night in Bethany. Maybe He hadn't had any breakfast, or maybe He just wanted a snack. Or maybe...His Father told Him to do something that would become a vivid physical prophetic sign that the Disciples (and His followers today) would easily grasp.

And this vivid physical prophetic act was to approach a fig tree, and when He saw that it had no fruit, He cursed the tree, and it dried up, and died quite quickly.[148]

As for what Jesus did to the fig tree, the Disciples were confused. They didn't understand WHY Jesus did this. But not ready to explain the reason He did what He did, Jesus merely tells them HOW He did it. And He does this by reminding them that He can only do what He sees the Father doing (John 5:19), and because the Father told Him to do it, He had the power to do it. This is what He's talking about when He tells them about trusting in order to cast a mountain into a sea.[149]

However, this is not THE lesson of the fig tree, as we'll see in a moment.

Jesus then arrives with His disciples into the city of Jerusalem and makes His way straight to the Temple, powerwalking as a person with a planned purpose. When He gets into the Temple's outer court He ONCE AGAIN wreaks havoc, tearing up the people and the Temple in the same way He had at the beginning of His ministry. In other words, after three or more years of Jesus' ministry, including the preparative ministry of His cousin John, NOTHING had changed in the spiritual life of the nation, the city of Jerusalem, the Temple, and in the leaders as a result of the Living Word (John 1:1, 9-11) being among them.

And that is NOT acceptable to Jesus.

What a scene! Jesus of Nazareth destroying the business of religion, for He hates Churchianity as there is NOTHING in it that pleases Him or is of His doing. And while He is doing this, as if to provide some musical melody and beat to His zeal, some children – the innocent who had eyes to see and ears to hear – are chanting over and over that He is the son of David and the Savior (Matthew 21:15b)! How ironic.

---

[148] Mark informs us that it was not the season for figs, but as we will see shortly, Jesus expects fruit from His people in and out of season.

[149] IF Jesus tells a person to cast a mountain into a sea, he or she can do so, knowing it will happen. IF Jesus does not tell a person to cast a mountain into a sea, that mountain isn't going anywhere. The issue isn't some sort of name-it-and-claim-it faith, a Christian witchcraft. The issue is the trust to obey what one is told to do.

It is clear: Jesus is pissed. And so are the leaders. The leaders got angry the first time Jesus did this, but this time the spirit of murder is on the edges of their hearts (John 11:53)! They questioned His authority to do what He did the first time, and Jesus responded by prophetically telling them that they would crucify Him the next time He did this (John 2:18-21). Which is now going to come to pass.

For Jesus, on the one hand He is very angry because of the lack of change despite of all He has done. But on the other hand, He also knew there wasn't going to be any change. Jesus knew His ministry was going to have the same result as Isaiah's.

You will be ever hearing but never understanding; you will be ever seeing but never perceiving. For this people's heart has become calloused; they hardly hear with their ears, and they have closed their eyes. Otherwise they might see with their eyes, hear with their ears, understand with their hearts and turn, and I would heal them. (Matthew 13:14-15).[150]

After the mayhem Jesus unleashes in the Temple this second time, the leaders are more prepared to confront Him, for what follows is a much longer conversation about Jesus' authority to do this than on the first occasion in which He did it. And their choice of "weapons" for this combat is a game of Who Knows the Bible Best. Then as the livid leaders try to pin Jesus with their Bible questions, Jesus' responses are like humiliating slaps to the face, but slaps that are intended to wake them up from their religious slumber. For example, Jesus says things like:

I tell you the truth, the tax collectors and the prostitutes are entering the Kingdom of God ahead of you. For John came to you to show you the way of righteousness, and you did not believe him, but the tax collectors and the prostitutes did. And even after you saw this, you did not repent and believe him. Therefore I tell you that the Kingdom of God will be <u>taken away from you and given to a people who will produce its fruit</u>. He who falls on this stone will be broken to pieces, but he on whom it falls will be crushed. (Matthew 21:31b-32, 43-44)

---

[150] Paul too knew his ministry among the Jews would have the same lack of results as Isaiah's and Jesus' – Acts 28:26-27.

Could Jesus have said anything more insulting...and true?!?

And yet, Jesus' words are having absolutely NO impact. His lips are moving, weighty things are coming out of His mouth, and the leaders cannot – as in being unable – hear them. The scene is like that of a jack-hammer with its pounding, pounding, pounding, and the leaders are getting nothing, nothing, nothing except angrier, angrier, and angrier.[151]

In everything Jesus says to these leaders He is confronting, exposing, and demeaning them in front of the people. And in every way, no matter which approach the leaders take, Jesus utterly shuts them down, thus we clearly can see who knows the Bible best. Again, this is embarrassing to these leaders as well as infuriating.

It's as if...in these heated exchanges...Jesus is DELIBERATELY provoking them...to kill Him. Could this be? Yes. This IS exactly what He's doing.

———————

And as if what Jesus has already said isn't strong enough so far, we come to Matthew, chapter twenty-three.

Matthew, chapter twenty-three begins with a scathing indictment of the spiritual leaders as Jesus rips them for who and what they actually are. His favorite words for them are "hypocrites," "blind guides," "blind fools," "blind men," and ultimately, "snakes" and "brood (i.e. family) of vipers,"[152] all of which He uses repeatedly in an attempt to pierce their hearts to bring about repentance.

Pause. Look at what Jesus is doing. He is calling these guys names, hard names, bad names. He's not just talking about their actions; He's labeling them themselves! He's telling them what they are! Clearly, in this LONG monologue Jesus holds nothing back, unleashing a torrent of truth about what is in these leaders' hearts as well as the foolishness of the things they do.[153]

But, the most outstanding thing Jesus does in Matthew, chapter twenty-three is that He pronounces seven – the number of perfection – curses ("Woe!") upon the leaders and upon the nation of Israel. In short, Jesus curses the "fig tree," that is, Israel, with a Perfect Curse. And one of the ways we know He is cursing Israel the "fig tree," is that

---

[151] Jeremiah 23:29
[152] A reference to the snake in the Garden. Jesus is saying that they are of Satan's lineage and family! Churchianity is demonic.
[153] There is much in this chapter twenty-three that applies to most leaders in this country.

in verse thirty-eight He prophesies the utter destruction of the nation, saying it too will end up like the actual fig tree – dried up and dead.

Look, your <u>house</u> is left to you <u>desolate</u>.

In 70 AD Rome fulfilled this prophesy, and the nation of Israel was no more. The people were either killed or taken captive and dispersed throughout other regions. Jerusalem, as well as other communities, were completely destroyed. By the time Rome was done, Palestine was in fact a desolate wasteland.[154]

I imagine that at these two final prophetic statements at the end of Matthew, chapter twenty-three a heavy silence fell upon them all – the leaders, the crowd, and the disciples. No one daring to speak, no one knowing what to say, a very uncomfortable moment as the weight of Jesus' pronouncements presses down hard on everyone.

For Jesus, there was nothing more to say. So maybe He looked at the Disciples and said, "Let's go." And with that He turned to leave with the Disciples trailing behind Him in single file, heads down, not wanting to make eye-contact with anyone.

If there was any doubt, all doubt has been removed. Jesus is a dead man! He purposely picked a fight, and in this fight He verbally beat the Hell out of His opponents, exposing and shaming them as much as He could. There is now NO question. They're going to kill Him! They are going to get even. They're going to do whatever they have to do to regain their honor and their status in the eyes of the people. And to do this they must do more than just prove that Jesus is false. They must eliminate Him.

True, the Jews used a variety of tactics to get the weak-willed, politically unstable politician, Pilate, to do their dirty work. And true, Pilate the politician tried to maneuver around the Jews' manipulations, even presenting them with a choice of freeing either Barabbas (Hebrew for "son of the father") or Jesus of Nazareth (THE Son of the Father). And it is also true that the Romans nailed Jesus to a cross.

---

[154] And just as Jesus' prophecy of Israel's destruction came to pass, so will there be a day when the city of Jerusalem will once again be threatened by the enemies of the Jews. Jesus of Nazareth, having been seen by every single person as He circled the globe in His return to this planet, will seat Himself on the familiar Mount of Olives to patiently wait. In time a delegation of the city's governmental and spiritual leaders will make their way to Jesus, stand before Him, and finally say to Him – **"Blessed is He who comes in the Name of the Lord"** – just as He prophesied.

But...the whole truth is this: EVERY human being, ALL of whom are sinners (Romans 3:22b-23), nailed Jesus to the cross, for He came to give His life as a ransom for many, making Him the ONLY way to know the God of Abraham, Isaac, and Jacob, the God of Israel, the One, True, Living God (Matthew 20:28; John 14:6).[155]

We're now at the beginning of Matthew, chapter twenty-four.

As I said, I can see the Disciples walking, but not talking, behind Jesus as He exits Jerusalem on His way to take a breather on the Mount of Olives, a peaceful place removed from the harsh things that just happened. Then, maybe out of some desire to try to lighten the heavy mood, a couple of the disciples turned to look at the city. The sun is setting in the west, and at its angle in the sky it seems to be illuminating the city's structures in a beautiful way. So they call Jesus' attention to this, again, maybe hoping this will touch His angry heart and calm Him. But instead of being calmed, Jesus points at the city and continues His prophetic words of doom:

Do you see all these things? I tell you the truth, not one stone here will be left on another; everyone will be thrown down. (vs.2)

Jesus had expressed His compassionate passion at the end of His scolding of Israel's leaders:

O Jerusalem, Jerusalem, you who kill the prophets and stone those sent to you, how often I have longed to gather your children together, as a hen gathers her chicks under her wings, but you were not willing. (23:37)

But the time for tenderness has passed. Divine judgment is to come. Jerusalem and the nation of Israel are done...JUST like the fig tree. And they won't just be done for four hundred years as in Egypt, nor for seventy years as in Babylon, nor for four hundred years from Malachi[156] to John the Baptist. But nineteen hundred years, nearly two millennia.

---

[155] An excellent work on The Cross is John Stott's The Cross of Christ.
[156] This messenger's message has MUCH that applies to The Church in this country! And 1:10-11 is a good place to begin.

171

As Jesus continues His prophetic words of judgment, the Disciples are getting the seriousness of what is unfolding this second day of Jesus' last week. And even though a couple of them had tried to lighten the weight of it, the somber mood takes over. And in this moment they ask the questions of all questions, the questions everyone has and to which everyone wants clear answers:

Tell us <u>when will this happen</u> and <u>what will be the sign</u> of your coming and of the end of The Age? (vs.3)

The Disciples question is twofold: when and what. They're asking when will Jesus return and how will they know what's happening is related to His return. And Jesus absolutely answers them...plainly. There is nothing in Jesus' answer that is difficult to understand. So everything Jesus says about the End Times and His return is crystal clear and easy to comprehend. Jesus is NOT being cryptic. He's being concise.

———————

But first I need to provide some personal background here.

Back in the early 1980's as a young Christian I read a popular book that was about the End Times. Even as little as I knew of the Bible at that time, a few things bothered me in this book.

How could The Church suffer so much at the beginning while The Church at The End is removed from any persecution and even martyrdom? Is The Church at The End weaker? Also, even as a new Christian I already had some sense that Christians are supposed to suffer, and that martyrdom is an honor (Matthew 5:10-12). Lastly, the earth is going away? I thought the Messiah is coming here!

However, everyone around me thought this was a great book and a great teaching, so I assumed something was greatly wrong with me. And as I learned about some other teachings on the End Times all this did was to confuse me more. In frustration I took the Pan-View of things, that is, that it didn't matter if I understood any of this for everything would pan-out in the end.

Well, it is true that everything WILL pan-out in the end. The question is: Will it pan-out for me? And will it pan-out for you? This is one of Jesus' concerns when He staunchly warns, **"Watch out that no one deceives you,"** for He knew that much confusion and deception about the End Times would proliferate.

So for many years I held to the Pan-View and avoided dealing with the End Times, other than to say, yes, Jesus is returning. Then the Spirit began a process which gave me some simple clarity about the End Times, especially as it relates to the assignment of a forerunner – to prepare the Bride for her Bridegroom-King.

Now back to Matthew, chapter twenty-four.

As I said, Jesus' response to His disciples' questions is plain and easy to understand. So much so that is one reason some have tried to explain away what He says, for what He says troubles the complacent, those who want some sort of insurance policy that assures them nothing bad will happen to them if they're living during this time, and especially if they're living a life of compromise. It's as if some want to live for the world, and yet not be "left behind" from "going to heaven."

And yet, Jesus has two clear overarching issues in all that He says that are completely contrary to the attitude of wanting to escape difficult times: First, as I already noted, He warns about not being deceived. This is a BIG one! Secondly, He admonishes His followers to be ready by being prepared. Not prepared to be removed, as if one needs preparation for that, but rather prepared for the intensely difficult things that will happen in the last few years leading up to His return.

Don't be deceived and be prepared.

And in speaking about the deception, Jesus describes it as deceivers multiplying and their deceptions permeating, using the word "many" to describe its influential scope. There will be many – both Christians and non-Christians – who will claim to know how to fix the world. There will also be many false prophets/teachers/leaders in The Church teaching many false things. That's heavy. Rightly and deeply knowing the Real Jesus, His Word, and having the Holy Spirit are going to be critical. Lacking in any of these will be disastrous. That's not my opinion. This is what Jesus is saying.

Jesus even prophesies what is going to be the result for those who don't know Him well: "Most" will be deceived, and as a result "most" will turn away from Him, for what He will be doing won't fit with the watered-down Jesus MOST have been told about (24:5, 10-12).[157]

---

[157] The Greek word in these verses is *polus*, which can be translated "many" or "most". I believe some of the English translators chose the word "many" to describe the results of false versions of Jesus, false leaders, and increased wickedness because "most" being led astray, "most" falling away, and "most" hearts growing cold just seems too extreme. (See NIV versus NKJV of 24:13.) But I believe Jesus is describing reality as when He talked about "most" choosing the Wide Way that leads to destruction. See Appendix I.

And as for those who do know the Real Jesus rightly and deeply, He says the following about what they can count on happening to them in the final years leading to His return to this planet:

Then you will be handed over to be persecuted and put to death, and you will be hated by all nations because of me. (24:9)

Because of the increase of wickedness... (24:12a)...For then there will be great distress, unequaled from the beginning of the world until now – and never to be equaled again. If those days had not been cut short, no one would survive, but for the sake of the [called-out-ones] those days will be shortened. (24:21-22)

For false Christs and false prophets will appear and perform great signs and miracles to deceive, if possible, even the [called-out-ones].[158] See, I have told you ahead of time. (24:24-25)

Next, Jesus says that His return will be an extremely visible and audible event!

So if anyone tells you, "There He is, out in the desert," [i.e. in some secluded compound or underground bunker or away from populated areas] **do not go out; or, "Here He is, in the inner rooms,"** [i.e. some private or personal place – one's car or bedroom] **do not believe it. For as lightning that comes from the east is visible even in the west, so will be the coming of the Son of Man. Wherever there is a carcass, there the vultures will gather.[159] Immediately after the distress of those days "the sun will be darkened, and the moon will not give its light; the stars will fall from the sky, and the heavenly bodies will be shaken." At that time the sign of the Son of Man will appear in the sky, and all the nations of the earth will mourn. They will see the Son of Man coming on the clouds of the sky, with power and great glory. And He will send His angels with a loud trumpet call,[160] and they will**

---

[158] With the idea of "if possible," Jesus IS saying that things are going to be SO awful that even the called-out-ones will be pressured to deny Him, which some will do.

[159] This statement is about how all these false prophets, teachers, and messiahs try to take advantage and cash in on the fears of people.

[160] In response to the concern of the Christians in Thessalonica that the rapture had already happened and they had missed it (maybe eluding to some sort of "secret" event), Paul's answer was that they would know when it happens for he says Jesus' return is an extreme-

gather His elect from the four winds, from one end of the heavens to the other. (24:26-31)[161]

———————

Now Jesus is going to tell the Disciples the reason and the purpose as to WHY the Father had Him curse the fig tree. And Jesus begins His explanation with a command, not a suggestion:

Now <u>learn this lesson</u> from the fig tree. (24:32a)

And here is THE lesson He commands His followers to learn from what the Father had Him do to the fig tree:

As soon as its twigs get tender and its leaves come out (i.e. the fig tree is reborn, come back to life), you know that summer is near. Even so, when you see all these things, you know that it [as in Jesus' return, or "He" Himself] is near, right at the door. <u>I tell you the truth</u>, this generation will certainly not pass away until all these things have happened. Heaven and earth will pass away, but my words will never pass away. (24:32b-35)

The Disciples get that Jesus is not giving them (nor His followers today) a horticulture lesson about how new leaves on a tree are due to the warmer weather of spring and summer. The Disciples grasped with the vivid visual of Jesus that morning cursing the fig tree, it drying up, and even dying, that it was a sign of what they then heard Him do to the nation of Israel, the "fig tree," when He cursed the leaders seven times perfectly that afternoon. For in this brief statement Jesus is clearly connecting what He did to the fig tree that morning with what He did to Israel later that day.

Then, using a phrase He used many times – I tell you the truth – He says that the generation that sees the "fig tree" (i.e. Israel) come back to life will not pass away until THAT generation sees His return. And as if to put His kingly seal on what He just said, He says that all He created can pass away, but what He just said will NOT pass away. His point: we can absolutely take to the bank what Jesus just told us, for He just gave

———————

ly noisy event – 1 Thessalonians 4:16.
[161] Clearly the "rapture" is not a secreted event.

175

us the timeframe of His return. He absolutely answered the Disciples' question about when He will return.

So first, has Israel been reborn, has she come back to life? Yes she has! When? On May 14th, 1948. Thus, the answer to the questions, **"Who has ever heard of such a thing? Who has ever seen such things? Can a country be born in a day or a nation be brought forth in a moment?"** (Isaiah 66:8). The answer? Unquestionably!

Secondly, how long is a generation? Is it like the so-called Greatest Generation? Is it the Baby-Boomer Generation? Is it the generations of the 1960's or 70's or 80's? Is it like Generation X? Or the Millennial's Generation? No. The Bible tells us how long a generation is. It is between eighty (Psalm 90:10) to one hundred years (Genesis 15:12-16).

Let's do some math that even I can do. One hundred years from 1948 is 2048. And eighty years from 1948 is 2028. We now have the timeframe of Jesus' return to this planet: sometime between about 2028 and 2048. In the same way that the Bible gives us the timeframe of Jesus' first coming, so Jesus Himself gives His followers the timeframe of His second coming.

There is no fancy manipulation of Bible texts here. No basing the End Times on Fox News or CNN or the Internet in an attempt to make modern connections to explain biblical descriptions. No lifting snippets of this verse and that verse to build a teaching that sounds good to American infected ears, minds, and hearts.

All I've done is to keep Jesus' words in the context of Matthew, chapters twenty-one through twenty-five. For what is recorded here of what Jesus said about the End Times and His return, in response to the Disciples' questions, is plain and simple, not complicated and convoluted with human conjecture.

After giving the disciples, and us, the lesson of the fig tree, that is, the timeframe – not the day and the hour – of His return, Jesus then begins to emphasize keeping watch SO THAT one is prepared.

He says that this preparedness is what it means to be a faithful and wise servant, for the unprepared are the ones who will become unfaithful to Him due to the pressures to deny Him. He says they will become unwise in their choices, which will make them hypocrites who end up in a place where there is weeping and gnashing of teeth (24:42-51).

Again, the reason for Christians falling away during this time will be due to being deceived and not being prepared. They will be deceived by false teaching about the End Times and about Jesus of Nazareth and about the Bible. Additionally, they will not have built their lives on the things Jesus and the writers of the New Testament taught. Thus, when The Storm hits, their lives will come down with a great crash![162]

If you doubt this, note Jesus' first parable at the beginning of Matthew, chapter twenty-five in which He vividly illustrates His points about not being deceived and being prepared with the Parable of the Ten Virgins. The main point of this parable? Five virgins (i.e. followers) were not deceived and were prepared and five virgins (i.e. followers) were deceived and were not prepared.[163] And notice what the Bridegroom in this parable says to those virgins who were deceived and not prepared.

I tell you the truth, I don't know you.

Notice also Jesus' admonition to those virgins who were not deceived and were prepared:

Therefore keep watch, because you do not know the day or the hour.[164]

There one more important timing-thing Jesus tells His disciples, and us, in verse fourteen.

And this Gospel of the Kingdom will be preached in the <u>whole world as a testimony to all nations</u> (i.e. ethnic groups), and <u>then</u> The End will come.

One last thing.

---

[162] See Matthew 7:24-27. This entire talk (chapters 5, 6, 7) is Jesus presenting the constitution of His Kingdom that has eight foundational principles.
[163] In all three of Jesus' concluding parables about the End Times the endings all have a warning to those who are deceived and not prepared being shut out (25:10), thrown out to where there is darkness and weeping and gnashing of teeth (25:30), and being sent away to eternal punishment (25:46). Clearly these are VERY serious warnings to HIS followers!
[164] But we do know the timeframe, thus why Jesus holds His followers accountable for not keeping watch.

There is a little comment Jesus makes here in Matthew, chapter twenty-four that can easily be missed even though I quoted it and underlined it above.

See, I have told you ahead of time. (vs. 25)

What He told the Disciples and is telling all of those who claim to be His followers down through the centuries, is that they are all without any excuses. In other words, He warned them (and us) and instructed them (and us). And as if that isn't clear enough, Jesus ends His comments about the End Times with two potent parables, one about what it means to be a faithful servant and one about what serving Him looks like (Matthew 25:14-46). And note Jesus' final words to the unfaithful servants and to those who failed to serve others:

…throw that worthless servant outside, into the darkness, where there will be weeping and gnashing of teeth.

Then they will go away to eternal punishment, but the righteous to Eternal Life.

And so, Jesus is being clear about what He tells the Disciples, as well as His followers today, about the signs and the season of His return. And He's doing this SO THAT those who want to avoid being deceived and those who want to be prepared can take action now. NO ONE will have an excuse for being deceived and unprepared at Jesus' return…just like the virgins who did not have any oil for their lamps when the Bridegroom showed up. Why? Because Jesus told everyone ahead of time the details and the timeframe of His return.

———————

As I said earlier, as a young Christian I found the teachings on the End Times to be so confusing (something Satan loves) that I opted for the neutral position of a Pan-View of the End Times.

Well, there is a very deceptive and very dangerous teaching related to the End Times that has become something of the standard belief among mostly Christian in Western Culture. It's called the Pre-Tribulation (before the Great Tribulation) Rapture (removed from). And in this twenty-fourth chapter of Matthew is one of the major texts used to support this terrible teaching.

> **Two men will be in the field; one will be taken and the other left. Two women will be grinding with a hand mill; one will be taken and the other left.** (24:40-41)

Even though according to the Pre-Tribulation Rapture, the rapture is a somewhat secret event, which Jesus and Paul say it is not, one of the main points of this teaching is that Christians are going to be taken off the earth before the Great Tribulation. And one can see how this may seem to be true based on the above passage...until this passage is put into context. Then it becomes perfectly clear that this passage does NOT support this teaching. Here is the passage in context.

> **<u>As it was</u> in the days of Noah, <u>so it will be</u> at the coming of the Son of Man. For in the days before the flood, people were eating and drinking, marrying and giving in marriage, up to the day Noah entered the ark; and they knew nothing about what would happen until the flood came and took them all away. That is how it will be at the coming of the Son of Man. Two men will be in the field; one will be taken and the other left. Two women will be grinding with a hand mill; one will be taken and the other left.** (24:37-41)

Quite simply, what happened in the days of Noah?

Was Noah and his family taken to Heaven? We're they removed in any way from the judgment of The Flood? No. They went through the judgment of The Flood. Certainly they had some protection from the flooding in the ark, which they would not have had if they had been deceived and unprepared for it. But Noah and his little family were still IN the worldwide judgment of The Flood, for they had jobs Yahweh wanted them to do.[165]

Secondly and MOST importantly, who was taken away by the flood? Well, even if one isn't familiar with the story in Genesis, Jesus tells us who was taken away by the flood in THIS passage. It was the people who were eating and drinking, marrying and giving in marriage,

---

[165] The Church at The End also has jobs Jesus wants her doing, which is why she will be here on the earth for the majority of the Great Tribulation.

that is, just going about their normal daily lives, even planning for the future while not knowing what was about to come upon them due to being deceived and unprepared. And it is THESE people, NOT Noah and his family, who The Flood took all away.

So as it was in the days of Noah, so it will be at Jesus' return: Two men will be in the field and two women will be grinding meal, and the ones who did not watch out that they weren't deceived and neither did they prepare themselves to endure and to overcome (e.g. Revelation 2:7, 11, 17, 26, 3:5, 12, 21) will be taken away (i.e. destroyed) by what unfolds (i.e. Matthew 7:26-27).

There is absolutely NO rapture, no removal from this planet of Jesus' followers before the Great Tribulation in this passage. In fact, it is clear that the taken-away-ones are the deceived and the unprepared, NOT those who weren't deceived and thus prepared to follow Jesus at all costs. Christians are not exempt from The Storm Jesus spoke of (Matthew 7:24-27). Neither is Jesus applying the issue of The Storm only to the Lost. Everyone, Christians and non-Christians are going to experience The Storm when it comes. Those who survive it will be those who built their lives on Jesus' words and not on anything else.

Note also Jesus doesn't speak in terms of IF The Storm comes, but WHEN it comes. So again, the issue is: What have the followers of Jesus of Nazareth in this country built their house/lives on?

Here's a brief history of this unbiblical and perilous teaching.

In the mid-1800's, as the Industrial Revolution was at its peak of cataclysmic upheaval and destruction of the simple culture and society of England, a time when people were leaving their villages and flocking to the cities and factories to find work, a time in which thousands of orphans were deposited onto the streets of the major cities because parents could not afford to take care of them (thus the rise of George Mueller's ministry), people were downtrodden and languishing in squalid living conditions. There were no unions, so pay was low and hours were long. Driven by greed, the factory and business owners had been successful in creating a new form of slavery and serfdom. People were profoundly struggling, to say the least.

It was into this very, very fertile soil of despair and desperation in which people were yearning for some sort of relief and salvation, some glimmer of hope of something different than the shabbiness and the stress they were living in, that this false teaching came.

Hope had been crushed by the money-worshipping wealthy who had no care or concern for their workers, so to hear that a woman had received a prophecy in which the End Times were about to begin and that The Church was soon to be secretly removed from any suffering... well...that seemed like great news, like a longing fulfilled!

As you probably can imagine, due to the people's physical and spiritual famine, this false teaching jumped to life and blazed like a fire through a field of dry grass. Everyone loved it! I mean, who wouldn't? We humans are not big on suffering, we Western Culture humans, even Western Culture Christians, really don't like suffering. Anything that will eliminate suffering...count us in![166] Forget that the eighth foundational principle of Jesus' Kingdom:

Blessed are those who are persecuted because of righteousness, for theirs is the Kingdom of Heaven. (Matthew 5:10)

And also forget about Jesus' explanation of this principle.

Blessed are you when people insult you, persecute you and falsely say all kinds of evil against you because of me. Rejoice and be glad, because great is your reward in Heaven, for in the same way they persecuted the prophets who were before you. (Matthew 5:11-12)[167]

In Jesus' motivational speech to His disciples before He sent them out to do ministry (Matthew, chapter ten), among the many things He told them was this:

Do not be afraid of those who kill the body but cannot kill the soul. Rather, be afraid of the One who can destroy both soul and body in Hell. (vs. 28)

Since this is how it was at the beginning of The Church, how can The Church in this country today promote a clearly unbiblical teaching in which Christians at The End are spared suffering and martyrdom?

---

[166] Which is why this false teaching is so popular here in this country!

[167] Consequently, this is a level of reward The Church in this country will not be receiving.

Truly, such people are wimps at the best and cowards at the worse.[168] Does The Church in this country think itself better than the early Church that suffered so much? The answer? Yes. Yes she does. The Church in this country arrogantly thinks she's special, even promot-ing a false teaching that makes people feel safe...in spite of the fact that the message of "peace, peace when there is no peace" is CLASSIC false teaching (i.e. Jeremiah 6:14).

———————

During the time when my dad was trying to get me back into Juda-ism, and on one of his trips here to the States, he was willing to have coffee and conversation with me. Very upset about "this Jesus thing" and in an attempt to get me to deny Jesus and return to Judaism, he took out his checkbook, made out a check to me for $25,000, and offered it to me in exchange for my rejection of This Jesus.

As I looked at the check I had thoughts about how much of a financial help this would be for my little family and me. For example, a few years later we bought our first house. At the time my dad offered me the $25,000 that same house sold for about $30 to $35K. With my dad's money we could have had a tiny house payment, which would have made a HUGE difference to us financially.

I then had thoughts of the fact that he was living in Israel and that I'm here in the States. I could say that I "tried" to deny Jesus and to do Judaism, but just couldn't. Of course I'd still have the money. This seemed like a plausible idea. But something just didn't seem like this was the right thing to do. So I turned down my dad's offer.

I didn't realize for many years that the temptation to say I would deny Jesus, even knowing I didn't mean it, and that I was only doing it so as to have a better financial situation for my family, is EXACTLY the sort of thing that the followers of Jesus are going to face in the End Times. Christians will seek to save their life or the lives of those they love by making similar seemingly innocent choices. But, denying Jesus, even pretending to, has profoundly negative eternal consequences.

Accepting the teaching of a Pre-Tribulation Rapture is similar to this, for it is a teaching that says your life will be spared, that you won't have to stand loyal to Jesus when, not if, it costs you. For one of the main points of the End Times is to purify The Church. ANY compromise-

---

[168] And if cowards, note what Jesus says in Revelation 21:8a.

ing of one's relationship with Jesus, no matter the threat, no matter the reason, is serious, just as it was in the early Church (e.g. Hebrews 6:4-6).

If there is anything to prepare oneself for this is certainly one very, very important one. No one shows up to run a Marathon without many months of serious training and preparation. How much more should there be preparation even now of oneself, one's spouse, one's children, one's grandchildren, etc. for what is going to come upon the earth very soon! Obviously the time to build an ark is not when it begins to rain. So learn the lesson of the five foolish virgins.

Would you like a biblical example of this preparation before The Storm hits? How about Shadrach, Meshach, Abednego, and Daniel?

For years Jeremiah warned the people that Babylon was coming (just as today forerunners are warning that the spirit of the Harlot-Babylon is already here). Most did not heed his warning. But, we know that a few did. How? Because there were four young men whose parents believed Jeremiah and began teaching their sons how to fast and how to pray, as well as how to stand firm even in the face of death.

These are things that need development in a person's life. They don't just suddenly show up when the pressure comes.[169]

So, in this country in which the national symbol is not the bald eagle but rather the microwave oven, the teaching that Christians will not be on the planet during the Big Trouble, having the privilege to suffer and the honor to die for the sake of Jesus, is more than welcomed as good news. It's being planned on!

Think: All of the warnings about watching and being prepared have no meaning if Christians are going to be suddenly and secretly removed ...even though ALL the warnings about watching and being prepared are addressed TO Christians. The apostles understood this, thus they taught people to be faithful in persecution.

And besides the clear biblical teachings which utterly invalidate this awful teaching, how about just one very practical point?

---

[169] I recommend the following book, Night, by Elie Wiesel. Wiesel is a Jew who went through the Holocaust. He tells the reader that before the Holocaust he "believed profoundly" in the God of Abraham. And yet the Antichrist-like horrors he experienced crushed his relationship with the Almighty. Granted, he was not a born again by the Spirit Christian. But what he went through emotionally and spiritually is EXACTLY what the real followers of Jesus are going to face.

IF it happens that I'm wrong and The Church is raptured before anything bad happens...I'm good with that. Suffering and martyrdom don't sound like fun to me, and I'm glad to be exempted from such things. And if as we're all rising up to meet Jesus in the sky you see me and say, "See, I told you so," I'm going to shrug my shoulders and say, "Oh well, my bad," and I'm still spared from the issues of the Great Tribulation.

BUT...if I and plenty of others are right, that The Church isn't going anywhere, she is going to be here working in conjunction with her Bridegroom-King, and thus experiencing tremendous pressure to deny Jesus to avoid suffering and dying because of Him, and you and those you love are not prepared for this...well...good luck!

————————

I hate to burst your American bubble...but many people who claim they belong to Jesus of Nazareth need to know the following historical facts and spiritual truths.

To the Greeks, generally speaking, the flesh and the material world were evil, and the spirit and the spiritual realm were good. This is why so many Greeks had a problem with Paul's preaching about a resurrection. Why would anyone want to have a body of flesh and to live on the earth, for to the Greeks that would be a bad thing.

And because Western Culture and The Church in Western Culture has taken up so much of Greek thinking, typically Gentile Christians want to get out of here and go to Heaven. Contrarily, in Jewish thinking Jewish Christians tend to long for the Messiah to come here to rule and to reign. So the truth is that Jesus, a Jew and not a Greek, a Gentile, or an American, isn't trying to get His followers out of here; He's coming here to establish His Kingdom.

And in this He is going to combine Heaven and Earth, ruling all His Creation from the actual city of Jerusalem in Israel as well as the new city of Jerusalem that descends from Heaven.

Further, this process of Jesus taking over the Earth will be a very natural thing in which His followers will have an important part, for He's not doing it all alone. He's not just waving His hand to supernaturally destroy His enemies, seeming to prefer hand-to-hand combat (see Isaiah 63:3 & Revelation 19:11-19).

The truth is, Jesus likes the natural realm. He created it. He also likes the natural process. It's not going away.

So stop trying to go Heaven to sit on a cloud and play a harp and start preparing for Heaven to come to Earth in which you will have work to do. Humans were created to work, also to think and to be creative, to experience pleasure and to have a sense of accomplishment in which one hears Jesus say, "Good job." Just as Adam had a job in the Garden, which was an example of the combined natural and spiritual realms, so will human beings in Jesus' Kingdom.

In short, Jesus didn't give human beings their personalities and abilities to then waste them by doing nothing in Eternity except singing songs. This would be a good time to read Matthew 25:14-29, which is part of the things Jesus said about the End Times.

So if the Pre-Tribulation Rapture is right, there's NO downside to people like me. But, if this teaching is in fact false, there is an ENOR-MOUS downside for those who are deceived by it and thus do not prepare.[170]

Oh, and by the way, the Tribulation is NOT about the Antichrist and his followers tribulating Christians.

The Great Tribulation is about the Lamb of God tribulating the Antichrist and his followers with eighteen or so judgments which increase in intensity, but always aimed at reaching the most people at the deepest heart-level to produce genuine repentance. Does the Antichrist and his followers retaliate, do they take out on Jesus' followers what Jesus is doing to them? Well, yes! It's a war. The enemies of Jesus don't just sit there and take it on the chin. They fight back. And since they can't hurt Jesus, they're going to hurt His followers...and that hurt is a privilege and an honor (Acts 5:41).

Truly, as it was at the beginning, so it will be even more so at The End. So here is a snapshot of The Church at The End as she participates with her Bridegroom-King in removing Evil from Creation:

On their release, Peter and John went back to their own people and reported all that the chief priests and elders had said to them. When they heard this, they raised their voices together in prayer to God. "Sovereign Lord," they said, "you made the Heaven and the Earth and the sea, and everything in them. You spoke by the Holy Spirit through the mouth of your servant, our father David: 'Why do the nations rage and the peoples plot in

---

[170] Being prepared does not mean building a bunker and stocking it with food and other supplies. Being prepared to endure persecution in The End is about one's heart, as in what and who one truly loves.

vain? The kings of the earth take their stand and the rulers gather together against the Lord and against his Anointed One.' Indeed Herod and Pontius Pilate met together with the Gentiles and the people of Israel in this city to conspire against your holy servant Jesus, whom you anointed. They did what your power and will had decided beforehand should happen. Now, Lord, consider their threats and enable your servants to speak your Word with great boldness. Stretch out your hand to heal and perform miraculous signs and wonders through the Name of your holy servant Jesus."[171] After they prayed, the place where they were meeting was shaken. And they were all filled with the Holy Spirit and spoke the Word of God boldly. (Acts 4:23-31)

———————

One of the false teachings of the Pre-Tribulation Rapture is that Jesus could return at any moment.

Nope. NOT true!

Why?

Because the Word of God says so.

While it is true that when Jesus does come He will come as a thief in the night, that is, at a day and time no one knows, ALL who want to avoid being deceived and who want to be prepared need to know the Real Jesus really, really well so that they do not encounter Him as a thief in the night.

It is to those who get deceived, who don't know Jesus of Nazareth as He is who will experience Jesus' coming as a thief in the night. In other words, like five of the virgins, they got deceived and were not prepared. Thus, these people will suffer great loss in the way that someone who doesn't prepare to thwart a thief is shocked when the thief causes him loss.

But, more than this, here is what the Word of God says about Jesus' return and how we know it will not be at any moment.

———————

[171] The declaration of the Gospel is to be followed by demonstrations of the Kingdom, showing that the Kingdom of Light is in fact here to drive away the kingdom of darkness. Again, the Kingdom of Jesus is not a matter of talk, of wise and persuasive words, or of the supposed wisdom of men, but of demonstrations of the Living God's power (1 Corinthians 2:4-5, 4:20)!

Jesus Himself says at least these two things about timing which tell us that His return is NOT at any moment. One, the Gospel of the Kingdom must be preached to every ethnic group on the planet.

And this Gospel of the Kingdom[172] **will be preached in the whole world as a testimony to all nations, and then The End will come.** (Matthew 24:14)

While The Church may be close to accomplishing this, but it has not been accomplished yet. So no, Jesus cannot come at any moment or He's a liar.

Two, there must be a Jewish Temple in Jerusalem for the Antichrist to set up an idol of himself in which he claims to be God and demands people everywhere worship him (Daniel 11:31).

So when you see standing in the Holy Place[173] (i.e. the Temple) **"the abomination that causes desolation," spoken of through the prophet Daniel – let the reader understand –** (Matthew 24:15)

For Jesus' words here to be fulfilled, the Muslim Mosque with the golden dome must come down, for it is sitting on the very spot where the Jewish Temple should be.

Certainly, this mosque could be destroyed today, whether on purpose or by an accident or by an act of nature. However, just consider the political implications of this, for however this mosque is removed – the Israelis tear it down on purpose, an accidental off-course missile destroys it, an earthquake brings it down – there is going to be LOTS of turmoil associated with its removal! And when Israel moves to build a Jewish Temple in its place, the Muslim world is going to resist this quite violently. So again, although this mosque IS going to come down and a Jewish Temple WILL BE built in its place as Scripture indicates, at the time of this writing, we're some years out from this happening.

Paul too says there are at least two things that must happen before Jesus can return (1 Thessalonians 4:13-18, 2 Thessalonians 2:1-12). The Christians in Thessalonica had been given a false teaching about the return of Jesus, specifically about a secret rapture[174], and Paul sent them a second letter to correct this:

---

[172] Notice, the Good News is that there is a King who is looking for and inviting people to be subjects in His Kingdom, not merely a savior trying to save people.
[173] Mark 13:14 – **"where it does not belong"**.

187

Concerning the coming of our Lord Jesus Christ and our being gathered to Him, we ask you, brothers, not to become easily unsettled or alarmed by some prophecy, report or letter supposed to have come from us, saying that the Day of the Lord has already come. <u>Don't let anyone deceive you in any way</u>, for [that Day will not come] (#1) until the rebellion (i.e. the falling away – Matthew 24:10) **occurs and (#2) the man of lawlessness is revealed….** (2 Thessalonians 2:1-3)

According to Paul the two things that must happen before Jesus of Nazareth returns to this planet to establish His Kingdom: The Falling Away and the man of lawlessness must come to power. Obviously neither of these has happened yet. To Paul, anyone who teaches differently is teaching deceptively.

So, at least four things must happen before Jesus returns to this planet: the Gospel must be preached to every ethnic group, a Jewish Temple must be built in Jerusalem on the very spot where there is a Muslim Mosque, the Falling Away of actual Christians, and the Antichrist comes to power.

Now, how will The Church know Jesus' return is imminent? Simple. When Jesus' battle plan outlined in the Revelation begins to unfold. Of course, Jesus' followers will need to recognize these events, knowing that she has a role in play in them[175] and thus will be here remaining faithful to Jesus in spite of enduring great suffering, persecution, and even martyrdom until the final trumpet (1 Thessalonians 4:16-18; Revelation 11:15-19).

———————

Matthew, chapter ten, has some simple instructions which can be helpful to Jesus' followers in The End.

As you go, proclaim this Message: The Kingdom of Heaven has come near. Heal the sick, raise the dead, cleanse those who have leprosy, drive out demons. Freely you have received; freely give. Do not get any gold or silver or copper to take with you in your

---

[174] Which the false teaching of a Pre-Tribulation also teaches.
[175] Just as Noah and his family did in the Flood.

belts – no bag for the journey or extra shirt or sandals or a staff, for the worker is worth his keep. Whatever town or village you enter, search there for some worthy person and stay at their house until you leave. As you enter the home, give it your greeting. If the home is deserving, let your peace rest on it; if it is not, let your peace return to you. If anyone will not welcome you or listen to your words, leave that home or town and shake the dust off your feet. Truly I tell you, it will be more bearable for Sodom and Gomorrah on the Day of Judgment than for that town. I am sending you out like sheep among wolves. Therefore be as shrewd as snakes and as innocent as doves. Be on your guard; you will be handed over to the local councils and be flogged in the synagogues. On my account you will be brought before governors and kings as witnesses to them. But when they arrest you, do not worry about what to say or how to say it. At that time you will be given what to say, for it will not be you speaking, but the Spirit of your Father speaking through you. Brother will betray brother to death, and a father his child; children will rebel against their parents and have them put to death. You will be hated by everyone because of me, but <u>the one who stands firm to The End will be saved</u>. When you are persecuted in one place, flee to another. Truly I tell you, you will not finish going through the towns of Israel before the Son of Man comes. The student is not above the teacher, nor a servant above his master. It is enough for students to be like their teachers, and servants like their masters. If the head of the house has been called Beelzebub, how much more the members of his household! So do not be afraid of them, for there is nothing concealed that will not be disclosed, or hidden that will not be made known. What I tell you in the dark, speak in the daylight; what is whispered in your ear, proclaim from the roofs. Do not be afraid of those who kill the body but cannot kill the soul. Rather, <u>be afraid of the One who can destroy both soul and body in Hell</u>. Are not two sparrows sold for a penny? Yet not one of them will fall to the ground outside your Father's care. And even the very hairs of your head are all numbered. So don't be afraid; you are worth more than many sparrows. Whoever acknowledges me before others, I will also acknowledge before my Father in Heaven. But <u>whoever disowns me before others, I will disown before my Father in Heaven</u>. Do not suppose that I have come to bring peace to the earth. <u>I did</u>

not come to bring peace, but a sword. For I have come to turn "a man against his father, a daughter against her mother, a daughter-in-law against her mother-in-law – a man's enemies will be the members of his own household." Anyone who loves their father or mother more than me is not worthy of me; anyone who loves their son or daughter more than me is not worthy of me. **Whoever does not take up their cross and follow me is not worthy of me. Whoever finds their life will lose it, and whoever loses their life for my sake will find it.** Anyone who welcomes you welcomes me, and anyone who welcomes me welcomes the one who sent me. Whoever welcomes a prophet as a prophet will receive a prophet's reward, and whoever welcomes a righteous person as a righteous person will receive a righteous person's reward. And if anyone gives even a cup of cold water to one of these little ones who is my disciple, truly I tell you, that person will certainly not lose their reward.

Lastly, there is a biblical writing whose thesis is ALL about remaining faithful in persecution, and thus is extremely helpful in preparing for The End: the letter to some Hebrew Christians. And because the author develops his thesis of remaining faithful in persecution from a variety of angles, a better title for this letter would be: A Manual on How to Endure In Persecution. So read it and study it carefully.

Here's the bottom-line for The Church in The End: It is not just answering the question of who Jesus is (Matthew 16:15). That's important. But what's critical is the First and the Greatest Commandment. Does one love Jesus with all their heart (*eros*), mind (*phileo*), and strength (*agape*)? And IF one does love Jesus first and most, then one major way a person expresses this is by being faithful to love Jesus WHEN it is HARD to love Him (John 14:15, 23, 24, 15:10).

For example, the mark of the Beast is put upon the hand and the forehead (Revelation 13:16-17). Although the Beast's mark is an actual and literal thing, the placing of the mark has meaning. The hand speaks of what one does. The forehead speaks of what one thinks.

Therefore, those who are compromised and lukewarm, not knowing the difference between Apostolic Christianity and Churchianity, or the difference between the Tree of Life and the Tree of Knowledge of Good and Evil, those who love Money, Democracy, Psychology, secular music, etc., those who are currently trying to walk the fence between the Kingdom and the World are those who are even NOW prepared to receive the mark.

Why? Simple. Because the things they're currently doing, the way they are living this life, their views of life and this world are ALREADY like that of the Harlot-Babylon and the Antichrist. Even if some of these know about the mark, they will be deceived into taking it, for it will just flow right along with what they are ALREADY thinking and doing. This is what John says concerning the Beast's mark:

This calls for Wisdom. (Revelation 13:18a)

NOT human wisdom, not worldly wisdom, NOT Tree of Knowledge of Good and Evil wisdom, NOT Churchianity's wisdom. But the Living God's Wisdom! So…

The Spirit and the Bride say, "Come!" And let him who hears say, "Come!" He who testifies to these things says, "Yes, I am coming soon." Amen! Come, Lord Jesus! (Revelation 22:17a & 20)[176]

I will tell of your mercy and your unfailing Love
I will be, to the glory of your Name
Like a banner they will see you lifted high above
They will speak, of the One upon the throne

And your glory, will cover the Earth
Like the waters, cover the seas
And the Earth, will sing your praises
Forevermore, your Kingdom shall be

Sing aloud your song

---

[176] See Appendix J

Give praise to the One
The Deliverer has come
It's the Bridegroom come

I believe Heaven's coming down
Jesus will reign, on the Earth
The two, shall become one
Forever united in the Son

This is reality, He is coming to reign on the Earth
And the increase, of His government, will know no end[177]

---

[177] "Glory Will Cover the Earth" by Justin Rizzo

THE CONCLUSION

The Conclusion

This message is NOT for the Lost, the ungodly, the un-regenerated here in the United States of America. If someone in this category happens to come upon this, reads it, is convicted by the Holy Spirit, repents, and seeks to pursue Jesus of Nazareth that is certainly a good thing!

This message is also NOT for Christians living outside of the United States. But again, if some follower of Jesus of Nazareth outside this country happens upon this message and it helps them, that too is a good thing.

This message IS for those who consider themselves to be followers of Jesus of Nazareth and who live in this country.

In Donald Miller's book, <u>Searching for God Knows What</u>, he cites the following true story.

A torrential storm came crashing into a community one night that was so strong that it caused a bridge over a swelling river to collapse. There was a man who lived along the river at this very spot. When he heard the loud cracking sound of the bridge tearing apart, he ran out into the dark night and the pouring rain to see for himself the damage.

As he stood there looking at the wreckage of the bridge with his flashlight, he saw the headlights of oncoming vehicles on the other side of the river. The man quickly realized that with the combination of the heavy downpour and the darkness, the drivers were not going to see that the bridge was out in time to stop.

Thinking swiftly, the man ran and got his boat's flare gun, and with it he began shooting flares AT the vehicles as they approached the broken bridge. This tactic worked, as each vehicle stopped before it could plummet over the edge into the rubble and the river.

The next morning the local news station was interviewing several of these drivers about what had happened. To a person, they each said that at first they thought some nutcase was trying to hurt them by shooting flares at them...that is, until they saw the danger the person was trying to save them from.

Maybe, IF you've read this far, you feel like those drivers.

And I'm with you in this. Some of the things I've expressed offend ME, for I understand the implications not only to The Church in this country, but also to myself and to those I love.

Unlike Isaiah, although I have received prophetic revelation I didn't ask for or seek, once I experienced it I did not say, "Oh send me, please, please, please!" For I recognized relatively quickly that most people would not like this message. Further, I identify much with Jeremiah. At the beginning, when I was young in the Lord, I thought, "Cool! This prophetic stuff is awesome!" But as things progressed, well, let's just say the message doesn't make me popular.

In short, I am the opposite of those who preach happy-clappy messages, the messages of the false prophets who say, "Beer, beer, plenty of beer!" (Micah 2:11). Those who tell people everything is wonderful, and that life is good, and that they should go for their dreams are leading people astray, to their doom really.

I'm like Jeremiah when he told Hananiah that he liked his prophetic word and sincerely hoped it would come to pass (28:5-6). But like Jeremiah who also told Hananiah that the whole purpose of a prophet, especially a prophetic forerunner who is charged with preparing the Bride for her Bridegroom-King, is not to say, "Hey ya'll, God just wants you to know He soooo loves ya." The MAIN reason Jesus sends prophets and prophetic forerunners is that things are NOT great, not even good, not even okay, and that repentance had better happen, or there will be terrible consequences (28:7-9).[178]

One of my personal issues in anything, but especially in spiritual things, is ALWAYS this: Is this you Jesus?

And the more serious something is, the more intense I become with: Is this you Jesus?!?!? I can't help myself, for I do NOT want to be a Joseph Smith who has led millions to spiritual destruction with Mormonism. Neither do I want to be a Jim Jones or a David Koresh who also led many to spiritual destruction...and physical death. I do not want to be a false person with a false message!

---

[178] I.e. Removal of light and revelation (Revelation 2:5b), Jesus fighting against us, as in judging us strictly by the standards of His Word (Revelation 2:16), sickness and death (Revelation 2:22-23), being allowed to be deceived and unprepared at Jesus' return, thus suffering great losses (Revelation 3:2-3), and of course, being vomited out of Jesus' mouth (Revelation 3:16).

Hopefully, what I have expressed here is correct, and if it is, that Jesus of Nazareth and His Bride are in the end blessed by it.

The Kingdom of Heaven is like treasure hidden in a field. When a man found it, he hid it again, and then in his joy went and <u>sold all he had</u> and bought that field. Again, the Kingdom of Heaven is like a merchant looking for fine pearls. When he found one of great value, he went away and <u>sold everything he had</u> and bought it. (Matthew 13:44-46).

When I survey the wondrous cross
On which the Prince of glory died,
My richest gain I count but loss,
And pour contempt on all my pride.

Forbid it, Lord, that I should boast,
Save in the death of Christ my God!
All the vain things that charm me most,
I sacrifice them to His blood.

See from His head, His hands, His feet,
Sorrow and [charity] flow mingled down!
Did e'er such [charity] and sorrow meet,
Or thorns compose so rich a crown?

Were the whole realm of nature mine,
That were a present far too small;
[Charity] so amazing, so divine,
Demands my soul, my life, my all.[179]

---

[179] Song by Isaac Watts.

THE APPENDIX

Appendix A

So what is a Christian?

Let's begin with what is not a Christian.

Jesus is not offering a Get-Out-Of-Hell-Free coupon and neither is He selling Fire Insurance for the Lake of Fire. That is, He is not merely trying to save people from their deserved judgment and its consequences. Or another way to say this is, Jesus is not merely a savior. He is the Savior, but He is also FAR more than that, for if Jesus is not a person's King (i.e. Lord, Boss, the One they want to love and obey – John 14:15, 21a, 23-24a, 15:10), then He is not that person's Savior.

Jesus isn't looking for people to "believe in Him" so they can avoid Hell yet have no desire to turn from living this life their own way.

Now, what is a Christian?

A Christian is someone who is willing to (1) repent – to turn from Sin and to turn toward obeying Jesus, and (2) who keeps on believing/ trusting the Jesus of Nazareth, and (3) who is immersed in water, and (4) who receives the Holy Spirit, which is THE main ingredient of the New Covenant (the Messianic Covenant – Ezekiel 11:19-20a, 36:26-27; John 3:5-6; Acts 2:16-18) and which is a real encounter with Him.

Then this Christian continues to be filled with the Holy Spirit for power purposes – both the power to love and obey Jesus and the power to further the Kingdom.

Need more information? I suggest The Normal Christian Birth, by David Pawson.

Appendix B

In what Jesus did to us and among us in this congregation we were faced with having to learn many critical lessons.

Believe it or not, we had some stupid theology, which Jesus regularly corrected. This was to our chagrin, as we thought we knew what we knew, only to find out that we knew very little. This shouldn't be a surprise, for the Pharisees and the Teachers of the Law also had some stupid theology Jesus tried to correct, and to which they did not respond well. The issue is humility and especially the willingness to be corrected...and...to change.

So to me, I don't care if Jesus asks me to stand on my head and to spit quarters. My only question is: How many? For when the Presence of the Living God shows up, He does many things that just don't fit into the human version of "decently and in order" (1 Corinthians 14:40 – NKJV). For there is the order of the dead bodies in a cemetery and there is the order of lively children in a nursery.

Also, once a person has tasted Living Water they KNOW the difference between it and sewage. Sadly those who have never tasted Living Water have no idea that they're being served sewage. For me, I WILL NOT drink sewage just to "survive." I'd rather die of thirst.[180]

Therefore, leaders are faced with two choices: Try to control to make things seem reasonable out of fear, or to back-off and let Jesus do what He wants to do, letting the One who owns the sheep have His way with His sheep, even when (not if) one doesn't understand it. Not that leaders shouldn't be careful in this, for there are false things that happen. Our approach was to "let the bush grow wild for a while, and then trim it back." This gave the Lord time to teach us about what He was doing, and most importantly it helped to minimize the possibility of us quenching Him out of biblical ignorance.

When the Pharisees demanded Jesus explain Himself and what He was doing, His answer was, "Do what I'm saying and then you'll know if it's true" (John 7:17). American thinking revolts at this Wisdom. Amer-

---

[180] I've read that dying of thirst is a difficult way to go, taking several days. But dying of dysentery from drinking dirty water is far worse, for being eaten from the inside out by bugs can take months with excruciating pain and filth!

ican thinking wants to completely understand something before doing it. Unfortunately for Americans, Jesus isn't an American.

Here's what I mean.

Jesus encounters a blind man, and to heal him Jesus SPITS in the man's eyes (Mark 8:22-26). (Jesus also put mud in another blind man's eyes – John 9:1-34.) He then asks the man what he sees, and although the man's eyesight is improved, it's not perfect. So Jesus puts His hands on the man's eyes and now his eyesight is completely restored to him.

I have some questions.

First, what healing power is there in Jesus' spit or in Palestinian dirt? Secondly, what did this blind guy, who had no idea who was speaking to him, do when he felt this stranger SPITTING on his eyes? Thirdly, why wasn't the man healed the first time?

The point is...this is weird. Jesus simply could have said, "Be healed," as He did in lots of other situations. Why did Jesus do what He did in this situation? Answer? Because that's what Jesus saw the Father doing (John 5:19). And in case you didn't know, the Father is not concerned with what we humans, especially we American, "enlightened," scientific, smart, Bible expert humans think about what He does, or even if what He does fits into our puny theology. As a wise man used to say, "This God offends the mind to reveal what's truly in the heart."

So, when the actual Presence of the Living God manifests among a people, it is definitely not "business as usual." Remember the parable by Brennan Manning I read in an earlier episode in which he compared the Holy Spirit to a buffalo hunter. Manning's analogy is more accurate than those immersed in Churchianity can even imagine.

The thing is, I think most people have some sense that if the Presence of the Living God did show up in their midst they would be blown away. And they don't want to be, for they like their comfortable and religious Sunday morning ice cream parties. For those who truly want the Presence of the Living God coffee and cookies are distractions. For those who are only interested in Churchianity there is never enough coffee and cookies.

So as news of what Jesus of Nazareth was doing in this congregation spread, two things happened. Those who were hungry for Jesus Himself, some living many miles away, spontaneously began to show up, for as D.L. Moody used to say, "You don't have to advertise a fire; a fire is its own advertisement." The other thing that happened was that far more people stayed away. Truly, as Jesus said, only a few want Him on His terms, and most don't (Matthew 7:13-14).

Appendix C

The Bible: probably THE most misunderstood and manipulated document in all of human history.

———————

Let's take a look at Shakespeare's play, "Hamlet."

The story begins with the unusual death of the king, Hamlet's dad. But then, his dad's death becomes suspicious when his mother quickly marries his dad's brother, Hamlet's uncle.

Hamlet concocts a plan to conceal his attempts to discover the truth by pretending to have gone insane with grief. The uses this cloak of being crazy to ask probing questions, and if the person he's questioning become concerned he falls back to claiming to just be crazy.

Finally, Hamlet's girlfriend, Ophelia, comes to him out of her concern for him, telling him how much she loves him and how much she wants to help him with his grief.

In response, and attempting not to expose his charade, even to his girlfriend, Hamlet says a well-known line: "Get thee to a nunnery."

If one does not know the culture of the Elizabethan Era in England, one may think, "Awe, how sweet. He's telling her to go spend time with a house of godly women in prayer."

But this is NOT what Hamlet is saying.

Queen Elizabeth I was quite concerned that her subjects behaved morally. So this was a time when, for example, women's clothes covered them from their ankles to their wrists to their chins. The problem for society was this: laws don't make people moral. People are going to find a way around these morality standards. And one of the ways people did this was to use verbal irony – saying one thing but meaning the complete opposite.

This is what Shakespeare is doing in what he has Hamlet say to Ophelia. Thus, the opposite of a house of nuns is...a house of whores. Hamlet is telling Ophelia to go prostitute herself. Thus, shortly after this exchange with Hamlet, Ophelia commits suicide from a broken heart. If one does not understand the culture at the time Shakespeare is writing, one will not understand why Ophelia did what she did.

Well, this is exactly the case with the Bible, a book with sixty-six writings spanning many centuries for the first thirty-nine and nearly a century for the final twenty-seven. And ALL of these were written in the ancient culture of the Hebrews.

Hebrews are NOT like Gentiles, Moderns, or Americans. Hebrews don't think like people in Western Culture who think like Greeks, since Western Culture was birthed out of the Renaissance, the Enlightenment, and the Age of Reason, all of which were based on Classic Greek Philosophy, for the leaders of these movements believed the Greeks (the Greeks!?!?) represented the high point of human development.

Then add in the fact that the Bible is reflecting the ANCIENT culture of Hebrews...and it is easy to read INTO the text meaning from one's modern culture (eisegesis) instead of pulling OUT of the text (exegesis) what is actually meant by the writer.

Eisegesis has been so prolific for so long, it seems people don't even consider its danger, and the resulting false teaching. And with the prolific propensity among some groups to claim that "God told" them... and some of the most ignorant and unbiblical things are claimed and taught utterly unashamedly.

How one handles the Bible matters!

It's not that any of us have perfect theology or knowledge, certainly not this writer, but that does not excuse us from doing all we can to be truly careful in how we read and understand all of the aspects of the Word of God, such as the language (i.e. Hebrew and Greek)[181], the historical background, the Hebrew cultural, the major themes (i.e. the covenants), etc.

Being sincere is important, but one can still be sincerely wrong. Integrity matters. Rightly dividing the Word of God also matters.

Do your best to present yourself to God as one approved, a worker who does not need to be ashamed and who correctly handles the Word of Truth. (2 Timothy 2:15)

Not many of you should become teachers, my fellow Believers, because you know that we who teach will be judged more strictly. (James 3:1)

---

[181] One doesn't have to be a Hebrew and Greek expert, for there are lots of language tools available.

Appendix D

The truth is, the Song Of Songs is only marginally helpful to a married couple. C'mon, how much marital help have you actually gleaned from this Song for your marriage? And the title immediately tells us why, for this Song's main purpose is far more than human marriage.

Just as the Holy of Hollies is not just one holy place among many holy places, but rather the holiest place of all holy places, and just as Jesus is not just one king among many kings, but rather the King of all kings, so this song is not just one nice song among many nice songs, but rather THE Song of all songs, the all-time, number one hit, the song that is eternally at the very top of the charts!

Therefore, the Holy Spirit has been extremely focused upon the Song Of Songs, highlighting it and illuminating it and revealing its treasures for many, many years now. If you haven't been aware of this, if you know little to nothing about this song, you are missing something incredibly important. You should seriously wonder if you and the leaders you're following are hearing from the Holy Spirit. Seriously.

For the overall point of the Song is how Jesus matures a member of the Bride in Real Love.[182] And this process begins with the person responding to the Holy Spirit's prompting in them to truly want to know the Bridegroom-King as deeply and as intimately as possible (1:2). And it ends with the person head-over-heels lovesick for the Bridegroom-King (8:1b & 6-7).

Note also the Bride's repeated comment:

"Do not arouse or awaken Love until it so desires" (2:7, 3:5, 84).

What she means is, this Love is NOT something a person can produce (i.e. arouse or awaken) by their own human efforts. This Love is Real Love and can ONLY be had from the One who is Love. In other words, acquiring Real Love is something Jesus does to His Bride. It is NOT something a person can do to themselves. Therefore, the whole point of the Song is to show the process He uses to develop His Love in a person who longs to have it...and...Him.

---

[182] The major reason Jesus gave for those who don't make it in the final years is because their love grew cold. Being immersed in the SOS process right now is critical to being prepared for that time when the pressure to not love Jesus will be great.

As an example of the Holy Spirit opening the eyes of a person's heart so he or she can "see" what passion the Bridegroom-King has for His Bride, note just these two statements the Bridegroom-King makes about His Bride:

You have stolen my heart, my sister, my Bride; <u>you have stolen my heart with one glance of your eyes</u>. (4:9)

Turn your eyes from me; <u>they overwhelm me</u>. (6:5a)

———————

Below is a possible outline of this process.

1. The Divine Kiss and the Bride's Life Vision -- 1:2-4
2. Her Journey Begins with the Paradox of Grace -- 1:5-11
3. Understanding Her Identity in God's Beauty -- 1:12 - 2:7
4. Challenging the Comfort Zone -- 2:8-17
5. She Experiences God's Loving Discipline -- 3:1-5
6. A Fresh Revelation of Jesus as a Safe Savior -- 3:6-11
7. The Prophetic Heart of the Bridegroom God -- 4:1-8
8. The Ravished Heart of the Bridegroom God -- 4:9 - 5:1
9. The Ultimate Test of Maturity -- 5:2-8
10. The Bride's Response to the Test -- 5:9 - 6:3
11. Jesus Praises Her after the Testing -- 6:4-10
12. The Vindication of the Persecuted Bride -- 6:11 - 7:9a
13. The Bride's Mature Partnership with Jesus -- 7:9b - 8:4
14. The Bridal Seal of Mature Love -- 8:5-7
15. The Bride's Final Intercession and Revelation -- 8:8-14

Appendix E

The Essential Nature of Holiness in Regard to Salvation
Do the warnings in Scripture mean anything to the Believer?

I. THE BIBLE TEACHES A "REMNANT THEOLOGY"

1. Jesus said in Matthew 7:13-23:

Enter through the narrow gate. For wide is the gate and broad is the road that leads to destruction, and most[183] enter through it. But small is the gate and narrow the road that leads to life, and only a few find it. Watch out for false prophets. They come to you in sheep's clothing, but inwardly they are ferocious wolves. By their fruit you will recognize them (use of a tree metaphor – Psalm 1). **Do people pick grapes from thornbushes, or figs from thistles? Likewise, every good tree bears good fruit, but a bad tree bears bad fruit. A good tree cannot bear bad fruit, and a bad tree cannot bear good fruit. Every tree that does not bear good fruit is cut down and thrown into the fire. Thus, by their fruit you will recognize them. Not everyone who says to me, "Lord, Lord," will enter the Kingdom of Heaven, but only he who does the will of my Father who is in Heaven. Many will say to me on That Day, "Lord, Lord, did we not prophesy in your Name, and in your Name drive out demons and perform many miracles?" Then I will tell them plainly, "I never knew you. Away from me, you evildoers!"**

2. The author of the Letter to the Hebrews wrote in 5:13 – 6:8:

Anyone who lives on milk, being still an infant, is not acquainted with the teaching about righteousness. But solid food is for the mature, who by constant use have trained themselves to distinguish good from evil. Therefore, let us leave the elementary teachings about Jesus and go on to maturity, not laying again the

---

[183] The Greek word is *poulos*. It can be translated either with the English word "many" or "most," depending on the translator. Here the translator chose the word "many," but in Matthew 24:12 he chose "most." I believe the word "most" fits best here as a contrast to "few." Plus, Jesus was not one to soft-pedal things, as the fact that He said "most" people's hearts will grow cold.

foundation of repentance from acts that lead to death, and of faith/trust in Him, instruction about baptisms, the laying on of hands, the resurrection of the dead, and eternal judgment. And God permitting, we will do so. It is impossible for those who have once been enlightened, who have tasted the heavenly gift, who have shared in the Holy Spirit, who have tasted the goodness of the Word of God and the powers of the Age To Come, if they fall away, to be brought back to repentance, because to their loss they are crucifying the Son of God all over again and subjecting Him to public disgrace. Land that drinks in the rain often falling on it and that produces a crop useful to those for whom it is farmed receives the blessing of the Living God. But land that produces thorns and thistles is worthless and is in danger of being cursed. In the end it will be burned.

II. THE REMNANT EVIDENCE OF GEORGE BARNA'S POLLS

- 86% of people living in the United States say they are Christians.
- 9% say they have a biblical worldview, that is, they have some Christian theology.
- 4% say they seriously seek to live their lives by the Word of God.

III. SOME BASIC EXEGITICAL QUESTIONS

- To whom is Jesus speaking in the Gospels and The Revelation of Jesus?
- To whom are the Apostles writing in their letters?
- To be in Jesus' Kingdom, does a person have to: Love the Lord? Obey Jesus? Abide in Christ? Believe/trust in and thus follow Jesus, being His disciple, living life His way?
- Can someone be saved from Hell if he is not saved from his Sin, or continues to purposely Sin?
- Does repentance, free will, and holy living play any part as evidence of a True Conversion?

IV. A BIG QUESTION

What is the eternal estate of the majority of people who claim to be born-again by the Spirit but who live immoral, or unfaithful, or blatantly disobedient, hypocritical lives?

1. They are saved no matter how they live.

If we claim to have fellowship with Him yet walk in the darkness, we lie and do not live by the Truth. If we claim to be without Sin, we deceive ourselves and the Truth is not in us. If we claim we have not sinned, we make Him out to be a liar and His Word has no place in our lives (1 John 1:6, 8, 10).

2. They never were saved; they only have a semblance of true faith.

But mark this: There will be terrible times in the Last Days. People will be lovers of themselves, lovers of money, boastful, proud, abusive, disobedient to their parents, ungrateful, unholy, without love, unforgiving, slanderous, without self-control, brutal, not lovers of the good, treacherous, rash, conceited, lovers of pleasure rather than lovers of God – having a form of godliness but denying its power (2 Timothy 3:1-5).

3. They were saved, but then fell away due to Sin or other issues.

I tell you. . .unless you repent, you too will all perish (Luke 13:5).

That same day Jesus went out of the house and sat by the lake. Such large crowds gathered around Him that He got into a boat and sat in it, while all the people stood on the shore. Then He told them many things in parables, saying: "A farmer went out to sow his seed. As he was scattering the seed, some fell along the path, and the birds came and ate it up. Some fell on rocky places, where it did not have much soil. It sprang up quickly because the soil was shallow. But when the sun came up, the plants were scorched, and they withered because they had no root. Other seed fell among thorns, which grew up and choked the plants. Still other seed fell on good soil, where it produced a crop – a hundred, sixty,

or thirty times what was sown. Whoever has ears, let them hear."
(Matthew 13:1-9)

Listen then to what the parable of the sower means: When anyone hears the message about the Kingdom and does not understand it, the evil one comes and snatches away what was sown in their heart. This is the seed sown along the path. The seed falling on rocky ground refers to someone who hears the word and at once receives it with joy. But since they have no root, they last only a short time. When trouble or persecution comes because of the Word, they quickly fall away. The seed falling among the thorns refers to someone who hears the Word, but the worries of this life and the deceitfulness of wealth choke the Word, making it unfruitful. But the seed falling on good soil refers to someone who hears the Word and understands it. This is the one who produces a crop, yielding a hundred, sixty, or thirty times what was sown. (Matthew 13:18-23)

V. THE FALSE AND TRUE ASSURANCE OF SALVATION

1. The False: simply confess Jesus as savior, receive Jesus in your heart, pray a prayer, make a general confession of being "a sinner"

2. The true: confess the Real Jesus as Lord, Master, and King, actually take steps to repent of specific Sin, grow in a personal relationship with Jesus in which one falls more and more in love with Him, and out of that love choosing to live holy (John 14:15, 23, 24, 15:10) (being a sheep versus being a pig)

CAN A BORN-AGAIN PERSON...

1. ...fall away from God and His Grace?
    Romans 11:22; Hebrews 3:12, 6:4-8; Galatians 5:1-7; 2 Peter 3:17-18; 2 Thessalonians 2:3; 1 Timothy 4:1; Matthew 13:21, 24:12; Revelation 2:5

2. ...neglect his salvation and drift away?
    Hebrews 1:14 - 2:3

3. ...stray from the truth?
    James 5:19-20; Matthew 18:15-17; 2 Peter 2:15-22

4. ...as a tree bear no fruit and be cut down?
    **Matthew 3:7-10, 7:17-23; Luke 3:7-9, 13:1-9; John 15:1-6;
    Romans 11:17-22**

5. ...be declared unworthy?
    Matthew 10:35-39, 22:1-14; Luke 12:46ff; Revelation 3:1-6

6. ...having believed in vain?
    **Galatians 3:1-4, 4:8-11; 2 Corinthians 5:20 – 6:2; 1
    Thessalonians 3:5**

7. ...go on sinning willfully?
    Hebrews 10:26-27

8. ...no longer having a sacrifice for sins?
    Hebrews 10:28-31

9. ...deny Jesus in word or deed and be denied?
    Matthew 10:28-39; Mark 8:34-38; Titus 1:15-16; 1 Timothy 5:8

10. ...be a castaway or disqualified?
    1 Corinthians 9:23-27, 10:1-13

11. ...be declared unfit for the Kingdom?
    Luke 9:62; Matthew 10:37-39

12. ...have dead, useless faith?
    James 2:12-26; Galatians 5:5-7

13. ...come short of Grace?
    Hebrews 4:1, 12:12-17

14. ...receive another gospel?
    Galatians 1:6-10; Jude 3-4

15. ...receive the Grace of God in vain?
    2 Corinthians 5:20 – 6:2

16. ...possess only a form of godliness?
    2 Timothy 3:5-10

17. ...be a hypocritical, lazy, and wicked servant?
    **Matthew 24:42-51, 25:14-30, 25:34-46; Philippians 3:17-19;
    Titus 1:10-16**

18. ...be severed from Christ?
    Galatians 5:1-7

19. ...not be in the faith, failing the test?
    2 Corinthians 13:5-6
20. ...and as a result receive no inheritance?
    **1 Corinthians 6:9-11; Galatians 5:19-21; Ephesians 5:5-7;
    Romans 8:12-13; Revelation 21:7-8**
21. ...not love the Lord and be accursed?
    Matthew 5:13; Mark 9:50; Luke 14:34
22. ...have his religion declared worthless?
    **James 1:19-26; Matthew 25:30; Luke 19:22; Titus 1:16;
    Hebrews 6:8**
23. ...not repent and overcome?
    Revelation 3:5
24. ...having his name erased from Book of Life?
    Revelation 2 and 3
25. ...love the World and not have the Love of the Father?
    1 John 2:15-17
26. ...live in wanton pleasure, being dead already?
    1 Timothy 5:5-7; James 5:1-6
27. ...love money, things, and Self more than God?
    **Matthew 10:25, 16:24-26; Luke 12:13-21, 16:19-31; John 12:24-
    26; Revelation 6:14-17**
28. ...have lips near God but a heart far from Him?
    Matthew 7:21-23; 1 John 1:2, 8, 10, 2:4, 6, 9
29. ...fail to do the will of God?
    **Matthew 7:21, 12:46-50; Mark 3:31-35; Luke 8:19-21; Hebrews
    10:36-39; 1 John 2:15-17**
30. ...and practice lawlessness?
    Matthew 13:41, 23:28, 24:12; 1 John 3:4
31. ...be entangled in the World and overcome?
    1 John 2:15-17; 2 Peter 2:20-22
32. ...turn away from the holy commands given them?
    2 Peter 2:20-22
33. ...fail to keep God's Word?
    John 8:31, 51-52
34. ...soil his garments?
    Revelation 3:1-6
35. ...turn his ears away from the Truth?
    2 Peter 2:20-22

36. ...turn away from the Faith?
Titus 1:13-14; 1 Timothy 5:14-15

37. ...not obey the Truth, being a son of disobedience?
Colossians 3:5-11

38. ...not follow Jesus and perish?
John 10:27-29

39. ...shrink back in shame at His appearing?
Hebrews 10:38-39

40. ...and go into outer darkness and destruction?
Matthew 8:12, 22:13, 25:30

41. ...be overcome and enslaved by Sin?
John 8:34-36; 2 Peter 2:18-19

42. ...be judgmental and be cut off?
Romans 1:31 – 2:11, 11:17-22

43. ...forsake the way of righteousness?
2 Peter 2:15; Joshua 24:20

44. ...not pursue peace and holiness, and not see the Lord?
Hebrews 12:14-17

45. ...not persevere to the end?
Matthew 24:13; Mark 13:13; 1 Timothy 4:16; 2 Timothy 2:10-12

46. ...be unforgiving and handed over to the tormentors?
Matthew 6:9-15; Matthew 18:15-35

47. ...be a foolish virgin?
Matthew 25:1-13

48. ...distort the Scriptures to their destruction?
2 Peter 3:16

49. ...not repent and perish?
Luke 13:1-5; the seven churches of Revelation 2 and 3

50. ...be lukewarm and vomited out by Jesus?
Revelation 3:14-22

51. ...be excluded from the Tree of Life?
Revelation 22:18-19

VI. THE PARABLES OF JESUS MAKE SENSE IF THE ABOVE LISTED ITEMS ARE RESPONDED TO IN THE AFFIRMATIVE

- The Sower – Matthew 13, Mark 4, Luke 8
- The Dragnet – Matthew 13:47-50
- The Unmerciful Servant – Matthew 18:21-35
- The Two Sons – Matthew 21:28-32
- The Wedding Banquet – Matthew 22:1-14
- The Faithful and Unfaithful Servants – Matthew 24:45-51
- The Five Foolish Virgins – Matthew 25:1-13
- The Using of Talents – Matthew 25:14-30
- The Sheep and Goats – Matthew 25:31-46
- The Rich Fool – Luke 12:13-21
- The Ready and Unready – Luke 12:35-48
- The Counting of the Cost – Luke 14:25-35
- The Ten Minas – Luke 19:11-27

VII. JESUS' ATTITUDE TOWARD SIN AND HOLINESS

1. Warning of Sin from the Sermon on the Mount

   - The pure in heart will see God – Matthew 5:8
   - Tasteless salt is thrown out – Matthew 5:13
   - Unless one's righteousness exceeds – Matthew 5:20
   - Angry words endanger a person's eternal welfare – Matthew 5:22
   - Better to gouge-out eye and/or cut off hand than to sin and go to Hell – Matthew 5:29-30
   - Danger of unbiblical divorce and remarriage – Matthew 5:31-32
   - No false vows, give freely, love enemies to be sons of the Father in Heaven – Matthew 5:33-48
   - If you do not forgive, your Father will not forgive you – Matthew 6:9-15

2. Possibility of Hell by denying Jesus and not living worthy of Him – Matthew 10:37-39

3. His angels will gather out of His Kingdom all stumbling block and those who commit lawlessness – Matthew 13:40-43

4. Seven woes (curses) spoken to people who are outwardly religious and inwardly corrupt – Matthew 23

5. Warning of disciples falling away due to a variety of things, and only those who endure to the end are saved – Matthew 24:10-13

6. Whoever is ashamed of Jesus and His Words, He will be ashamed of him – Matthew Mark 8:38

7. Many will seek to enter the Kingdom, but will not be able, for evildoer will have to depart from Him – Luke 13:22-28

8. A person cannot be Jesus' disciple unless he or she (Luke 14:25-35:

    - hates his father, mother, etc.
    - carries the cross and follows Him.
    - calculates the cost and finishes.
    - gives up his possessions.
    - does not lose his saltiness.

9. It is an absolute truth that anyone who deliberately sins is a slave of Sin – John 8:34

10. If anyone does not abide in Him, he or she is thrown away and burned – John 15:1-6

11. Hebrews 1:8-9

Your throne, O God, will last for ever and ever, and righteousness will be the scepter of your Kingdom. You have loved righteousness and hated wickedness; therefore God, your God, has set you above your companions by anointing you with the oil of joy.

12. Revelation 21:5-8

He who was seated on the throne said, "I am making everything new!" Then He said, "Write this down, for these words are trust-

worthy and true." He said to me: "It is done. I am the Alpha and the Omega, the Beginning and the End. To him who is thirsty I will give to drink without cost from the spring of the Water of Life. He who overcomes will inherit all this, and I will be his God and he will be my son. But the cowardly, the unbelieving, the vile, the murderers, the sexually immoral, those who practice magic arts, the idolaters and all liars — their place will be in the fiery lake of burning sulfur. This is the second death."

13. Revelation 22:12-15

"Behold, I am coming soon! My reward is with me, and I will give to everyone according to what he has done. I am the Alpha and the Omega, the First and the Last, the Beginning and the End. Blessed are those who wash their robes, that they may have the right to the Tree of Life and may go through the gates into The City. Outside are the dogs, those who practice magic arts, the sexually immoral, the murderers, the idolaters and everyone who loves and practices falsehood.

VIII. JESUS' WARNINGS TO THE SEVEN CHURCHES

Ephesus – Revelation 2:4-7

Yet I hold this against you: You have forsaken your First Love. Remember the height from which you have fallen! Repent and do the things you did at first. If you do not repent, I will come to you and remove your lampstand from its place. He who has an ear, let him hear what the Spirit says to the churches. To him who over-comes, I will give the right to eat from the Tree of Life, which is in the paradise of God.

Smyna – Revelation 2:10-11

Do not be afraid of what you are about to suffer. Be faithful, even to the point of death, and I will give you the Crown of Life. He who has an ear, let him hear what the Spirit says to the churches. He who overcomes will not be hurt at all by the Second Death.

Pergamum – Revelation 2:14-17

You have people there who hold to the teaching of Balaam, who taught Balak to entice the Israelites to sin by eating food sacrificed to idols and by committing sexual immorality. Likewise, you also have those who hold to the teaching of the Nicolaitans. Repent therefore! Otherwise, I will soon come to you and will fight against them with the sword of my mouth. He who has an ear, let him hear what the Spirit says to the churches. To him who overcomes, I will give some of the hidden manna. I will also give him a white stone with a new name written on it.

Thyatira – Revelation 2:20-29

You tolerate that woman Jezebel, who calls herself a prophetess. By her teaching she misleads my servants into sexual immorality and the eating of food sacrificed to idols. I have given her time to repent of her immorality, but she is unwilling. So I will cast her on a bed of suffering, and I will make those who commit adultery with her suffer intensely, unless they repent of her ways. I will strike her children dead. Then all the churches will know that I am He who searches hearts and minds, and I will repay each of you according to your deeds. Now I say to the rest of you in Thyatira, to you who do not hold to her teaching and have not learned Satan's so-called deep secrets (I will not impose any other burden on you). Only hold on to what you have until I come. To him who overcomes and does my will to the end, I will give authority over the nations – "He will rule them with an iron scepter; he will dash them to pieces like pottery" – just as I have received authority from my Father. I will also give him the morning star. He who has an ear, let him hear what the Spirit says to the churches.

Sardis – Revelation 3:1-6

I know your deeds; you have a reputation of being alive, but you are dead. Wake up! Strengthen what remains and is about to die, for I have not found your deeds complete in the sight of my God. Remember, therefore, what you have received and heard; obey it, and repent. But if you do not wake up, I will come like a thief, and you will not know at what time I will come to you. Yet you have a few people in Sardis who have not soiled their clothes. They will walk with me, dressed in white, for they are worthy. He who overcomes will, like them, be dressed in white. I will never blot out his name from the Book of Life, but will acknowledge his name before my Father and His angels. He who has an ear, let him hear what the Spirit says to the churches.

Philadelphia – Revelation 3:10-13

Since you have kept my command to endure patiently, I will also keep you from the hour of trial that is going to come upon the whole world to test those who live on the earth. I am coming soon. Hold on to what you have, so that no one will take your crown. Him who overcomes I will make a pillar in the temple of my God. Never again will he leave it. I will write on him the Name of my God and the Name of the city of my God, the new Jerusalem, which is coming down out of Heaven from my God; and I will also write on him my new Name. He who has an ear, let him hear what the Spirit says to the churches.

Laodicea – Revelation 3:15-22

I know your deeds, that you are neither cold nor hot. I wish you were either one or the other! So, because you are lukewarm — neither hot nor cold — I am about to spit you out of my mouth. You say, "I am rich; I have acquired wealth and do not need a thing." But you do not realize that you are wretched, pitiful, poor, blind, and naked. I counsel you to buy from me gold refined in the fire, so you can become rich; and white clothes to wear, so you can cover your shameful nakedness; and salve to put on your eyes, so you can see. Those whom I love I rebuke and discipline. So be earnest, and repent. Here I am! I stand at the door and knock. If anyone hears my voice and opens the door, I will come in and eat with him, and he with me. To him who overcomes, I will give the right to sit with me on my throne, just as I overcame and sat down with my Father on His throne. He who has an ear, let him hear what the Spirit says to the churches.

IX. THE APOSTLE'S TEACHINGS OF JESUS

The Apostle Paul

- Romans 2:1-16
- Romans 6:15-23
- Romans 8:12-13
- Romans 11:17-23
- 1 Corinthians 9:24-27
- 1 Corinthians 10:1-12
- 2 Corinthians 6:14 – 7:11
- Galatians 5:2-1, 19-21
- Galatians 6:7-8
- Ephesians 5:1-10
- Philippians 2:12-16
- 2 Thessalonians 1:6-12
- 1 Timothy 4:16
- 1 Timothy 5:6-8, 11-15
- 2 Timothy 2:8-13, 16-19

The Apostle Peter

- 1 Peter 1:14-19
- 2 Peter 1:5-11
- 2 Peter 2:17-22
- 2 Peter 3:1, 8-15

The Apostle John

- 1 John 1:5 – 2:11
- 1 John 2:15-17, 23-24, 28-29
- 1 John 3:4-24
- 1 John 4:17-20

The Apostle James

- James 1:12-16
- James 2:14-26
- James 4:1-10

- James 5:1-6, 19-20

The Writer of the letter to some Hebrews

- 2:1-3
- 3 and 4
- 5:9
- 6:7-8
- 9:27-28
- 10:19-39
- 12:14-17, 25-29
- 13:4

X. THE LITTLE WORD "IF" IS A HINGE UPON WHICH THE DOOR OF SALVATION SWINGS

- Forgiveness – Matthew 6:14-15
- Restoration – Matthew 18:12ff
- Forgiveness – Matthew 18:35
- Holiness – Mark 9:43-47
- Fruitfulness – Luke 13:9
- Holiness – Luke 13:34-35
- Abiding – John 15:6
- Behavior – Romans 8:13
- Tree of God – Romans 11:21-23
- Salvation – 1 Corinthians 15:2
- Legalism – Galatians 5:2
- Endurance – Galatians 6:8-9
- Resurrection – Philippians 3:11
- Endurance – Colossians 1:23
- Family – 1 Timothy 5:8
- Neglect – Hebrews 2:3
- Endurance – Hebrews 3:6, 14
- Barrenness – Hebrews 6:8
- Willful Sin – Hebrews 10:26
- Turning Away – Hebrews 12:25
- The Tongue – James 1:26

- Wandering – James 5:19-20
- Fearful Hope – 1 Peter 4:18
- Diligence – 2 Peter 1:10
- Worldliness – 2 Peter 2:20
- Confession – 1 John 1:9
- Abiding – 1 John 2:24-25
- The Mark – Revelation 14:9-12
- Tampering – Revelation 22:18-19

XI. THERE ARE ONLY THREE POSSIBILITIES:

1. One has been born-again, and thus out of his or her love for Jesus he or she seeks to obey Him by living by His Spirit or walking with His Spirit, as well as keeping in step with His Spirit (Galatians 5:16-18 & 22-25).
2. Or, one has been born-again by the Spirit, but is sowing to the Flesh, thus reaping the fruit of the Flesh (Galatians 5:19-21), and eventually Hell.
3. Or, one has never actually been born-again by the Spirit and is simply religious with a form of "godliness" but without the reality, which also results in Hell (2 Timothy 3:5).

———————

The pig versus sheep metaphor is a good way to describe the difference between those who are simply Christianized participating in Churchianity versus those who are faithful, lovesick followers of Jesus of Nazareth, the Jewish Bridegroom King.

Pigs like and even love the mud (i.e. Sin). They live deep in the mud. They call the mud good. They don't see any problems with the mud. They rationalize the mud.

Sheep sometimes accidentally, or even on purpose, get into some mud (i.e. Sin). However, the moment they do they know that the mud is mud, and they ultimately don't like the mud. They don't make excuses for or rationalize the mud. They call the mud what it is – mud. And whether they accidentally got into the mud or whether they deliberately got into the mud, they truly do not want to be in the mud. So they call out to the Shepherd to come help them out of the mud.

None of Jesus of Nazareth's followers are perfect and sinless. All of us make mistakes, act immaturely, misbehave, make wrong choices, and commit Sin. Hopefully, and ideally, as a follower of Jesus of Nazareth matures and grows in True Love he or she does less and less of such things.

However, no one – NO ONE – ever completely arrives at perfect sinlessness in this life. Paul called himself the "worst of sinners" (1 Timothy 1:15-16). He confessed that sometimes he did things he knew not to do and didn't do things he knew he should do (Romans 7:14-20). He also admitted that he struggled with covetousness (Romans 7:7-8) and lust (2 Corinthians 11:29). And yet he wrote this:

If someone else thinks they have reasons to put confidence in the flesh, I have more: circumcised on the eighth day of the people of Israel, of the tribe of Benjamin, a Hebrew of Hebrews; in regard to the Law, a Pharisee; as for zeal, persecuting The Church; as for righteousness based on the Law, faultless. But whatever were gains to me I now consider loss for the sake of Christ. What is more, I consider everything a loss because of the surpassing worth of knowing Christ Jesus my Lord, for whose sake I have lost all things. I consider them garbage, that I may gain Christ and be found in Him, not having a righteousness of my own that comes from the Law, but that which is through faith in Christ – the righteousness that comes from God on the basis of faith. I want to know Christ – yes, to know the power of His resurrection and participation in His sufferings, becoming like Him in His death, and so, somehow, attaining to the resurrection from the dead. Not that I have already obtained all this, or have already arrived at my goal, but I press on to take hold of that for which Christ Jesus took hold of me. Brothers and sisters, I do not consider myself yet to have taken hold of it. But one thing I do: Forgetting what is behind and straining toward what is ahead, I press on toward the goal to win the prize for which God has called me heavenward in Christ Jesus. (Philippians 3:4b-14)

As mentioned at the beginning, Jesus said:

Enter through the narrow gate. For wide is the gate and broad is the road that leads to destruction, and most enter through it. But small is the gate and narrow the road that leads to life, and only a few find it.

Jesus also warned that because of the incredible level of wickedness, the hearts of most of those who consider themselves to belong to Him will grow cold, resulting in their falling away.

Because of the increase of wickedness, the love of most will grow cold, but the one who stands firm to the end will be saved. (Matthew 24:12-13)

The apostle Paul also affirms this.

Don't let anyone deceive you in any way, for That Day will not come until the rebellion occurs and the man of lawlessness is revealed, the man doomed to destruction. (2 Thessalonians 2:3)

These people are not the Lost who fall away. These are people who consider themselves to be Christians. Which is why Paul's advice in 2 Corinthians 13:5 is important.

Examine yourselves to see whether you are in The Faith; test yourselves. Do you not realize that Christ Jesus is in you – unless, of course, you fail the test?[184]

---

[184] Also see David's Pawson's, <u>Once Saved, Always Saved?</u>.

Appendix F

When looking at the five covenants the Living God is in – which are the ONLY covenants He is in – there are six areas each covenant addresses.[185] And these six areas are:

1. Who is the covenant with?
2. What is the covenant offering?
3. What does the covenant expect?
4. What happens if the covenant is failed?
5. How long is the covenant good for?
6. What is the purpose of the covenant?

So, let's consider the Mosaic Covenant.

Number One: The Mosaic Covenant is ONLY for the Jewish people. The only way for it to possibly apply to a Gentile is if the Gentile wanted to convert to Judaism and adhere to the Law of Moses...ALL the Law of Moses, not just the parts one likes. But even in this, I'm not so sure the Living God would allow it, for He made this covenant specifically with the people of Israel. Gentiles are not allowed. Sorry? I mean, really, does anyone WANT to be under the Law of Moses...ALL the Law of Moses?

Number Two: This covenant offered provision and protection to the nation of Israel while Israel occupied the Promised Land. For being out of the Land was one of the consequences for disobedience to this covenant. Thus, this covenant is for the nation of Israel and it is tied specifically to the Promised Land.

Number Three and Four: This covenant expects the nation of Israel to obey all of the Law of Moses. And when the nation, not merely individuals, obeyed or disobeyed this covenant the entire nation was either blessed with health and prosperity or cursed with disasters, occupation, and even exile.[186]

---

[185] I am indebted to David Pawson's little book, By God, I Will: The Biblical Covenants.
[186] For example, there were those in the ten northern tribes who had not given themselves to idolatry, and yet, they were taken captive and removed from the Land by the Assyrians. There were also those in Judah who were responding to Jeremiah's message, but they too were taken to Babylon. Again, this is because the Mosaic Covenant is for the Jewish nation as a whole. It is NOT individual as is the Messianic Covenant.

Number Five: This covenant is a temporary covenant, as it was supposed to be replaced when the Messiah came and offered the New Covenant, the Messianic Covenant, which Jesus came and did.

Number Six: This covenant's purpose was to show what Righteousness looks like, and that no one could or would ever meet such standards. Thus, it also showed the need for a better way:

"This is the covenant I will make with the House of Israel after that time," declares the LORD. "I will put my Law in their minds and write it on their hearts. I will be their God, and they will be my people. No longer will a man teach his neighbor, or a man his brother, saying, 'Know the LORD,' because they will all know me, from the least of them to the greatest, for I will forgive their wickedness and will remember their sins no more." (Jeremiah 31:33-34).

So take the issue of tithing, which is a Mosaic Covenant command that says if one tithes the Living God blesses and if one does not tithe He curses.

First, if one is not a Hebrew living in Israel – that is, one is a Gentile – lost or born-again by the Spirit – the issue of tithing has no application to that person. There is no divine requirement for anyone, other than a Jew living in Israel who wants to be under the Law of Moses, to tithe.

Thus, if one is a born-again by the Spirit follower of Jesus of Nazareth, that is, one is in the Messianic Covenant, tithing is NOT only NOT an issue, there is NO blessing for doing it and no curse for not doing it. The followers of Jesus are to avoid serving the god of Money, they are to live a simple, non-materialistic, fasted lifestyle, and they are to give joyfully and generously to help others.

That's it. No curse for disobedience and no blessing for obedience, for the motive for ANY obedience in the Messianic Covenant is not for material and physical blessing as it is in the Mosaic Covenant. The motive for ANY obedience in the Messianic Covenant is to remain in Jesus' Love (John 15:10) and to receive future rewards (e.g. Matthew 6:19-20, 25:19-23).

I know, I know. Leaders have either blatantly or subtly given the message that Christians are supposed to tithe. The truth? They don't do this because they're just SO concerned that you're okay financially.

They do this because they are SO concerned that they and their ministry are okay financially. It's called a guilt-trip.

But now, IF you're looking for an "old testament" (which isn't accurate to say it this way) thing to do so as to receive blessings from what you do, how about the Abramic Covenant? This covenant guarantees – no joke – that anyone who blesses Abraham's descendants will be blessed, and anyone who curses Abraham's descendants will be cursed (Genesis 12:3a). In case you don't have a descendant of Abraham readily available, I'm a descendant of Abraham. I was circumcised on the eighth day (Genesis 17:9-14). So...would you like my mailing address so you'll know where to send your checks?

In short, Woe to those who change the New Covenant by teaching ANY sort of blessing-for-obedience and curse-for-disobedience! Christians are NOT under the Mosaic Covenant, much less a blending of it with the Messianic Covenant. The apostle Paul would have a kanipshin fit if he knew The Church was teaching such a thing!

Just for a little more clarity, I want to make sure I mention what Jesus said in Matthew 5:17-20.

Jesus is not talking about the rituals and legal requirements of the Mosaic Covenant, such as tithing[187], when He said He would never, ever abolish anything from "the Law and the Prophets." In fact, He's not even referencing the Mosaic Covenant. He's talking about the entire Bible, which for Him was Genesis through Malachi.

The things Jesus did not come to abolish and that will stand forever and ever are the moral codes and standards of the Word of God. In other words, He is not doing away with the Ten Commandments, or the sexual standards of Leviticus, chapter eighteen, etc. The moral issues contained in the Word of God are NEVER going away. The Mosaic rituals and legal requirements are, but NOT the moral standards for holiness.

How do I know Jesus is talking about the moral standards ONLY as never going away and not the Mosaic Covenant rituals and legal requirements (such as tithing)? Simple. Read the specific examples He expounds upon beginning in 5:21.

---

[187] He will address the issue of the god of money and the spirit of materialism in 7:19-34.

So, not only are His moral standards as contained in Genesis through Malachi never, ever going away, but Jesus explains that His followers are held to a higher standard, one that exceeds the holiness of the Pharisees. For example, it's not good enough for His followers not to actually commit murder, Jesus' followers are not even to hate, and not only are they not to hate, they are to love their enemies.

The rituals and the legal requirement of the Mosaic Law are done. They served their purpose. Now, a New Covenant, the Messianic Covenant, with its higher standard for holiness that is in one's heart has replaced it. Inner holiness versus outward performance as empowered (i.e. Grace) by the Holy Spirit is what's being offered to Jews and Gentiles alike.

Appendix G

There is ONLY one nation that is special to the Living God – Israel.

And Israel did NOT choose the Living God, the Living God chose them. And He did NOT choose them because they were great and mighty, and like Americans who have a can-do, never count-us-out, we're-winners-not-losers attitude. If anything, the Living God chose Israel because they were nothings and nobodies, the least of all peoples, stiff-necked even.

Theologians have a term for what the Living God did by choosing ONLY Israel to who He would reveal Himself. It's called the Offense of Particularity. That is, the Living God chose a particular people – the sons and daughters of Abraham, the Hebrews, the Jews – to not only reveal Himself to, but also for them to reveal Him to the rest of the peoples on the earth. And the facts of history are that this irks Gentiles, even Christian Gentiles, both of whom want to be special instead of the Jews.

In short, The Living God's choice of Israel, of having them as His special people, a people with whom He has a permanent covenant, offends EVERYONE who isn't Jewish. And while the colonists and then the people of the United States want to believe that THEY are special and that THEY have a unique calling and purpose...THEY DO NOT.

There is ONLY one nation that is special to the Living God and with whom He has a permanent covenant: the nation of Israel.

———

Now, remember that to whom much is given, much is required, and because of Israel's special place before the Living God they have had a HUGE responsibility...at which they have miserably failed. And just one of their major failures was crucifying Jesus of Nazareth, their Messiah.

In a biblical sense everyone, every human being, crucified Jesus because He came the first time to be the ultimate payment for Sin and ALL of us are sinners. But the Jews forced the issue, thus the Living God has held them responsible for that.

When **"all the people"** standing before Pilate called for the release of Barabbas (Hebrew for "son of the father") instead of Jesus of

Nazareth, the King of the Jews (and the actual Son of the Father), they even went so far as to say, **"Let His blood be on us and on our children!"** (Matthew 27:25). And the Living God has honored that request for nearly 2,000 years, which includes the Holocaust.

Truly, to whom much is given, much is required, and Israel blew it big time, and they have paid dearly for it!

And yet...

In The End Israel is going to have a prominent part.

For example, when the day comes in which Jesus' prophecy in Matthew 23:39 is fulfilled and all of Israel says, **"Blessed is He who comes in the Name of the Lord"** to Jesus of Nazareth Himself, and as a result of their public repentance, when the Gentile nations see this Jesus showing mercy to the very ones who called for His crucifixion, when the Gentile nations see His compassion for His murderers...Israel will be lifted up for all the world to see the Living God's great Mercy being offered to a people who clearly do not deserve it.

And since He will be willing to show the Jews Mercy, how much more will He be willing to be merciful to the Gentiles IF they are willing to repent!

Also, although The Church is made up mostly of Gentiles today, Gentiles should NEVER forget that they have been grafted into the Jewish root.

> **If some of the branches have been broken off, and you, though a wild olive shoot, have been grafted in among the others and now share in the nourishing sap from the olive root, do not boast over those branches. If you do, consider this: You do not support the root, but the root supports you. You will say then, "Branches were broken off so that I could be grafted in." Granted. But they were broken off because of unbelief, and you stand by faith. Do not be arrogant, but be afraid. For if God did not spare the natural branches, He will not spare you either.** (Romans 11:17-21)

Appendix H

Chapters one, two, and three of the Revelation have the most con-
centrated descriptions of Jesus of Nazareth in the entire Word of God.
Truly, this writing is the greatest revealing (apocalypse) of Jesus of
Nazareth who is the Christ (1:1a).

And since we are rapidly approaching the time of Jesus' return to
this planet, just as Jesus warned, there are many deceptive deceptions
about who Jesus of Nazareth is, what He is like, and what He is doing.
So doing some in-depth study on each of these descriptions of the Real
Jesus for heart-revelation (i.e. Ephesians 1:17-18a) is important to do
right NOW! And in doing this ask the Holy Spirit to take the information
and to make it revelation to your heart, so that it does not remain as
nothing more than mere head-knowledge or theology:

1. The Faithful Witness – 1:5a
2. The Firstborn from the dead – 1:5a
3. The Ruler/King over the kings of the Earth – 1:5a; 17:14
4. The One who loved us – 1:5b
5. The One who washed us – 1:5b
6. The One who made us kings and priests – 1:6
7. The Alpha and the Omega – 1:8
8. The Beginning and the End – 1:8
9. The Lord – 1:8; 17:14
10. The One who is, was, and is to come – 1:8
11. The Almighty – 1:8
12. The One whose voice is like a trumpet – 1:10
13. The First and the Last – 1:11
14. The Son of Man – 1:13
15. The One clothed in a garment down to His feet – 1:13
16. The One who is girded about with a golden band – 1:13
17. The One whose head and hair are white – 1:14
18. The One whose eyes are like a flame of fire – 1:14
19. The One whose feet are like finely refined brass – 1:15
20. The One whose voice is as the sound of many waters – 1:15
21. The One holding the seven stars – 1:16

22. The One out of whose mouth comes a sharp two-edged sword – 1:16
23. The One whose countenance is like the sun – 1:16
24. The One who lives – 1:18
25. The One who has the Keys of Hades and of Death – 1:18
26. The One who walks amid the seven lampstands – 2:1
27. The Son of God – 2:18
28. The One who holds the seven spirits of God – 3:1
29. The One who is Holy – 3:7
30. The One who is True – 3:7
31. The One who has the Key of David – 3:7
32. The Amen – 3:14
33. The Beginning of Creation – 3:14

Next, it is no accident that Jesus put these letters He dictated to John in the Revelation, the document which contains His battle plan for taking over the earth. In other words, these letters have some of the critically important behaviors Jesus is warning His people to avoid AND to have in the Last Days.

So, as important as it is to SEE Jesus of Nazareth rightly, as in who He is and what He is truly like, it is also incredibly critical that His followers clearly comprehend what behaviors He expects from them so that they overcome and remain faithful to Him at all costs.

We know that we have come to know Him if we obey His commands. The man who says, "I know Him," but does not do what He commands is a liar, and the truth is not in him. But if anyone obeys His Word, God's Love is truly made complete (i.e. mature) **in Him. This is how we know we are in Him: <u>Whoever claims to live in Him must walk as Jesus did</u>.** (1 John 2:3-6) (See also John 14:15-23, 15:10.)

1. With ears to hear, hear what the Spirit is saying right now to His Church, His Bride – 2:7, 2:11, 2:17, 2:29, 3:6, 3:13, 3:22
2. Repent of anything Jesus tells us to repent of – 2:5, 2:16, 2:25, 3:3, 3:19

To The Church in Ephesus:

3. Stand for the truth and the exposing of false and deceptive ministries – 2:2
4. Persevere with patience – 2:3
5. Labor for the sake of Jesus' Name without becoming weary – 2:3
6. Hate the false grace message – 2:6

To The Church in Smyrna:
7. Be faithful in True Ministry despite severe suffering and debilitating poverty (both of which make us wealthy) – 2:9
8. Do not fear suffering – 2:10

To The Church in Pergamum:
9. Hold fast to Jesus' Name (character and message) – 2:13
10. Do not deny our relationship with Jesus even unto death – 2:13

To The Church in Thyatira:
11. Press into more mature works of service: Real Love, trust in the Lord, and patience – 2:19
12. Hold fast to the things we know are true and right until Jesus returns – 2:25

To The Church in Sardis:
13. Be watchful (prayer) to strengthen the things that have a tendency to become weak in our lives, for we are to seek to be perfect (mature – Matthew 5:48) – 3:2
14. Remember the lessons we received and heard and be obedient to them – 3:3
15. Walk in a worthy way, a way that honors Jesus – 3:4

To The Church in Philadelphia:
16. In whatever circumstance (door) the Lord has put us in, and even in great weakness (which Jesus loves), we're to keep God's Word and to not deny Jesus' Name (character and message) – 3:8
17. Because Jesus is returning very soon, hold fast to Him (intimacy) and to His ways (obedience) – 3:11

To The Church in Laodicea:
18. Buy from Jesus fire-refined gold that we may be truly rich, white garments that the shame of our nakedness be not revealed, and the True Anointing that we may truly see and hear – 3:18

19. When repenting, do it with hot zealousness (Matthew 18:8-9) – 3:19
20. Listen for Jesus' knock and His voice, and don't delay in opening the door for intimacy with Him – 3:20

Here are some things not to do.

1. Ignoring and/or refusing to hear (not having ears that hear) what the Spirit is saying right now to His Church, His Bride
2. Ignoring and/or refusing to repent of what Jesus tells us to repent of

To The Church in Ephesus:
3. Putting increased ministry before cultivating Love for Jesus – 2:4
4. Putting anything before the First and the Greatest Commandment – 2:5

To The Church in Smyrna:
5. Fearing the reality of suffering due to living for Jesus without compromise – 2:10

To The Church in Pergamum:
6. Accepting or acquiescing to the teachings of Balaam – greed and sexual immorality which lead to idolatry, a false version of God, a god of our own making – 2:14
7. Allowing false teachings on Grace (Jude 4) – 2:15

To The Church in Thyatira:
8. Allowing false prophetic ministry (Matthew 7:15-23) – 2:20
9. Allowing teachings which lower standards of obedience and morality – 2:20, 24

To The Church in Sardis:
10. Pretending to be alive with God's Presence when the reality is the opposite – 3:1
11. Not watching (praying), thus not being prepared for Jesus' return – 3:2
12. Walking in an unworthy, dishonoring way to the Name of Jesus – 3:3-4

To The Church in Laodicea:

13. Being lukewarm, passive about and compromising in our relationship with Jesus – 3:15
14. Being found rich in worldly things which cause us to be arrogant, selfish, wretched, miserable, poor, blind, and naked – 3:17
15. Having a zeal-less, earnest-less repentance – 3:19

If it helps, here is a list of consequences for not doing the things Jesus of Nazareth says to do or not do.

1. Being deceived by false teachers which results in not having ears to hear what the Spirit is saying right now to His Church, His Bride (Matthew 24:4-5, 10-12; 1 Timothy 4:1-2)
2. Anything from not actually being known by Jesus (Matthew 7:21-23), to falling away (2 Thessalonians 2:3), to losing eternal rewards due to works being revealed for what they are (1 Corinthians 3:10-15)

To The Church in Ephesus:
3. Jesus Himself quickly removing our light and influence – 2:5

To The Church in Pergamum:
4. Jesus coming quickly to fight against us with the power of His Word – 2:16

To The Church in Thyatira:
5. Being cast upon a sickbed – 2:22
6. Experiencing the wrong kind of tribulation – 2:22
7. Death (i.e. Joshua 7; Acts 5:1-10) so that The Church knows that the Real Jesus is watching and does deal with us according to righteousness – 2:23

To The Church in Sardis:
8. Not being prepared for Jesus' return and losing rewards at the best or falling away at the worst – 3:3

To The Church in Laodicea:
9. Not truly seeing Jesus for who He is and what He's doing – 3:18
10. Making Jesus sick to His stomach – 3:16

And, if it helps, here is a list of rewards Jesus of Nazareth promises to those who do what He says to do.

1. Hearing truly and accurately what the Spirit is saying right now, and thus being empowered to follow Him in what He is doing right now
2. Being an overcomer

To The Church in Ephesus:
3. Hating what Jesus hates; prioritizing with Jesus' priorities – 2:6
4. Being given fruit from the Tree Of Life – 2:7

To The Church in Smyrna:
5. Being given the crown of life – 2:10
6. Not being hurt by the second death – 2:11

To The Church in Pergamum:
7. Being given some Hidden Manna – 2:17
8. Being given a White Stone that has a new name for us that no one knows but Jesus and us – 2:17

To The Church in Thyatira:
9. Being given power over nations, even participating with Jesus in doing what He's doing to restore the nations in the Millennium – 2:26-27
10. Being given the morning star – 2:28

To The Church in Sardis:
11. Walking with Jesus as worthy followers clothed in white garments – 3:4-5
12. Not being blotted-out of the Book Of Life – 3:5
13. Having our name confessed before the Father – 3:5

To The Church in Philadelphia:
14. Having the Lord Jesus Himself forcefully vindicate us, even compelling our enemies to acknowledge how much He loves us – 3:9
15. Being kept in the hour of trial that the entire Earth is going to experience – 3:10
16. Not losing one's crown – 3:11
17. Being made a pillar in God's Temple – 3:12

18. Never not being in God's House – 3:12

19. Having Jesus write on us the name of God, the name of the city of God, as well as Jesus' new name – 3:12

To The Church in Laodicea:

20. Jesus coming in among us, sitting with us, making His home with us, communing with us, and giving us the right to rule the Earth with Him – 3:20-21

Appendix I

One of the main issues of the End Times has to do with Jesus purifying His Bride. For He will NOT have a compromised, unfaithful Wife! He is looking for a people who will give it all and lose it all because they are so lovesick for Him.

Therefore, one of the challenges in the End Times for the followers of Jesus concerns being offended...by Jesus of Nazareth! That's right. Not just by the world, society, or the Antichrist and his followers, but by Jesus. And in Matthew, chapter eleven, Jesus addresses this possibility, for it is true that This God offends the mind to reveal what is actually in the heart...even the hearts of His people.

Here's the situation.

John has been imprisoned. And he knows what's going to happen to him, for he is literally going to decrease, as in depart this earth, so that Jesus can increase. And because he knows this is going to happen he wants his disciples to make the transition away from him and to Jesus. So to do this he sends them on an assignment to find out for THEMSELVES whether Jesus is the Messiah or not.

John, THE forerunner to the Messiah is NOT having doubts himself.[188] The reason he was conceived, brought into this world, and made the forerunner with the spirit of Elijah was to be the forerunner to the Messiah (Luke 1:13-17). John isn't now doubting. So his words are what he's telling his disciples to say to Jesus about whether He is the One. These are not his words expressing his doubt.

Well, John's disciples obey him and go to Jesus and ask Him the question John told them to ask: Are you the One? And Jesus absolutely answers them. And not merely with words, but with actions.

Go back and report to John what you <u>hear and see</u>: The blind receive sight, the lame walk, those who have leprosy are cleansed, the deaf hear, the dead are raised, and the Good News is proclaimed to the poor. (Matthew 11:4-5)

---

[188] How do we know that John isn't having a crisis of faith? Note what Jesus says about him in Matthew 11:11-15!

Jesus' answer to the question of whether or not He's the One? He restores the sight to the blind. He causes the lame to walk. He cleanses those with leprosy. He opens the ears of the deaf. He proclaims the Gospel to the physically and spiritually poor. Why, He even raises some dead people![189] And all this right there in front of John's disciples (note Jesus told them to go tell John what they heard and SAW). With such really wonderful things, why then does Jesus conclude by saying:

Blessed is anyone who does not stumble (i.e. offended) **on account of me.** (Matthew 11:6)

Stumble? Offended? At THIS Jesus? How or why would ANYONE be offended at a Jesus who does such awesome things??? Healing people, delivering people, raising people from the dead...why would such things result in a person being offended at the One doing these???

The answer?

When He doesn't deliver His own cousin, John, from the executioner's ax.

When Jesus does not step up to help John, John's disciples are going to question this Jesus' care and provision. His lack of action to help John is going to cause John's disciples to doubt that He is the Messiah. And this is exactly the kind of thing that is going to happen in the final years. Jesus of Nazareth is going to do things and not do things that can offend His followers' minds and hearts. And yet, this Jesus will be looking for His followers to still love Him and trust Him and obey Him.

Part of the problem is that no one, like Peter, thinks that something can happen that will offend us, make us deny Him. "Oh not me, Lord! I'll die for you"...until, for example, you are left to live having seen those you love killed, or some other terrible thing. Like with Job, and Peter, the enemy knows how to get to each of us. And the more Jesus has a hold of a person's life, the more that person is attacked.[190]

The moment one thinks he or she won't fall, something happens to bring them down. The truth is, ALL of us are susceptible to falling to the pressure to question, doubt, and deny Jesus. Thus, not being deceived and being prepared are not optional as we rapidly approach the time Jesus of Nazareth returns to this planet to establish His Kingdom.

---

[189] All of these are not only physical issues. They're all also spiritual issues: spiritual blindness, unable to walk-out the spiritual life, spiritual numbness (which is what Hansen's Disease is), unable to hear spiritual truth, etc.

[190] I.e. 2 Corinthians 12:6-7

Appendix J

An Outline of the Revelation of Jesus

CHAPTER 1: **John's CALLING to prophesy about the End Times:** John was given truths about Jesus' majesty that formed the way he prophesied about the End Times. These truths are meant to equip The Church as to the Real Jesus.

CHAPTERS 2-3: **Jesus dictated LETTERS to seven congregations:** The instructions Jesus gave to these congregations about overcoming Sin gives The Church practical insight into what she must also overcome.

CHAPTERS 4-5: **Jesus takes the SCROLL:** It contains the Earth's title deed and His battle plan to cleanse it.

CHAPTERS 6-22: **Jesus' BATTLE PLAN:** Jesus reveals His main storyline to cleanse the Earth of Evil. His battle plan is seen in **five chronological sections** that describe events that unfold in sequential order. Each section is followed by an **explanation** to help understand that section. These **five chronological sections** tell The Church what happens to the Antichrist's followers in some eighteen or so judgment events (Seals, Trumpets, and Bowls). The **five explanations** function as a parenthesis, putting the storyline on "pause" so as to answer questions arising from the chronological events in each section: Why is This God's wrath so severe? What will happen to His followers? Etc.

> CHAPTER 6: **Chronological Section #1:** the **SEAL JUDGMENTS** against the kingdom of darkness.
> CHAPTER 7: **Explanation #1:** Christians undeceived and prepared receive **PROTECTION** from judgments.
>
> CHAPTERS 8-9: **Chronological Section #2:** the **TRUMPET JUDGMENTS** against the Antichrist's empire.
> CHAPTERS 10-11: **Explanation #2:** Christians receive **DIRECTION** by a great increase of prophetic ministry.

CHAPTER 11:15-19: **Chronological section #3:** the **SECOND COMING PROCESSION** and the Rapture at the seventh and last trumpet (1 Corinthians 15:52; Revelation 10:7; 1 Thessalonians 4:16). Jesus replaces all governmental leaders on Earth in a hostile takeover.
CHAPTERS 12-14: **Explanation #3:** the **CONFRONTATION** against the saints by the Antichrist's system requires that all his governments be taken over.

CHAPTERS 15-16: **Chronological section #4:** the **BOWL JUDGMENTS** destroy evil infrastructures in society.
CHAPTERS 17-18: **Explanation #4:** the **SEDUCTION** of Babylon's evil religion and economic system will permeate and infiltrate all the structures of society, requiring that Babylon be totally destroyed.

CHAPTERS 19-20: **Chronological section #5:** Jesus' **TRIUMPHAL ENTRY** to Jerusalem (Revelation 19:11 - 21:8).
CHAPTERS 21-22: **Explanation #5:** the **RESTORATION** of all things (Acts 3:21; Revelation 21:9 - 22:5).

The Seven Main Symbols
All events and numbers are to be taken in their plain literal meaning unless specifically indicated not to (Revelation 1:20; 5:6; 11:8; 12:1, 3, 9; 17:7, 9, 15-18, etc.). And as for the few symbols, they are all explained by the angels.

Dragon: Satan (12:3, 4, 7, 9, 13, 16, 17; 13:2, 4; 16:13; 20:2)
First Beast: the Antichrist (13; 14:9-11; 17:3-17; 19:19-21; 20:4, 10)
Another Beast: the False Prophet called "another Beast" just once (13:11)
Seven Heads: the seven empires that persecuted Israel (Egypt, Assyria, Babylon, Persia, Greece, Rome, and the revived Roman Empire (Daniel 2:41-42; 7:7; Revelation 12:3; 13:1; 17:3-16)
Ten Horns: a ten-nation confederation that serves the Antichrist (17:12-13)
Harlot Babylon: a worldwide demonically inspired religious and economic system based in the re-built city of Babylon, near Baghdad in Iraq (17-18; Jeremiah 50-51)
Woman with a Male-child: the faithful remnant of Israel throughout history (12)

NOTES AND PRAYERS

NOTES

PRAYERS

NOTES

PRAYERS

Made in the USA
Columbia, SC
30 June 2023

19765449R00143